CM 1449

D1172774

The Senator
and the
Sharecropper's Son

"Dishonorably Discharged," *Harper's Weekly*, November 8–10, 1906.

The Senator and the Sharecropper's Son

Exoneration of the Brownsville Soldiers

JOHN D. WEAVER

TEXAS A&M UNIVERSITY PRESS
College Station

The paper used in this book meets the minimum requirements
of the American National Standard for Permanence
of Paper for Printed Library Materials, Z39.48-1984.
Binding materials have been chosen for durability.

Library of Congress Cataloging-in-Publication Data

Weaver, John Downing, 1912–

    The senator and the sharecropper's son : exoneration of the
Brownsville soldiers / John D. Weaver. —1st ed.

    p.   cm.

    Includes bibliographical references and index.

    ISBN 0-89096-748-2

    1. Afro-American soldiers—Texas—Brownsville—History—20th
century. 2. Brownsville (Tex.)—Race relations. 3. United States—
Race relations. 4. United States. Army—Afro-American troops—
History—20th century. 5. United States. Army. Infantry Regiment,
25th—History—20th century. 6. Riots—Texas—Brownsville—
History—20th century. 7. Willis, Dorsie W. 8. Foraker, Joseph
Benson, 1846–1917. 9. Roosevelt, Theodore, 1858–1919. I. Title.

F394.B88W43   1997

355.1'332—dc21   96-29637

                                                            CIP

*For
Chica,
Who makes the
day begin.*

Contents

Illustrations

Preface

I grew up with my mother's anecdotes of a cross-country train trip from her native Washington, D.C., to Brownsville, Texas, in the early years of her marriage, when she had no children underfoot. My father was a court reporter in that first decade of the new century, and long after I had forgotten what caused my young parents to go so far from home, I had come to assume that a trial of some sort—a murder, perhaps—had led them to that scruffy Mexican border town.

In the early fall of 1968, when I completed a writing assignment in Washington, D.C., a friend drove me down to Front Royal, Virginia, where Mother had taken a small apartment within walking distance of the hillside cemetery where my father and his family are buried. As I was mixing drinks, Mother made a casual reference to Brownsville, and my friend asked what had taken her to Texas.

"Some Negro soldiers shot up the town," she said, "and Teddy Roosevelt kicked them out of the Army."

"Did Dad report their trial?" I asked.

"They didn't have any trial. He just kicked them out."

"But, Mother, not even the president can go around kicking people out of the army without a trial."

"Teddy Roosevelt did," she insisted.

When I got back to Los Angeles a few days later, I decided to look into the judicial proceedings my father had recorded three years before I was born. I had no trouble finding the *Report of the Brownsville Court of Inquiry* in the research library at the University of California at Los Angeles. The testimony and exhibits were bound in four sand-colored volumes of Senate Documents, Sixty-first Congress, Third Session, 1910–11. On the opening page I saw that the court's five generals were present at its first meeting in Washington, May 4, 1909, and that "Henry B. Weaver was duly sworn in as reporter."

I made a photocopy of the page and sent it to Mother, who lost little time responding to my request for information on the background of the proceedings:

> *Teddy Roosevelt was President and he had sent an entire Negro regiment to Brownsville with white officers and it had infuriated the people so that they harassed the soldiers every way they could. If they went to a soda fountain for a drink they were served and then they would break the glass they drank from right in front of them—there was a tiny little foot bridge you had to use to get into a rowboat to row across the Rio Grande—they charged 6 cents Mex and 3 cents USA money— when a Negro would get on this bridge often they would shake it so they fell into the water. . . . This treatment incited the colored boys and they planned to do something about it so one night when the officers were all playing cards, a small segment of the soldiers got together to shoot up the town.*[1]

Mother's account was written more than sixty years after the midnight shooting spree. Errors had crept in, but not so many or so far-fetched as some I was finding in standard reference works at UCLA. Three companies (B, C, and D) of the 1st Battalion, 25th Infantry, not an "entire Negro regiment," had been sent to Texas in the summer of 1906, and the ten- to twenty-minute raid had occurred around midnight on August 13, when the outfit's five white officers were asleep.

By the time I received Mother's letter I had discovered *Notes of a Busy Life*, the memoirs of Joseph Benson Foraker, the Republican senator from Ohio who emerged as the Zola in this "Black Dreyfus Affair" and died in 1917 still believing that "if the Government had spent the one-tenth part to discover the men who shot up Brownsville that it did to convict the innocent soldiers of a crime they never committed, the truth would have been easily and long ago established."[2]

In the first week of spring, 1910, the court of inquiry wound up their hearings, the five generals agreeing unanimously that Brownsville had indeed been assaulted by Negro soldiers stationed at Fort Brown in the summer of 1906. For reasons known only to themselves and possibly their Maker, they permitted 14 men to apply for reenlistment. They closed the case on the other 153 infantrymen.

It was still closed on New Year's Day, 1971, when I flew to Chicago to plug *The Brownsville Raid* on Bob Cromie's television program, *Book Beat*. In the course of the interview I explained that I wanted to launch a campaign to clear the records of the black battalion. That night the exoneration crusade was taken up by Fred Wall, publisher of the *Chicago Courier*, and his editorial columnist, Doris Saunders, who had read an advance copy of the book.

Doris and I met at my hotel following the Cromie interview and hurried off to the studios of Channel 7 to sit in on the taping of a television show, "Black on Black," produced by Vernon Jarrett. Fred Wall dominated the show, looking back in anger at what had happened to black Americans in the past year and looking ahead with the same indignation and eloquence to what was likely to happen to them in the next twelve months.

When the taping session ended, Fred and Doris whisked me off to a South Side hangout for Chicago's black journalists. There, seated at a long table with a lively, articulate group of writers, editors, and publishers, including Herbert Nipson of *Ebony* and Pierre Guillmant of the *Defender*, we got to talking about a crusade to clear the army records of the Brownsville soldiers. Fred turned to Doris and, in a thundering voice that might have sounded familiar to Moses, proclaimed: "Let it begin right here, right now."

"It is too late to help the men, who suffered unjustly," Doris wrote in the *Courier* (February 6), "but it is not too late for their names to be vindicated and justice, even tardily, to be done."

When I got back to Los Angeles, Frank Terry, a genial spokesman for the Department of Labor (he later defected to Veterans Affairs), suggested I gather up some Brownsville material, including Doris's column, and send it to his sister, Mrs. Juanita Terry Barbee, administrative aide to Gus Hawkins, a black congressman from Los Angeles.

"I am deeply interested in doing something on this," Juanita wrote back.[3]

Frank and Juanita's grandfather, John Sayers, a runaway slave, had joined the Union Army and fought for his freedom. He had also taught himself to read and seen to it that his children grew up with books and music. One of his daughters, Jessie, a schoolteacher, left Kentucky in 1910 and settled in Los Angeles, where she married Woodford H. Terry, a building contractor.

While rearing her three children, Jessie Terry found time to sponsor Sunday afternoon concerts at her church, work for the desegregation of public schools, help recall a corrupt mayor, and serve as the first black member of the City Housing Commission. She was also an active Democrat at a time when black Americans were veering away from their traditional loyalty to the party of Abraham Lincoln.

One of her young disciples, Augustus Freeman Hawkins, a mild-mannered, light-skinned economist who could have slipped unnoticed across the color line, entered politics in 1934 as a twenty-seven-year-old New Deal Democrat bent on unseating Fred Roberts, a black Republican who had held his Assembly seat since 1918.[4]

The editor of the *California Eagle* saw the race as a contest "between experience and lack of experience, between calm, proven judgment and hot-headed radicalism." A week later, after Gus had won handily, the black community paper praised him for having waged "a clean and educational campaign, confining his statements to facts and a frank discussion of principles."[5]

Assemblyman Hawkins proceeded to work quietly and effectively for laws dealing with the greatest needs of his constituents: jobs, housing, schools, medical care. He was the chief architect of the state's Fair Employment Practices Act and of the law putting an end to racial discrimination in the sale of homes. No one was more adept at getting a bill through the Assembly, and no one cared so little about who got credit for its passage.[6]

He is not a man to move by impulse, but he had introduced more than one hundred bills in the legislature by 1962 when he was elected to the House of Representatives, where he continued to sponsor legislation for the poor, the lame, the halt, and the blind. He was vice-chairman of the newly formed thirteen-member Black Caucus headed by Charles C. Diggs, Jr., of Michigan at the time he read Doris Saunders's *Courier* article into the *Congressional Record* on March 18, 1971, and expressed the hope that it would "ignite an interest in my colleagues to delve further into this little-known incident in our nation's history."

Later that month (March 29) he introduced a bill, H. R. 6866, directing the secretary of defense to rescind "the effect of Special Order Numbered 266 issued by the War Department on November 9, 1906, and to rectify the injustice caused by such order with respect to all members of Companies B, C, and D, First Battalion, Twenty-fifth United States Infantry."

"This grievous injustice," he said, "will continue to gnaw at the nation's conscience until we correct it."[7]

After nearly ten months of deliberations, the army announced its opposition to H. R. 6866 in a report that treated the soldiers' guilt as indisputable historical fact. "Some sixteen to twenty unidentified soldiers of Companies B, C, and D furtively left the army garrison and ran amuck through town, firing into homes and stores," the January 24, 1972, report stated, and went on to add: "The incident was immediately investigated by the commanding officer of the Twenty-fifth Infantry, Major Charles W. Penrose. He found that, although the specific raiders could not be identified, the raid was definitely perpetrated by members of his command."

No mention was made of the tainted evidence on which Major Penrose had at first been led to believe the raiders were members of his command, nor of the fact that he and the black battalion's four other white officers later came to agree that none of their men had taken part in the midnight shooting spree.[8]

"If the proposed bill were enacted, it would serve only to reopen the investigation, once again, a matter which has been thoroughly investigated in every regard," the Pentagon report concluded, ignoring a significant detail. Each of the government's "thorough" investigations had been predicated on the unquestioned guilt of the soldiers, and none had turned up evidence on which a single enlisted man had ever been indicted, tried, and convicted. The army recommended that "the bill not be favorably considered."

The report was bucked to President Nixon's advisers in the Office of Management and Budget, who passed it along to the government's lawyers in the Department of Justice. It was mid-May before Management and Budget got a reply from Acting Attorney-General Richard G. Kleindienst. The army, he noted, had missed the point of the Hawkins bill, which was not to conduct still another investigation of the Brownsville Affray, as it was officially dubbed, but "to rectify the gross injustice involved in the mass discharge of 167 soldiers."[9]

Kleindienst's summary differed from the Army's by stating that persons "thought" to be black soldiers had shot up the town, and it reminded the Pentagon's historians that the government's repeated investigations had failed to establish the identity of a single raider. He recommended action by the army under existing law to set aside the summary discharges without honor "despite the administrative inconvenience involved."

"If that is done," he said, "enactment of H. R. 6866 would be unnecessary."[10]

Four months later, on September 28, 1972, as my wife and I were driving across Sunset Boulevard to have dinner with Gladwin Hill, who had spent a quarter-century covering Southern California for the *New York Times*, we picked up a half-dozen copies of the street edition of the *Los Angeles Times*. It carried a front-page headline in type that could have heralded the outbreak of World War III:

Army Clears 167
After 66 Years

Gus Hawkins was more amused than angry when the Pentagon publicists who cobbled the text announcing Secretary of the Army Robert F. Froehlke's exoneration of the Brownsville soldiers failed to mention his bill or the book that had inspired it. It also failed to mention the Republican president who had issued the order they were rescinding or the Republican president who, as secretary of war, had carried it out. With a straight face the Pentagon press agents explained that "an internal Army review of administrative and judicial policies brought this instance of mass punishment to the attention of the Secretary."

"It seems strange that many years later a Republican President releases this decision just before the election," Gus Hawkins pointed out. "The black vote may have something to do with it."

"Politics did not have a thing to do with it," I was later told by Colonel Robert W. Berry, a West Point law professor serving as the army's general counsel at the time of the exoneration. "An army officer in Personnel read your book and got interested in the injustice. I don't know how he got to the Secretary, but Bob Froehlke was the key to it. When the case was brought to him, a member of his staff said, 'It can't be done.' 'Why not?' Bob asked. 'Because it's never been done before,' he was told, and he simply said, 'Do it.'"[11]

In the summer of 1972, at the age of eighty-six, Dorsie W. Willis of Company D, whose name was the last to appear on the roster of the 25th Infantry's

1st Battalion, was still shining shoes in the same downtown Minneapolis barber shop where he had worked for the previous fifty-nine years. During that time the price of a shine had shot up from ten to fifty cents and two generations of young customers had gone off to fight a world war. John F. Kennedy had been born in Massachusetts and killed in Texas. Women had started voting, flying airplanes, and wearing pantyhose. American families had grown accustomed to such novelties as frozen vegetables, electric refrigerators, radios, tape recorders, color television, moon-walkers, Saran Wrap, and instant coffee. In all those years, Dorsie had taken only one vacation. Two weeks.

"And," he liked to point out, "I never got a dime's pay when I was sick."[12]

He had outlived two wives before he married Olive Allen in 1945 on his fifty-ninth birthday. She was thirty-one years younger. Her friends predicted the marriage would last no more than a year or two, but for the next twenty-seven years she dropped him off at the barber shop each morning at 5:30. After putting in an eight-hour day packing from seven thousand to ten thousand pounds of hamburger patties for a restaurant chain, she picked him up that evening at 6:30.

"If people came late," Ollie recalls, "He'd stay till the last one was gone. Then he'd sweep up the hair and mop the floor. I'd drive around the block or go over to my sister's house and wait. Sometimes I've brought him home with fifty cents in his pocket."

In a good week, Dorsie earned $60 and Ollie $95. His Social Security check added another $162.40 a month, of which $30 to $40 went for his various medicines. But the Willises dressed well, set a bountiful table for their friends, and took pride in being listed among the more dependable contributors to the Zion Baptist Church.

One of Dorsie's regular customers was Jack Cornelius, an advertising executive active in the work of the Boys Clubs of America.

"How much does it cost to send one of them poor boys to summer camp?" Dorsie asked one day.

"Fifty dollars," Cornelius said, and twice a year Dorsie started showing up at his office with $25 in silver coins.

"What I liked," Dorsie explained, "was they didn't ask about a boy's religion or care what color he was. Just so long as he was poor, they took him in."[13]

Toward the end of the summer of 1972, the barber shop changed hands, and the new owners told Dorsie they had found a younger man to take over his work. They gave him two weeks' notice. On the eve of the Labor Day weekend, Dorsie's last day on the job, Ollie called for him at the usual hour. She ached at the sight of his gnarled hands struggling to hold onto the mop handle as he moved slowly and painfully on legs crippled by arthritis.

He finished with the floor, checked the stainless steel wash basins, the towel racks, and the barber chairs. The shop was spotless when he turned in his keys and hobbled away from his life's work. No one saw him to the door, shook his hand, wished him well.

"On the way home I was crying so hard I could hardly drive," Ollie remembers.[14]

A few weeks after Dorsie's last day at the shoeshine stand, one of the barbers called him at home with the news that the army had cleared the records of the Brownsville soldiers. He had just heard about it on the radio, he said. Dorsie got in touch with Jack Cornelius, who dashed off a letter to his friend General Mark Clark, World War II commander of Allied forces in Italy.

"You may possibly remember Willis, the perfectly remarkable, very old Negro who undoubtedly has shined your shoes when you have been in the barber shop here in my building," Cornelius wrote, and went on to say that during the last forty years the old man had often spoken of his innocent involvement in the Brownsville incident. Now that he had been exonerated, the letter continued, "both Willis and I are under the impression that he might possibly be entitled to some back pay."

"Probably not, but I'll find out," the general replied, and forwarded the inquiry to some army friends in Washington who passed it along to the Pentagon.[15]

In granting the black battalion honorable discharges, the army had ruled out back pay, allowances, and benefits for "heirs and descendants" but had said nothing about "survivors." The subject was tossed into play when the Clark letter reached Secretary Froehlke's office accompanied by a one-page handwritten note from a man in Minneapolis who claimed to have been a member of the Brownsville battalion.

"I was certainly glad to read where you'd given us a honorable discharge," the man wrote, "which I tried to get fifteen or twenty years ago through the American Legion at the court house here."

When Paul Houston, a reporter in the Washington bureau of the *Los Angeles Times*, learned about the Brownsville survivor from a news release put out by Congressman Hawkins's staff, he called the Willis home and ended up with both Dorsie and Ollie on the phone. At breakfast, Saturday, December 2, I read his front-page report of their three-way conversation and was pleased to discover that Dorsie supported my thesis. "It was a frameup from the beginning," he had told the California reporter. I phoned Dorsie and told him I had come to the same conclusion.[16]

In Washington, where he was preparing legislation to provide appropriate benefits for the Brownsville victims, Gus Hawkins dismissed the Pentagon's handling of the exoneration as "a real disgrace" and went on to add, "The Army must have felt there was some wrong committed when it amended the discharges, but to do so without considering the human tragedies and factors is cold-blooded."[17]

Major General De Witt C. Smith, Jr., deputy chief of information, agreed. He was delighted with the nice things said about the army when it cleared the records of the black battalion, and he warned, "We must try to keep on the side of the angels rather than letting an initially good action deteriorate so that we become devils."

"Had a call from Washington Saturday and three men are coming here at my home Friday," Dorsie reported January 7, 1973, in a letter Ollie wrote for him, thanking me for a copy of *The Brownsville Raid*, which, he said, she was reading to him ("my eyes are not too good").

The three army officers dispatched to Minneapolis were told to carry out "low-key type interviews designed to assist Mr. Willis in his identification." They found him seated in his black leather chair, his wooden cane and Ollie's Doberman Pinscher within reach. His friend Jack Cornelius made the introductions. They were joined by C. E. Newman, a local newspaper publisher, the officers reported, and "the interview shifted to the dining room where Mrs. Willis served a home-cooked meal of Southern fried chicken."

When Cornelius and Newman alluded to the possibility of asking for congressional action to compensate their genial host, Ollie's Washington guests explained they had come to Minneapolis simply to determine whether her husband was the same Dorsie Willis who had signed up with the 25th Infantry in January, 1905. Once the guests had finished eating, a medical officer tactfully asked Dorsie if he might examine some scars that could help with his identification. Dorsie told him to go ahead.

Scars on both forearms and on the left cheek were compatible with those noted by an army doctor at the time Dorsie enlisted in Oklahoma Territory. His signature on the enlistment certificate, a Washington handwriting expert found later, matched the signature of Dorsie W. Willis on documents accompanying a 1954 application for an honorable discharge.

The information was submitted to BISID (Brownsville Incident Survivor Identification Board), which agreed unanimously that the alert, genial old man in Minneapolis was the same Dorsie W. Willis who had been sent home in disgrace in the fall of 1906 by an impulsive stroke of Theodore Roosevelt's pen. The board recommended that Dorsie be given an honorable discharge. However, he was not entitled to any back pay or allowances, Secretary Froehlke was advised, because at the time of his dismissal he had been paid in full and given train fare home.

"Mr. Willis will be entitled to burial in a national cemetery and a headstone," the military bureaucracy reported, standing grimly by army policy, which provided nothing more than a piece of paper, a hole in the ground and a stone to mark it.[18]

In view of Dorsie Willis's "notoriety," army press agents felt that a general should present his honorable discharge, and to avoid placing too much emphasis on "the racial aspects" of the case, it was decided not to send a black general to Minneapolis. The assignment fell to General Smith, whose humanitarian concerns were known to correspond with those of Secretary Froehlke.

The presentation ceremony was held at Zion Baptist Church on Sunday, February 11, 1973. It was Dorsie Willis's eighty-seventh birthday and the twenty-eighth anniversary of his marriage to Olive Allen, who had spent the early morning hours in the kitchen preparing for an afternoon spread of fried chicken, roast beef, sweet potatoes, spinach, and beans.

The church was overflowing with friends, well-wishers, television crews, and reporters as Dorsie stood before the congregation, flanked by Ollie and his sixty-five-year-old son Reginald. General Smith read from the notes he had jotted down on the flight from Washington that morning: "I appreciate this chance to come into your house of worship, and, in the house of God and before the friends of Dorsie Willis, make absolutely and officially clear what has always been true and clear in the minds of those who have known Mr. Willis—that is, that he rendered honest, faithful and entirely honorable service to his country while in the uniform of the United States Army."

This significant day, he reminded his audience, was the eve of Abraham

Lincoln's birthday and the beginning of what was then Black History Week.

"In Mr. Willis' case, we are trying to substitute justice for injustice, to make amends, to say how much we of this generation—white men as well as black—regret the errors of an earlier generation," he continued, and closed with a personal tribute to Dorsie Willis: "You honor us by the quality of the life you have led."

The old soldier was given a standing ovation. The choir sang *The Battle Hymn of the Republic*, and the *New York Times* reported, "Grown men wept."

"I had a feeling that this would happen eventually," Dorsie told an Associated Press reporter after the ceremony, and then spoke out against the government's apparent unwillingness to pay for the wrong it had done him. "If I made a mistake sixty-six years ago, I'd have to pay for it."[19]

I wrote *The Brownsville Raid* as a legal brief in narrative form designed to gain a hearing for the 167 black infantrymen summarily dismissed without honor by Theodore Roosevelt's Special Order 266, which was carried out in the fall of 1906 by Secretary of War William Howard Taft, who occupied the White House four years later when five retired generals sitting as a court of inquiry upheld the action of their two commanders-in-chief and closed the troublesome case.

In *The Senator and the Sharecropper's Son* I set out to place the Brownsville story in its historical context, bring it up to date and, at the same time, take a fresh look at the relationship between the popular president responsible for this massive miscarriage of justice and the Ohio senator who opposed him. Joseph Benson Foraker, as Allan Nevins pointed out in his foreword to Everett Walters's 1948 biography, was a "man of great gifts" and "unflinching courage," but historians have tended to be less charitable in dealing with him than with Roosevelt who, after reading the senator's memoirs in 1916, wrote to say, "I admire your courage and forthrightness."[20]

In his review of *The Brownsville Raid*, Lewis L. Gould, a University of Texas at Austin historian of the period, said Senator Foraker "may well have been too close to some large corporations, but he also retained some vestiges of the commitment of the Civil War generation in the North to the idea of human equality. . . . This prompted him to champion the cause of the Negro soldiers." It also prompted a powerful and vindictive young president to drive him from public office, leaving Gould to comment: "The biased, dictatorial, petty Roosevelt that emerges from the narrative is an unpleasant corrective to the usual picture of the man."[21]

"I have gotten the men I went after," Roosevelt boasted a few weeks before he left the White House, and the first name that came to mind was Foraker's.[22]

In the spring of 1909, when Roosevelt was slaughtering African wildlife and Foraker was practicing law in Cincinnati, the *Memphis Sentinel* called attention to the ex-senator's last official action, "his successful opposition to the enactment of the law forbidding the intermarriage of the two races in the District of Columbia, and making such intermarriage a crime. The Negroes of this country have not had such a faithful champion of their rights since the days of Charles Sumner."[23]

Foraker had been dead for fifty-five years when, in 1972, exoneration was finally decreed for the 167 soldiers who, in his words, had asked "no favors because they are Negroes, but only for justice because they are men." Along with the black Mississippi sharecropper's son who honored the Brownsville battalion by serving as its last survivor, the Ohio senator whom Theodore Roosevelt, late in life, came to regard as "the champion of people who had no champion," is also a candidate for exoneration.[24]

*The Senator
and the
Sharecropper's Son*

Chapter One

*"Slavery, so cruel to the slave, was fatal to the master," Alexis de
Tocqueville concluded after visiting Kentucky and Ohio during his nine-
month tour of the United States in 1830 and 1831. The two frontier
states, separated by the Ohio River, enjoyed the same healthy air and
temperate climate. There was only one significant difference between them,
the young French aristocrat noted. "Kentucky allows slaves, but Ohio refuses
to have them." On the river's left bank "one sees a troop of slaves loitering
through half-deserted fields," giving the impression that "society had gone to
sleep." On the right bank "a confused hum proclaims from afar that men are
busily at work; fine crops cover the fields; elegant dwellings testify to the taste
and industry of the workers." The contrasts between the two states "explain
the differences between ancient civilization and modern."*[1]

Joseph Benson Foraker was born July 5, 1846, in a two-story farmhouse
in Highland County, Ohio, where free Negroes were permitted to work as
laborers, servants, barbers, coachmen, janitors, and caterers, but were
denied the right to vote, serve on juries, join the militia, testify in court
cases involving whites, and send their children to schools their taxes helped
support.

At the time young Ben was reciting the alphabet and struggling with
arithmetic, the Free Soil Party used its balance of power in the legislature

to modify the state's infamous Black Laws, but Negro children, attending classes in shacks, churches, and abandoned white schools, rarely got more than basic training in reading, writing, and arithmetic. Their fathers could now testify against a white neighbor in a court of law but still were unable to vote, join the militia, or serve on juries. Of the public institutions Negroes supported with their tax payments, only the jails were open to them.[2]

Women, colored and white, also had few rights. "I wish women to have her voice among the pettifoggers," Sojourner Truth, a former slave who had lived in freedom for twenty-four years, told a women's rights convention in Akron, Ohio, in 1851, the year *Uncle Tom's Cabin; or, Life Among the Lowly* was appearing in weekly installments in the *National Era*. Harriet Beecher Stowe, its diminutive author, also had come to regard the legal position of married women as a form of slavery.[3]

When her book exploded on the country, young Foraker read it aloud to his mother, who was concerned less with slavery than with temperance. The self-taught farm boy went beyond the schooling he got in the winter months, reading up on history, especially Napoleon, the Indian Wars, and the Roman emperors.[4]

"I developed also from the beginning an aptitude for declamation," he noted in his memoirs.[5]

In 1856 the ten-year-old orator was a fervent supporter of the first Republican presidential ticket, Frémont and Dayton, running on the slogan "Free Soil, Free Speech, Free Press." He fabricated a Republican flag from homemade dyes and flew it from a tree he had moved to the top of a hillock on his father's farm near Reece's Mill. Later, looking ahead to the election of 1860, Ben Foraker became an enthusiastic supporter of New York's front-running abolitionist, Senator William H. Seward, but changed his allegiance when he heard Abraham Lincoln speak in Cincinnati.

"It was so clear, simple and straightforward, and so easily understood and so persuasive, that it completely captured me."

He was discussing the speech with an elderly miller who had become his "friend, adviser and guide," when Judge Nathaniel Delaplane, a Democrat, rode up to the door of the mill where the old man and the farm boy were talking. Foraker never forgot what happened next. "He made a remark of a rather deprecating character about my views on such matters, at which the old miller took offense. In a somewhat resentful manner he picked me up in his arms, and, holding me out toward the judge, told him in an earnest, energetic tone to take a good look at me, for some day I would be governor of Ohio. That was my first nomination."[6]

Julia Bundy, of Wellston, Ohio, was twelve years old when a company of U.S. Marines led by Colonel Robert E. Lee attacked a band of abolitionists who had seized the federal arsenal at Harpers Ferry, Virginia, in October, 1859. "I came riding home from school one early December dusk," she wrote seventy-odd years later. "A sullen red sky. Father was standing there. He lifted me off my horse. 'They've hanged John Brown,' he said." It was this dramatic happening, the elderly widow later recalled, that pierced "my childish unconsciousness of the volcano beneath our feet."[7]

The War of the Rebellion was in its second year, with memories of Union reverses at Bull Run and Ball's Bluff still fresh in memory when Ben Foraker signed up with the 89th Ohio Volunteers and set out for a beleaguered western Virginia valley held by rebel forces. As the train rolled across Jackson County, Ohio, it passed within view of the Wellston home of Hezekiah S. Bundy, a Republican state senator who was running for Congress (and who lost, but would win two years later). Sixteen-year-old Private Foraker took no notice of the house at the time, but eight years later he would know it well. He had become the congressman's son-in-law.[8]

Julia Bundy was born June 17, 1847, in a log house built by her maternal grandfather on land deeded to him in 1808 by President Madison. At the time Foraker passed by her home, the "Log House" had given way to the "Fine House," with its "immense" parlor and the first kitchen sink the neighbors had ever seen. Even so, Julia noted, "we were for all practical purposes as isolated as when Daniel Boone complained that a thirty-five-mile farm hardly gave a man elbow room."[9]

Looking back on her childhood from the days of platinum blondes, hip flasks, Sigmund Freud and Havelock Ellis, rumble seats, and trial marriages, Julia pointed out that "the epoch takes on picturesqueness now, but women were ground up in it, in the ceaseless concern with food, raiment and warmth. I am sure that the modern woman's bolt from the kitchen and home, so solemnly deplored, has very deep roots in woman's drudgery past, in a life that men would have gone down under, would, rather than keep it up, gratefully have seen their sex die out."[10]

Private Foraker was felling trees and constructing breastworks at Fort Shaler when he read a newspaper report that on Monday, September 22,

President Lincoln had signed a preliminary Emancipation Proclamation, notifying the Confederacy that on January 1, 1863, one hundred days away, all slaves in states still in rebellion against the Union would be "thenceforward, and forever free." There was no doubt among the 89th Ohio Volunteers as to the wisdom of the president's action, Foraker recalled, even though they knew the war would be prolonged and bloodier because it now involved "not alone the preservation of the Union, but also the abolition of slavery."[11]

When the unshackled slaves left the plantations to sign up for military service (180,000 by the war's end), "they helped transform the nation's treatment of blacks and blacks' conception of themselves." For the first time in their lives they could appear in court (military) and testify against a white man. The master's lash had given way to "the impersonal sovereignty of the law."

"No negro who has ever been a soldier," a Northern official wrote in 1865, "can again be imposed upon; they have learnt what it is to be free and they will infuse their feelings into others."[12]

Theodore ("Teedie") Roosevelt was born October 27, 1858, at 28 East Twentieth Street, to a wealthy, civic-minded twenty-seven-year-old New York City importer who had married an exquisite Southern belle reared on a Georgia plantation worked by slaves. On April 12, 1861, when rebel cannon fired on Fort Sumter, the frail, restless, asthmatic two-year-old and his six-year-old sister, Anna ("Bamie"), had been joined by a fourteen-month-old brother, Elliott ("Ellie"), and their pregnant mother was carrying the last of the flock, Corinne ("Conie"). Teedie found himself torn between love for his Lincoln Republican father, for whom he had been named ("the best man I ever knew"), and his Confederate mother ("a sweet, gracious, beautiful Southern woman"), whose two brothers were fighting under the Stars and Bars.[13]

From his mother and her sister, Annie Bulloch, the boy heard so many stories about Roswell, the family home, that when, as president, he visited the Georgia plantation for the first time, he recalled feeling "as if I already knew every nook and corner of it, and as if it were haunted by the ghosts of all the men and women who had lived there. I do not mean merely by my own family, I mean the slaves."[14]

The house, he recalled in his autobiography, "was on the line of Sherman's march to the sea, and pretty much everything in it that was portable was taken by the boys in blue, including most of the books in the library." Foraker

Private Foraker, Co. A., 89th O. V. I., Campaign Picture, 1883

was one of "the boys in blue" who marched across Georgia, but the route his outfit took spared him the temptation to "borrow" a book from the Bulloch library.[15]

None of the Roosevelts, including Teedie's godlike father, saw combat in the War Between the States. Theodore Senior, thanks to his young friend John Hay, Lincoln's secretary, obtained an appointment to an allotment commission created to persuade soldiers to send home a portion of their pay. The elder Roosevelt worked hard to improve the lot of the fighting men and their families, but he remained a civilian. He hired a substitute to do his fighting.[16]

"To know how dreadful war is you must see it for yourself," Foraker wrote his parents from Fort Donelson in early February, 1863, a few days after the 89th Ohio had reached Tennessee in time to rescue a battered Illinois regiment. The Ohio volunteers later were assigned to the Army of the Cumberland and took part in thirty-one skirmishes and battles, including Chickamauga, Missionary Ridge, and Atlanta.[17]

"A great piece of good fortune" spared Lieutenant Foraker the carnage of Chickamauga. He and two other officers had been dispatched to Ohio that fall to "escort back to the front our regiment's quota of the men who were then about to be drafted." When the recruiters reached Columbus, they discovered that opposition to the draft was so strong the government had decided it was better to try to make do with volunteers.[18]

A week after Lincoln's reelection, General William Tecumseh Sherman left Atlanta in flames and began his devastating march to the sea. The right wing followed the railroad to the southeast, toward Jonesboro. Major General Henry W. Slocum, with Foraker as his aide-de-camp, moved eastward, toward Madison. The two forces met at Milledgeville, the state capital, on November 23, a few hours after the governor and legislators had hastily decamped.

"Upon somebody's suggestion," Foraker recalled in his old age, "a mock special session of the legislature of Georgia was convened, composed of officers of Slocum's command. I sat as a member and voted for a resolution which was unanimously adopted, repealing an ordinance of secession and restoring the state to the Union. That was my first legislative experience, and it is needless to say I greatly enjoyed it."[19]

"I was not present at these frolics," General Sherman wrote in his *Memoirs*, "but heard of them at the time and enjoyed the joke."[20]

Slocum's forces were in Smithfield, North Carolina, when word of Lee's surrender arrived and in Raleigh when they learned of the president's death. The national press was running front-page stories of the trial of his "assassins" when Captain Foraker was mustered out of the army on June 14, 1865. He had served thirty-five months and traveled some 3,000 miles, more than 1,700 of them on foot, "with knapsack on the back and enemy in the front."[21]

General Sherman, his brother John recalled in his *Recollections of Forty Years in the House, Senate and Cabinet*, spoke of Foraker "in the highest terms of praise," recalling that at Missionary Ridge, the youthful lieutenant "commanded two companies and led them over the ridge into the enemy's works, being the first man of his regiment over the ridge."[22]

At a reunion of the Army of the Tennessee held in Cincinnati in 1889, General Sherman turned to Governor Foraker, who was running for re-election, and reminisced:

> *I well remember you as you rode into my quarters when Joe Johnson struck my left in North Carolina. You burst upon us in a grove of pines, with a message from Slocum, saying that he needed to be reinforced. I recall your figure, sir, splashed with mud, your spurs that were red, your splendid horse, hard-ridden and panting, and how you sat erect; and I shall not forget the soldier that you looked and were. . . . I marked you well then, and thought of the honors that were your due. You have gloriously attained them, and I believe and approve that higher, the highest honors, await you.[23]*

Of the more than 1,000 volunteers in his regiment who started out together, only 231, rank and file, returned home, "and among them all there could scarce be found a corporal's guard who could not show where at least one bullet of the enemy had struck them." Foraker came home to Hamilton County shortly before his nineteenth birthday. When he came of age, in 1867, he cast his first vote in favor of an amendment striking the word "white" from Ohio's Jim Crow constitution.[24]

"We had been heading towards an encounter for a long time, Foraker and I," Julia Bundy Foraker recalled long after her husband's death. "He had only a year's start on me in life and we grew up on farms but a short motoring distance apart today, but separated then, as by a continent, by the worst roads in the world."[25]

They met in 1868 in Delaware, Ohio, where Captain Foraker had signed up for the classical curriculum at Ohio Wesleyan University before moving on to Cornell to begin the study of law. The young veteran felt a strong commitment to see to it that "there should be no frittering away of the results of the struggle for the Union." With a Democrat, Horatio Seymour, running for president on a platform Foraker considered "hostile to all that had been done for the reconstruction of the [Southern] states," he felt obliged to speak up on behalf of General Grant, the Republican nominee. This, his first political speech, came when Republicans had set out to reconstruct the

South. Their reforms, a Democratic newspaper had vowed, would "last as long as the bayonets, which ushered them into being, shall keep them in existence, and not one day longer."[26]

Julia Bundy, a devout Republican enrolled at nearby Ohio Wesleyan Female College, was in the audience the night Captain Foraker spoke. He "was young and needed a haircut," she remembered, "but he inspired me with a curiously heightened interest in the campaign. I thought I'd attend all meetings."[27]

The two students were walled off from one another by Methodist morality. "There was to be no dancing; above all, there was to be no waltzing. 'Hugging up,' our preacher called it, 'two strangers huggin' up.'" Only on Saturday night, "Reception Night," were the young women allowed to receive gentlemen callers. "One hour! Girls who had no beaux to receive hung over the bannister—'reception door must always be left open'—and jeered with mischievous eyes. Mrs. Donelson, governess of the college, received with us during the whole of those racing sixty minutes. When nine o'clock struck, her hand was already on a bell—irreverently, the 'cow bell'; she rang it sharply."[28]

"When I speak of 'We 3,'" eleven-year-old Teedie Roosevelt wrote in his diary in December, 1869, "I mean Ellie, Conie and I. When I say 'they three' or the three big people I mean Papa, Mama and Bamie." Teedie considered himself a child, along with his younger brother, Elliott (who would become Eleanor Roosevelt's father), and his still younger sister, Corinne (Conie), but Bamie (a nickname dating back to an uncle's letter from Italy shortly after Anna's birth asking about the "bambina") was ranked among the "big people" even though she was less than four years older than the diarist. As a teenager, studying in France, she made the wistful remark, "I do not think I ever quite let myself be young."[29]

Conie's closest childhood friend, Edith Kermit Carow, was fond of Teedie. She "played house" with the young naturalist and put up with his dead birds, frogs, snakes, and mice. When the Roosevelts reached Paris on a European trip in 1869, the boy, who later would later use his "bully pulpit" on Pennsylvania Avenue to plump for simplified spelling, confided to his diary: "In the evening mama showed me the portrait of Eidieth Carow and her face stired up in me homesickness and longings for the past which will come again never, alack never."[30]

"Theodore," his father said in the fall of 1870, when the family returned from its European tour, "you have the mind, but not the body, and without the help of the body, the mind cannot go as far as it should. You must make your body. It is hard drudgery to make one's body, but I know you will do it."[31]

Teedie worked out every day at Woods Gymnasium, then came home to get in some additional exercise with the athletic equipment his father had fitted out in the second-floor piazza. In his diary during August, 1871, for the first time in years, there was no mention of illness. He continued the regimen that winter and, with private tutors, began studying English, French, German, and Latin. Edith saw no reason to join Teedie in his gymnastic workouts, but, he was pleased to note, "she was a girl you could talk to about books and birds and animals, and collecting specimens."[32]

Cincinnati's population had climbed to 200,000 in the summer of 1869, when Foraker, having graduated from Cornell, was reading law in the offices of Sloane and Donham. By the time he was admitted to the bar, in October, he and Julia were engaged and she had become captivated by a new fad—the sewing machine. "It was," she recalled in an age of radios and refrigerators, "complicated, awkward (the sewing plate was raised very high) and costly, but I spent entranced hours at it. I had a romantic feeling just then about neatly-hemmed sheets, towels and teacloths."[33]

When Foraker hung up his shingle in "The Queen City of the West" four years after the war's end, litigants could choose among three hundred lawyers. The young bachelor earned $600 that first year. When he married Julia the following fall (October 4), the bride's father, shaken by the prospect of losing his unsalaried housekeeper, offered the young couple half the family farm if the bridegroom could be persuaded to run it. Julia never forgot his prophecy: "If we stuck safely to the farm, he argued, my husband might, with luck, some day become judge of Jackson County."[34]

Foraker joked about the tears his father-in-law shed at his daughter's wedding. "Particularly, when you are doing so well," the bridegroom pointed out to him, and Julia agreed, but in the first year of their marriage the young lawyer brought home only $400 in fees, considerably less than his father-in-law had spent on the bride's trousseau. Coal deposits later put a $100,000 price tag on the land the bride and groom had turned down.[35]

After having spent their first two years in a Cincinnati boarding house on Elm Street, the Forakers were living in suburban Norwood at the outset of the 1873 depression. When reformers, radicals, and social workers demanded a public-works program designed to relieve unemployment by putting the jobless to work building city streets, parks, playgrounds, and rapid-transit systems, urban editors denounced the program's supporters as "disgusting," "crazy," "loud-mouthed gasometers," who were ready "to chop off the heads of every man addicted to clean linen." The unemployed were advised "to quietly abide their time till the natural laws of trade" restored prosperity.[36]

Julia Foraker rocked cradles, copied legal documents for her husband, and struggled with the Buckeye Cook Book, "buoyed by the pleasantest of convictions, that of getting ahead." Her husband attended his first Republican State Convention at Columbus in 1875 as a member of a Hamilton County delegation supporting Superior Court Judge Alphonso Taft for governor.[37]

The judge, taking a strong stand against state support for parochial schools, lost out to Rutherford B. Hayes, a popular ex-congressman and two-term governor with a splendid war record who had helped bring about ratification of the Fifteenth Amendment ("The right of the citizens of the United States to vote shall not be denied or abridged by the United States or by any State on account of race, color, or previous condition of servitude.")

In Philadelphia, birthplace of the Declaration of Independence, plans were afoot for a magnificent centennial exhibition when the first day of 1876 was greeted at midnight by bells, sirens, and whistles from the city's churches, ships, and factories. Millions of unemployed breadwinners awakened to another bleak winter day in the country's worst depression.

In the South, whites and blacks were caught up in a Reconstruction nightmare of white-hooded night riders; in the west the Sioux, sold out by President Grant's secretary of war, were six months from their confrontation with the 7th Cavalry in the valley of the Little Bighorn. In Jacksonville, Illinois, Silas Bryan's son Billy was trying to articulate more distinctly by taking to the woods near Whipple Academy and, like Demosthenes, reciting long, difficult passages with his mouth full of pebbles.[38]

Americans bundled their children off to Philadelphia to gorge on popped corn and stare at George Washington's false teeth, Mr. Bell's telephone, "a new floor-cloth called linoleum," and the latest thing in typewriting machines (for twenty-five cents a "type girl" would run off a personal letter). Mark Twain, the spiritual progenitor of present-day hackers, found his way around the machine's keyboard by tapping out the 1867 sentence devised by a court reporter, Charles E. Weller of Milwaukee: "Now is the time for all good men to come to the aid of their party."[39]

Women protested their inability to join those "good men" at the polling places despite a six-year-old Constitutional amendment providing access to the ballot regardless of "race, color, or previous condition of servitude." A dozen years after Emancipation, Negroes also were being disfranchised, particularly in states where their votes could control the outcome of an election.

In the fall of 1875, when General Hayes was campaigning for another term as governor of Ohio, a state in which the black vote was crucial, Mississippi Negroes were being slaughtered in Republican counties, a bloody prelude to a disputed national election of a Republican president whose critics would accuse him of "abandoning" the Negro. As H. Wayne Morgan points out, however, "The whole process of American history abandoned the Negro."[40]

Governor Hayes, Ohio's favorite son, was every delegate's choice for vice president when the Republican National Convention began its deliberations in Cincinnati on Wednesday, June 14, 1876, three days after James Gillespie Blaine, the strongest contender for the presidential nomination, had suffered "a stroke of apoplexy" on his way to church in Washington.

The charismatic Man from Maine, Speaker of the House and soon to be a United States senator, had just made a vigorous but less-than-convincing defense of his involvement with $64,000 in Union Pacific bonds. When he quickly recovered his health and sent his supporters a reassuring message in his own handwriting, his enemies accused him of play-acting. A story filed by a Washington correspondent of the *New York Sun* appeared under the headline "Blaine Feigns a Faint."[41]

Foraker sat in on the proceedings at Exposition Hall, a wooden structure with twin towers resembling "an ambitious and disappointed railroad depot." It was his first national convention, and, given his Free Soil heritage, he may have arranged to be present when Frederick Douglass came to the podium to describe what Emancipation and Constitutional enfranchisement had meant for the black man in the South. Freed from the slaveholder's lash only "to be subject to the slaveholder's shotgun," he called on the delegates to select a nominee who would give assurance that "black men shall walk to the ballot box in safety, even if we have to bring a bayonet behind us."[42]

Disfranchised women were represented by Sarah J. Spencer of the National Women's Suffrage Association, who reminded the delegates that their party had "emancipated 4,000,000 of human beings and established universal suffrage," but, she asked, "where were the 10,000,000 of women citizens of this Republic?" Mrs. Stowe agreed. "The question of Women and her Sphere," she had one of her *Chimney-Corner* characters point out, "is now, perhaps, the greatest of the age."[43]

To the end of his life, Foraker cherished the memory of Robert Ingersoll's nominating speech: "Like an armed warrior, like a plumed knight, James G. Blaine marched down the halls of the American Congress and threw his shining lance full and fair against the brazen foreheads of the defamers of his country and every maligner of his fair reputation. For the Republican Party to desert that gallant man now is as though an army should desert their general upon the field of battle."[44]

In the course of his political life the "Plumed Knight" was a prominent contender for the Republican nomination at five national conventions, but, a biographer writes, "the testimony of his family and friends corroborates that of his own letters and public utterances that it was only in 1876 that he really desired the nomination." Roscoe Conkling, the vain, virulent, overbearing New York Republican boss, was determined to block it. He had never forgotten or forgiven Blaine's sarcastic reference in a Congressional debate to "his majestic, supereminent, turkey-gobbler strut."[45]

Aside from Blaine and Conkling, the Ohio contingent backing Governor Hayes for the top spot on the national ticket had to contend with Oliver P. Morton of Indiana, the favorite of Negro delegates from the South, and Benjamin Helm Bristow, Grant's secretary of the treasury, who had initiated the exposé of the whiskey ring. Bristow was the candidate of sixty New York reformers, headed by Theodore Roosevelt, whose seventeen-year-old namesake, back home at 6 West 57th Street, was putting his spring dancing lessons to good use that summer while preparing to enter Harvard in the fall.

To the elder Roosevelt, bracing himself for the distasteful task of making his first political speech, virtually everything about Conkling was repugnant. No text of Roosevelt's talk survives, but he wrote his daughter: "The crowd cheered violently. We were all in perfect harmony." On the seventh ballot the delegates chose Governor Hayes, and Roosevelt returned home, pleased at having played a part in derailing Conkling's nomination.

He relaxed at Oyster Bay, seemingly unconcerned about having, like Blaine, incurred the enmity of New York's malevolent boss.[46]

The Democrats pitted Hayes against Samuel J. Tilden, "a sober, grey man, whose hallmark was a devious silence," which, like Grant's, was a shield, often mistaken "for strength and wisdom." He had grown rich in the practice of corporate law and on the same day could "endow a library and tell a clerk who asked about vacations: 'Your vacation will begin at once, and continue indefinitely.'" He had prosecuted the Tweed Ring, but his claim to be a reformer was regarded as "preposterous."[47]

When a group of Harvard freshmen were demonstrating for the Republican candidate in Cambridge that fall, chanting, "Hurrah for Hayes and Honest Ways!" a Democratic senior shouted from a second-floor window: "Hush up, you blooming freshmen!" Albert Bushnell Hart, an influential historian in the making (W. E. B. Du Bois and Oswald Garrison Villard would be among his graduate students) was impressed by the indignant reaction of a loyal Republican classmate, "small but firmly knit," who "slammed his torch to the street. His fists quivered like steel springs and swished through the air as if plunging a hole through a mattress. 'It's Roosevelt from New York,' someone said. I made an effort to know Roosevelt better from that moment."[48]

William Howard Taft, a year older than Roosevelt, was a Yale sophomore that fall. He would be affectionately remembered by classmates as the university's "most admired and respected man." Roosevelt, according to a biographer of both men, "did not conform to the Harvard pattern as Taft conformed to Yale. He was eager, hurried, and nervous, when it was the Harvard manner to be indifferent and composed. He bristled with ideas. He kept interrupting his instructors by asking questions. He rushed about the Harvard Yard at a half trot and was, to his classmates, a rather alien figure." Taft was "judicial beyond the comprehension of a Theodore Roosevelt." In 1878, when he graduated second in a class of 132, Taft prophesied that in the coming age there would be "no political giants because of the absence of emergencies to create them."[49]

In his diary on October 22, Hayes wrote, "Only two Sundays more before the Presidential election" and reflected on the dangers of "a contested result." On December 6, when members of the Electoral College gathered in state capitals to verify the outcome of the election, four states (Louisiana,

Florida, South Carolina and Oregon) submitted conflicting tallies, a contingency for which the Founding Fathers had made no provision. The electoral votes, under the Constitution, went to the president of the Senate, who in a joint session of Congress opened and counted them. No clue had been left as to whether the president of the Senate or the members of the two houses of Congress should decide how disputed votes were to be tallied.[50]

Conkling, who had taken no part in the campaign, sent word to Hayes in mid-December that the price of his support was repudiation of such meddlesome reformers as Carl Schurz, along with the understanding that the organization's New York customhouse appointees would not be disturbed. Hayes, aware of the boss's "lack of hearty support," responded with a bland promise to "deal fairly and justly by all elements of the party."[51]

Meanwhile, Ohio's Republican Congressman James A. Garfield informed Hayes, some "leading southern Democrats in Congress, especially those who were old Whigs," were ready to part company with northern associates who had been "invincible in peace and invisible in war." Garfield suggested that Hayes, "in some discreet way," let the Southerners know that he intended to show them "kind consideration," a euphemism for home rule and for patronage (a Democratic postmaster general in the Hayes cabinet would be appreciated).[52]

The outcome of the electoral commission's deliberations became apparent on February 9, when a tie-breaking vote gave Florida's contested ballots to Hayes. "The indications still are that I am to go to W[ashington]," Hayes noted in his diary Sunday, February 18, after he had been awarded Louisiana's electoral votes. "I talked yesterday with Fred. Douglass and Mr. [James] Poindexter, both colored, on the Southern question. I told them my views. They approved. Mr. Douglass gave me many useful hints about the whole subject. My course is a firm assertion and maintenance of the rights of the colored people of the South, as according to the 13th, 14th and 15th amendments."[53]

Within the first two months of the Hayes presidency, however, federal troops posted at the South Carolina and Louisiana statehouses were ordered back to their barracks, and a black Louisianan lamented that the whole South "had got into the hands of the very men who held us as slaves." The conservative *Chicago Tribune* proclaimed an end to "the long controversy of the black man," a sentiment echoed by the liberal editor of the *Nation:* "The negro will disappear from the field of national politics. Henceforth, the nation, as a nation, will have nothing more to do with him."[54]

Four months later the president returned from a nineteen-day tour through Ohio, Kentucky, Tennessee, Georgia, and Virginia. "Received everywhere heartily," he wrote in his diary. "The country is again one and united!" At the start of the 1878 campaign, however, he learned from Joseph H. Rainey, a black South Carolina congressman, that "the Whites are resorting to intimidation and violence to prevent the colored people from organizing for the elections." After the elections, Hayes noted that in both South Carolina and Louisiana, Negroes had been kept from the polls by "violence of the most atrocious character." The Democrats not only succeeded in retaining control of the House; they also won a majority in the Senate, which would enable them to kill Administration requests for money to enforce election laws.[55]

With the removal of federal troops from the doorsteps of lawmakers in South Carolina and Louisiana in the spring of 1877, Hayes could "hope for peace" and turn his attention to civil-service reform. That summer, while New York's Senator Conkling was in Europe, sneering at "President Rutherfraud" and his "snivel service crowd," a commission appointed by Secretary of the Treasury John Sherman and headed by John Jay, grandson of the first chief justice, wound up its investigation of the occasionally corrupt and generally inefficient New York customhouse, where department chiefs intimated that some of the men "appointed to perform the delicate duties of the appraiser's office, requiring the special qualities of an expert, were better fitted to hoe and to plow."[56]

On September 6, Sherman wrote New York's governor, informing him that the three leading officials in the customhouse would have to be replaced. And, he added, the Administration hoped that the politically powerful Collector of Customs Chester Arthur would be "recognized in a most complimentary way." When Arthur declined an offer to resign and take over a Paris consulship, Sherman pointed out that his resignation "might be inferred from your letters on file" and suggested it would "be better for you to tender it formally before your successor is appointed."[57]

Three weeks later, when New York Republicans convened in Rochester, Senator Conkling expressed his contempt for "the dilettanti and carpet-knights of politics," who "masquerade as reformers, while "their real object is office and plunder." Hayes waited almost a month before returning the senator's fire. On October 24 he nominated Jay's forty-six-year-old friend Theodore Roosevelt to replace Chet Arthur. The names of two other customhouse nominees were submitted to the Senate to serve as surveyor and naval officer. The nominations were referred to the Committee on Commerce, presided over by Roscoe Conkling.[58]

Hayes recorded his defeat on December 13: "In the language of the press 'Senator Conkling has won a great victory over the Administration.' My N.Y. nominations were rejected 31 to 25."[59]

"We cannot stand so corrupt a government for any great length of time," the elder Roosevelt wrote "Dear Old Theodore" at Harvard, and expressed "fear" for his son's future, leaving him in ignorance of the intestinal cancer that would bring his life to an agonizing end on February 9, 1878.[60]

Nine months after "the blackest day of my life," Theodore wrote his younger sister, Corinne, that he was "going to drive over to Dick Saltonstalls, where we shall go out walking with Miss Rose Saltonstall and Miss Alice Lee." He had met Alice Lee the month before, on October 18, "and loved her as soon as I saw her sweet, fair young face."[61]

In the spring of 1880, while Theodore and Alice were preparing for their fall wedding, Bamie and her friend Sara Delano were reconciling themselves to the probability of ending their lives as spinsters. At one of Mrs. Roosevelt's 57th Street dinner parties, Sara met James Roosevelt, a widower twice her age who, his hostess noted, "talked to her the whole time" and "never took his eyes off her!" The Hudson River squire invited Sara and Bamie to Hyde Park on May 7, and Franklin Delano Roosevelt grew up hearing his mother say that if she had not accepted that invitation to Hyde Park, "I should now be 'old Miss Delano' after a rather sad life!" They were married at the Delano estate on the Hudson that October.[62]

Theodore and Alice were married in the Unitarian Church at Brookline, Massachusetts, on October 27, the groom's twenty-second birthday. His bride was nineteen. "I have been living in a dream of delight," the bridegroom wrote his mother from Oyster Bay.[63]

Chapter Two

"The colored people of the South have been
robbed of their forty electoral votes."

—*Joseph Benson Foraker,*
1885

While Foraker was building his law practice and "dabbling along the edges" of Ohio politics in 1880, Theodore Roosevelt was working on his first book, *The Naval War of 1812*, and walking fifty-four blocks down Fifth Avenue to the Columbia Law School, where the young Harvard graduate "distinguished himself for his egotism and energetic questioning in lectures."[1]

On November 2 the bewitched bridegroom tore himself away from his bride long enough to be driven over to East Norwich, where he cast his first vote in a presidential election. It went, of course, to the Republican candidate, Senator-elect James Abram Garfield, one of the corpulent, bearded war heroes bred for the Executive Mansion in "The United States of Ohio," where, "with its polyglot population and varied economy, only the political compromisers stayed alive."[2]

Garfield's nomination had thrown the Democrats off stride. Looking forward to confronting a major figure of the Grand Old Party, as it had come to be called, they "counted on fights among Republicans to help their cause." As a result, when Democrats assembled in Cincinnati, the most impressive feature of their convention was its confusion. The delegates settled on General Winfield Scott Hancock, prompting the *New York Times* to ask its readers if any of them knew what the candidate "thinks about the principles of finance, about the tariff, civil service reform, interstate commerce or free ships?"[3]

President Hayes marveled at the peculiar constitution of a political "party which sends rebel brigadiers to Congress because of their rebellion, and which nominates a Union General as its candidate for president because of his loyalty."[4]

In the electoral college, Garfield won the presidency with a comfortable lead (214 to 155), but of the 9,200,000 popular votes cast, he received only 7,368 more than his Democratic opponent. Hancock carried no northern state and Garfield no southern state.[5]

White supremacist Democrats, running on a platform which called for a "free ballot" but made no mention of Negroes, had solidified the South. Republicans, backed by black voters in the North and the Middle West, had demonstrated their ability to win the presidency without support from below the Mason-Dixon line. The fate of the southern Negro had become incidental to a national victory for the party of the Emancipator.[6]

"The elevation of the Negro race from slavery to full rights of citizenship is the most important political change we have known since the adoption of the Constitution in 1787," Garfield said in his inaugural address, and pointed out that "it has liberated the master as well as the slave from a relation which wronged and enfeebled both."[7]

Replying to allegations that "in many places honest local government is impossible if the mass of uneducated Negroes are allowed to vote," he agreed that "bad local government is certainly a great evil, which ought to be prevented," but, he contended, "to violate the freedom and sanctities of the suffrage is more than an evil. It is a crime which, if persisted in, will destroy the Government itself."

Four months later, on July 2, as Garfield and Secretary of State Blaine were heading for a train in the Baltimore & Potomac railroad station, Charles Julius Guiteau, a demented, self-styled lawyer, theologian, and politician, whipped out "an ugly-looking weapon, of what is known as the five-barreled British bull-dog pattern, of 44-caliber, with a white bone handle" and fired two shots at the president. One bullet pierced a sleeve, the other lodged in the back muscle near the spinal column. The president might have survived the wound (hot bullets are self-sterilizing) had he not been done in by physicians poking about with nonsterile instruments.[8]

The tragedy would mean "work in the future for those who wish their country well," Roosevelt wrote in his diary while he and Alice were taking a European holiday. Back home, a political friend, Joe Murray, who had gained control of their silk-stocking legislative district, proposed Theodore as its candidate for the Assembly. He won by an impressive margin, leading the party's ticket by 600 votes.[9]

The twenty-three-year-old patrician, who later would point out in his memoirs that a "young man of my bringing up and convictions could join only the Republican party," found himself working with farmers, liquor dealers, mechanics, a butcher, a pawnbroker, three newspapermen, and thirty-five lawyers. He dismissed the Democrats as "vicious, stupid-looking scoundrels," wrote off a senior Republican as a "bad old fellow," and re-marked that another had "the same idea of public life and civil service that a vulture has of dead sheep." Murray, his political mentor, reared in the Tammany faith, devoutly believed that not to share the spoils when you got into office was "almost as dishonorable as not to pay your debts."[10]

An Albany reporter, observing the Manhattan dude, with his new gold-rimmed spectacles and gold watch fob, wondered, "What on earth will New York send us next?" In the Democratic press, he was "his Lordship" and "the exquisite Mr. Roosevelt." His trousers were cut so tight, the *World* reported, that when making his "gyrations," only the joints above the belt were bent. A reporter for the *New York Times*, however, assured his Repub-lican readers that the brash young legislator was "a good-hearted man to shake hands with, and he had a good honest laugh." Although "green as grass," he was a hard worker who "obviously cared and wanted to learn."[11]

On January 1, 1882, the day Roosevelt took office in Albany, Grover Cleve-land, a 280-pound Union Democrat who, like Theodore's father, had paid a substitute to fight his war, assumed his new duties as mayor of Buffalo and "quickly gained the reputation of being a no-nonsense executive who was an enemy of graft and the friend of the taxpayer." A year later, Governor Cleveland, after delivering a bromidic inaugural address at Albany, was turn-ing to the titular head of the "Roosevelt Republicans" for advice on legisla-tive matters.[12]

"The Governor would sit large, solid, and phlegmatic, listening gravely to the energetic utterances of the mercurial young man, but signifying neither assent nor dissent," the *Brooklyn Eagle* reported, and Cleveland remarked, "There is great sense in a lot of what he says, but there is such a cocksuredness about him that he stirs up doubt in me all the time."[13]

New York's "Cyclone Assemblyman" was fussing over a pregnant wife and drawing up plans for a three-story, hilltop mansion at Oyster Bay before he headed west to the Dakota Badlands, where he would shoot a buffalo and astonish his guide by doing an Indian war dance around the carcass. When he got back to New York with his buffalo head early in the fall of 1883, he sublet the brownstone and moved Alice into 6 West Fifty-seventh Street, where she was joined by her sister-in-law, Corinne Robinson, who had recently had a baby. They set up a third-floor nursery for both infants. The same matriarchal roof also sheltered Theodore's mother and his older sister, Bamie.[14]

The man of the house was in Albany on February 13, 1884, when he received a telegram at the Assembly's morning session. Alice had given birth to a daughter. After much handshaking and backslapping, he went back to his work with the Cities Committee and managed to report fourteen bills. Several hours later he received a telegram giving him the crushing substance of what his younger brother, Elliott, would tell their sister, Corinne, that afternoon, an hour before Theodore arrived: "Mother is dying, and Alice is dying too."[15]

"The light has gone out of my life," the young orphan-widower wrote in a February 14 diary entry otherwise bare except for a large X. He rephrased the sentiment in a privately printed memorial: "And when my heart's dearest died, the light went from my life for ever."[16]

On Sunday, February 17, three days after her mother's death, the baby was christened Alice Lee and turned over to Bamie, her beloved "Aunty Bye." Two days later her father went back to work in Albany. "I think I should go mad if I were not employed," he wrote his reformer friend Carl Schurz in reply to a letter of condolence. He could not bring himself to speak of his loss, then or later. Neither Alice Lee Roosevelt nor her acid-tongued daughter, Alice Roosevelt Longworth, appears in the *Autobiography*.[17]

By 1883, Foraker's law practice was sufficiently well-established to enable him to make his home in a quiet residential section of Walnut Hills. He had been elected to the Superior Court of Cincinnati and served three years of his four-year term before resigning because of illness. Some months later, fully recovered, he was back in his law office. Now a prominent and well-paid member of the bar, Foraker caught the eye of Ohio's Republican governor, "Calico Charlie" Foster, a prosperous dry-goods merchant who had decided not to run for a third term. His attempts to regulate the liquor traffic would focus the wrath of brewers, distillers, and thirsty constituents on any Republican candidate and make his defeat inevitable. Foster picked Foraker as his candidate rather than sacrifice a more eminent Republican.[18]

A tall, slender, boyish thirty-seven, sporting a fashionable drooping moustache, Foraker made the rounds of the state's political leaders and won over their most prominent members, including Major William McKinley, serving his third term in Congress. Foraker got the nomination, but when Republicans split over the liquor issue, he lost the election to a Cincinnati friend and fellow-member of the bar, George Hoadly, a "wet Democrat." Julia characterized him as "a sledge-hammer fighter, but a fair one."[19]

Foraker resumed his law practice which, he insisted, was now so prosperous he would give no more thought to politics. The following summer, however, he headed for Chicago to attend his first national convention as a participant (he had watched three others from the galleries). For the first time he met Marcus Alonzo Hanna, a rich, politically ambitious Cleveland, Ohio, iron merchant. Both men were backing Senator John Sherman, who had asked Foraker to place his name in nomination.[20]

Foraker also had his first encounter with Theodore Roosevelt and his erudite friend Henry Cabot Lodge, who at thirty-four, had been an editor, with Henry Adams, of *North American Review*, collaborated on a history of Anglo-Saxon law, and written biographies of Alexander Hamilton and Daniel Webster. He was currently chairman of the Massachusetts Republican Party and a congressional candidate. Foraker preserved a newspaper clipping describing the way the two upper-class Easterners "applauded with the tips of their fingers, held immediately in front of their noses." Roosevelt, according to another clipping, "may have ability, but he has also an inexhaustible supply of insufferable dudism and conceit, and he has a brassy impudence that will some day be fittingly rebuked."[21]

Roosevelt and Lodge had come to the 1884 convention opposed not only to President Arthur, who presided over a bitterly divided party, but also—even more vehemently—to James G. Blaine, whose "admirers are more numerous than those of any other man," the *New York Times* had noted. When Tom Platt, never one to miss a bandwagon, called on Conkling to tell him he was supporting the Man From Maine, the wealthy corporation lawyer reminded him, "You know what Blaine did to us," and wasted no additional words on the matter.[22]

On the second day of the proceedings, Foraker, Roosevelt, and Lodge joined forces in a move to challenge the national committee's choice of a temporary convention chairman committed to Blaine. "We would assert the right of the convention to name its own chairman by nominating for that office the Honorable John R. Lynch, a distinguished colored man of national prominence, who was a delegate from the state of Mississippi," Foraker recalled in his memoirs.[23]

Lodge made the nominating speech, and Roosevelt seconded it, invoking the memory of Abraham Lincoln, who "broke the fetters of the slave." Lynch was elected, and Foraker, facing the most important assemblage he had ever addressed, nominated Senator Sherman in a "carefully prepared extemporaneous speech." It was repeatedly interrupted with generous rounds of applause, but, his biographer notes, an "impulsive reference to 'that brilliant genius from Maine' precipitated a boisterous demonstration lasting almost fifteen minutes. Foraker stoutly maintained then and later that the Blaine reference was 'innocently' made; his political opponents contended that he said it purposely to show his own interest in Blaine and his willingness to lead the Ohio Sherman faction over to the Plumed Knight. Certainly an experienced politician would not have made such a statement."[24]

On the fourth ballot, when Blaine picked up the 411 votes he needed for nomination, McKinley asked Roosevelt to second a motion to make it unanimous. Roosevelt refused. When Foraker got back to his law office, he wrote Sherman a letter describing the New York Assemblyman as "a young man of rather peculiar qualities," who "has not quite as much discretion as he will have after a while." Lodge, pictured in the press as "a tall young man with crisp, short hair, full beard and an appearance of half-shut eyes," struck Foraker as "not only absolutely honest in all that he endeavored to do, but he is a man of culture and a man of most excellent judgment. There is nothing 'cranky' about him."[25]

Democrats assembled in Chicago's Exposition Hall in July, sedated by partisan clichés, came alive when General Edward S. Bragg of Wisconsin took over the platform and delivered a thundering oration in which he spoke up for young western Democrats who loved New York's governor "not only for himself, for his character, for his integrity and judgment and iron will, but they love him most for the enemies he has made." He concluded with two short, compelling sentences: "The party wants some new life. They have followed old leaders to death."[26]

Only two ballots were needed to choose Governor Cleveland as the party's candidate to reclaim the Executive Mansion after a hiatus of more than twenty years.

After a restful and reflective stay at his Dakota ranch, Roosevelt announced in Boston on July 19 that he would support the Republican ticket, but, he wrote Lodge the following month, "I do not think we need to take any active part in the campaign." Later that summer he was denounced for the first—but by no means the last—time by Joseph Pulitzer, the brilliant, moody owner of the *World*, New York's most influential Democratic paper. By voting for "a man he admits to be venal and corrupt, and for whom he blushes to speak," the *World* declared on August 26, Roosevelt had revealed himself as "a reform fraud and a Jack-in-the-box politician who disappears whenever his boss applies a gentle pressure to his aspiring head."[27]

Twenty-one-year-old William Randolph Hearst, a Harvard undergraduate, cast his first vote that fall, and when returns showed Cleveland overcoming Blaine's early lead, the exuberant young Democrat hired a brass band, organized a parade, and "bought wagon-loads of beer, set off fireworks in all directions, and raised such a red-blazing, ear-splitting, rip-roaring, all-night racket as to scandalize old Cambridge." He was suspended and spent what would have been his senior year at Harvard as a reporter for the *World*. He admired its mingling of lurid sex and crime stories with well-written, well-documented attacks on political and corporate corruption.[28]

The campaign took a nasty turn when the scavenger press feasted on Governor Cleveland's "woman scrape," as he called it. The bachelor candidate, in his earlier days, had taken up with a widow named Maria Halpin. When she gave birth to a son whose paternity was in doubt, Cleveland accepted responsibility for the child. He never saw the woman or her son again, but when Maria suffered a mental breakdown, he arranged for her institutional care.[29]

"Whatever you do, tell the truth," Cleveland instructed his campaign strategists, and in his diary he noted that "the policy of not cringing was not only necessary but the only way."[30]

A Baptist minister in Buffalo portrayed the Cleveland-Blaine campaign as a choice "between the brothel and the family . . . between the depredation of woman and due honor, protection, and love of our mothers, sisters and daughters." Republicans took to the hustings with baby carriages, calling out in falsetto voices, "Ma! Ma! Where's My Pa!"[31]

When the late returns confirmed Cleveland's victory, Democrats were chanting:

> *Hurrah for Maria! Hurrah for the kid!*
> *I voted for Cleveland,*
> *And damned glad I did!*[32]

Cleveland had carried Connecticut, Indiana, New Jersey, and Delaware along with the Solid South, which gave him 183 of the 201 electoral votes he needed to win the presidency. Thanks in no small measure to Pulitzer's *World*, Tammany Hall, and some backstage work by Roscoe Conkling, New York's 36 votes gave the Democrats their margin of victory. "I look upon the four years next to come as a dreadful self-inflicted penance for the good of my country," said the president-elect, and announced his intention "to cultivate the Christian virtue of charity toward all men except the dirty class that defiled themselves with filthy scandal."[33]

After more than two decades in the wilderness, the Democrats were now back in command of the Executive Branch and held a majority in the House of Representatives, where appropriations of federal funds originated. Southern whites were jubilant. "Not since 1876, when bayonet rule was overthrown and the people of the South regained their liberties, has this community been so profoundly moved," a New Orleans paper reported for the edification of its white readers, who, as a happy spokesmen put it, had now been offered "escape from captivity and humiliation."[34]

The Democratic party, as Hal Williams points out, "seemed woefully unprepared to rule, tired and fragmented, lacking focus and discipline, with neither a coherent national purpose nor experienced leadership." The Republican party, after a quarter-century of supremacy, had been left "with less fear than contempt for a party which one called 'a hopeless assortment of discordant differences, as incapable of positive action as it is capable of infinite clamor.'"

Republicans had prevailed in the two preceding national elections although the "Solid South" had assured the Democrats approximately 135 electoral votes, about fifty short of victory. To Henry Watterson, Kentucky's plain-speaking editor-statesman, a Unionist by conviction, a secessionist and Confederate soldier by heart, it was "a bad thing for the South that its fortunes were in any way tied to the lumbering bag of dry bones and dead language, which at the close of the war, was labeled the Democratic party."[35]

Unlike other industrialized nations of the time, "the United States did not witness a political marriage between the industrialists of the North and the planters of the South. The Civil War and Reconstruction created instead a two-party system that was in large part a two-region system, the Republicans representing the most powerful interests in the North, the Democrats representing the most powerful interests in the South. In such an arrangement the South could not hope to win much from the federal government. Southern planters, industrialists, farmers, artisans, merchants, professionals—all found themselves in one party, their divergent interests papered over by white unity."[36]

In his inaugural address, bowing to "the conscience of the people," President Cleveland gave assurance that in his administration there "should be no pretext for anxiety touching the protection of the freedman in their rights or their security in the enjoyment of their privileges under the Constitution and its amendments."[37]

Four years later, when Republicans regained the Executive Mansion, southerners were still counting Negro heads to determine how many representatives they would send to Congress but denying adult Negro males their right to vote for them.

"We have just seen a Democratic President elected because by violence and fraud the colored people of the South have been robbed of their forty electoral votes," Foraker wrote a black constituent a month before Cleveland's first inaugural.[38]

The Founding Fathers, in drawing up the Constitution, required the slave population to be counted by the census-takers and then three-fifths of that total number was to be used in determining the size of the state's delegation in the House of Representatives and, thus, how many electors it would send to the electoral college to ratify the election of the president and vice president.

In the years following ratification of the Fifteenth Amendment (1870), freedmen were counted along with whites in the state's population base, but gradually they had become disfranchised by the machinations of southern Democrats. Their numbers, however, still helped determine how many men the South would send to Congress and to the electoral college. White southerners, as Roosevelt had remarked in a Massachusetts campaign speech for Congressional candidate Lodge, "play this game to rule the Union with loaded dice."[39]

Foraker agreed, pointing out that "when a man deposits his ballot in Mississippi, or Georgia, or any other State in this nation for President, he is voting not alone for himself and the people of his State, but he is voting for the people of the State of Ohio; and when a man goes to the ballot box with a shotgun to keep somebody from putting his ballot in the box, he is interfering with the expression of the people that affects not only the citizens of his own State, but the citizens of Ohio as well."[40]

Foraker kept insisting he would not run for governor in 1885, but once the national election returns were in and Ohio Republicans began to look around for a candidate to deny Governor Hoadly a second term, his name inevitably cropped up. Well aware that it would be virtually impossible for the Republican nominee to win without Ohio's Negro vote, Foraker's enemies within the party revived charges made against him in 1883 by Democrats who had blanketed the state's black press with allegations that he had left Ohio Wesleyan when it admitted a colored student and had defended a white friend accused by a colored man named Gazzaway of having violated the Civil Rights law.

In a long letter to a Negro constituent who had asked for his side of the story, Foraker replied that the Ohio Wesleyan student had "left school at the end of his first term of his own free will and accord. I did not leave there until one year later." As for Gazzaway, Foraker explained that he had been represented in the case by "two colored men, both of whom had testified, and will testify again, that throughout the case I neither did nor said anything that was, or could be, in the slightest degree, disrespectful or offensive to the colored people."

In his first campaign for governor, when some of his youthful battlefield letters home found their way into print, Foraker had been "mortified," but now, in view of the racist charges from fellow-Republicans, he was delighted to quote a relevant passage from the correspondence his mother had preserved: "The war ought not to stop until slavery is abolished, and every colored man is made a citizen, and is given precisely the same civil and political rights that the white man has." The sentiments of the teenage infantryman were still held by the middle-aged politician.[41]

Addressing "audiences filled with Civil War veterans, Negroes, politi-

cians, and elements of the party out of office, this type of speech had tremendous appeal. Foraker knew what the Ohioans of the eighties wanted—
and he gave it to them." Despite Democratic gains in both houses of the
legislature, Republicans controlled the house, and their comfortable majority on the joint legislative ballot sent John Sherman back to the U.S.
Senate.[42]

Chapter Three

*"No rebel flags will be returned
as long as I am governor."*

—*Joseph Benson Foraker, June 15, 1887*

"Yesterday I was eighteen hours in the saddle," Roosevelt wrote Lodge June 5, 1885, when he was back in the Badlands, working on *Hunting Trips of a Ranchman*. He was also trying to stay away from his old flame, Edith Kermit Carow. Ever since Alice's death, Edith had discreetly avoided her childhood friend, calling on his sisters at times when she could be certain Theodore would not be home. This went on for nineteen months. Then one day, after visiting Bamie and little Alice, Edith descended the stairs and came face to face with Theodore in the hallway.[1]

He put off returning to his ranch, and on October 26, the eve of his twenty-seventh birthday, he invited Edith to the Meadowbrook Hunt Ball at Sagamore Hill, the Oyster Bay home intended for Alice Lee. During the hunt his horse fell and he crawled out from under it with a broken arm. It was still in a sling when he proposed on November 17. Edith said "Yes," but for the time being they agreed to tell no one.[2]

The following spring a decade of strikes and agitation for an eight-hour workday was climaxed by the explosion of a bomb in Chicago's Haymarket Square during a meeting called by strikers, socialists, and anarchists (many of them foreign-born) to protest police brutality. Police opened fire, and by the time order was restored, seven lawmen had been mortally wounded.[3]

Tammany Democrats and machine Republicans were shocked when, in the wake of the Haymarket bombing, Henry George agreed to run for mayor of New York as the candidate of organized labor. To the working man this scholarly, Utopian single-taxer, whose *Progress and Poverty* had sold millions of copies, was a heroic figure. Tammany got the jump on the Republicans when Boss Richard Croker selected an ideal candidate, Abram S. Hewitt, a wealthy, high-minded Democrat and old friend of the Roosevelt family. He had known Theodore as a young frog collector.[4]

The Republican machine could have assured George's defeat by endorsing Hewitt and dividing the spoils with the victors, as it had done before, but this time Tammany had fielded an honest man who could not be counted on to go along with such an arrangement. Republican strategists figured that in a three-way race, George might attract enough defectors from the ranks of Democrats, the self-styled "workers' party," to elect an independent Republican. The machine decided to sound out Roosevelt.

"With the most genuine reluctance I finally accepted," he wrote Lodge on October 17, 1886. It is, of course, a perfectly hopeless contest."[5]

The candidate was still trying to explain to his sisters why he and Edith Carow had withheld from them the news of their secret engagement. They had learned about it from a bit of gossip they'd spotted in the social column of the *New York Times*. Bamie accompanied her brother to London, where the wedding was to take place. They sailed on the SS *Etruria* four days after Theodore ran a bad third in Hewitt's successful race for mayor.[6]

At the close of the marriage ceremony at St. George's, Hanover Square, the bridegroom signed the registry with a flourish, identifying himself as "Rancher."[7]

As an elderly widow, looking back on her husband's political campaigns, Julia Foraker remembered getting the baby to sleep and the other children quieted down only to have a band of serenaders appear under her windows. Florence once strayed into a political gathering on her way home from primary school and discovered to her disgust that it was a Democratic rally.[8]

"They spit tobacco," she reported, "and they have never washed their hands." Louise, sent to the blackboard to write something from James Russell Lowell, asked her teacher, "Do you think anyone really cares what that old mugwump said?"[9] When Louise brought home a note from her teacher, her father replied, "Just wait till you get Julia."

Julia slept through her father's inaugural address when he became Ohio's thirty-seventh governor on January 11, 1886. The official reception was curtailed by a blizzard, but his parents managed to make their way to the ceremonies in the rotunda of the state capitol in Columbus. When retiring Governor George Hoadly paid their son a graceful compliment, his elderly mother replied, "If he only comes out with as much honor as he goes in I shall be satisfied."[10]

Foraker fired the three commissioners responsible for the selection of Cincinnati's police force and appointed a new board composed of two Republicans and two Democrats. He also pushed through legislation that created a state board of health, established the position of dairy and food commissioner, and set up a five-member board of managers to oversee the state penitentiary and to provide more humane treatment for inmates. Early in the new year, 1887, the last of the state's infamous "black laws," the one providing separate schools for colored children, was repealed.[11]

In the town of Xenia, three miles from Wilberforce University, where a few years later W. E. B. Du Bois would occupy the classics chair, one-third of the population was black. When a Negro girl, supported by a Negro lawyer, tried to enroll in the local high school, she was refused. A damage suit was filed and the school board lost, but eventually won out when gerrymandering restored separate and unequal schools.[12]

Dorsie William Willis was born to Corsey S. Willis, a strong-willed young black sharecropper, and his deeply religious wife, Dochie, in Mississippi. When he joined the army, in 1905, he said he was born in Jackson on November 13 between 1883 and 1886, but in the latter years of his life, he claimed to have been born in Vicksburg on February 11, 1886. His father and mother had been born free, but their parents and grandparents, with roots in some long-forgotten African village, had lived in bondage to a white slaveholder.[13]

"My great-grandmother worked in the boss's house," Dorsie recalled in his old age, "and, from all I can gather, my grandmother was his child. He was one of those tough guys that whatever he did was right and nobody had nothing to do with it. He was king of the forest. My grandmother never learned to write, but she could read. She picked it up from playing with the

Dorsie W. Willis, the last of the Brownsville soldiers. Courtesy *New York Times*,
December 31, 1972. Photograph by Boyd B. Hogen.

boss's white kids. That was the height of her ambition, an education for her
children.

"My father—C. S., they called him—was the only one of my grandmother's kids that taken after that white fellow. He never thought anybody,
white or black, was superior to him in any way, and he would speak his

opinions any place, any time. My mother used to get after him sometimes about the things he said, and he'd tell her, 'I might as well die today as tomorrow, die here as further down the creek.'"

In one of Dorsie's earliest memories he was sitting on the front stoop with his mother when a white man came riding up to the cabin on a big black horse. The man, named Pearman, owned the land C. S. worked in return for a share of each year's crop. When Pearman saw Dorsie's mother at home with her child, he wheeled his horse around and trotted off to the field where C. S. was working with his mule and his two horses.

"How come Dochie ain't working in the field?" Pearman asked, and C. S. countered: "How come Mrs. Pearman ain't working in the field?"

Eighty years later, Dorsie could still remember the cloud of dust in which his father and the white man fought that day.

"The white man slid down off'n his horse and my father unhooked the mule and taken the singletree, that was what he was fighting with. After they got through fighting, he rode the mule up to the house and he told my mother, 'Go out in the field and get the horses.' Mamma went out and got the horses and brought 'em in, while he rode over to his father's place on the mule. His father and his brother come back with him to the house. We was all hiding under the porch, lying on the ground, and I can remember my father telling my mother, 'If you hear any noise, don't say nothing, just pinch me.' His father and his brother stayed there with us a day or so, thinking the white people would be coming to get him and kill him, but they never showed up.

"My father was living pretty good for a colored man in those times. He had eighty acres to farm for himself and his family, but he had to leave; people all knew he couldn't stay there and sell nothing, so he had to just walk away from it all—the chickens, the cow, the mule, the two horses, everything."

Dochie's first letter from C. S. was mailed in Memphis, Tennessee. The next time she heard from him he was in Oklahoma Territory, which had been settled (1828–1846) by displaced Indian families who, like many of their former white neighbors in North Carolina, Tennessee, Georgia, and Mississippi, had held black men, women, and children in bondage. After the war the federal government contended that, because the five tribes (Cherokees, Creeks, Chickasaws, Choctaws, and Seminoles) had joined the rebellion, they had forfeited their lands and treaty guarantees. Provision was made for a territorial government that, it was hoped, would lead in time to the formation of a new state. A Choctaw delegate proposed its name, Oklahoma ("red people").

Dorsie was three years old when Oklahoma lands were opened with the first run of homesteaders in the spring of 1889. Six townsites were established, Guthrie, Oklahoma City, Kingfisher, El Reno, Norman, and Stillwater. Oklahoma City beat out Guthrie to become the capital. By 1900 the combined population of Oklahoma Territory and Indian Territory was 390,000. Ten years later the state had a population of 1,657,155.[14]

When C. S. found work in Guthrie, the largest of the new Oklahoma towns carved from Creek and Seminole lands, he sent for his family. His parents and one of his four brothers also decided to try their luck out west. Dorsie, in his eighties, recalled those pioneer days:

> *Oklahoma was young and there wasn't any houses around there for quite some time. We lived in a hole in the ground, what they called a 'starter cellar.' You dug yourself a hole, then you built onto it. All those new settlers coming in there, nobody was hardly able to help the other fellow. Nobody had anything. My father worked for a white fellow by the name of Massey, lived on a farm about a mile from town. His daughter was married to a school teacher and he taken me into his school, an all-white school just across the road. I was the only colored fellow.*

If C. S., like so many black southerners pouring into Oklahoma Territory, hoped to escape the indignities of a Jim Crow society, he was disappointed. When his family left the Massey farm and moved to Guthrie, the boy was not permitted to attend a white school two blocks from his home.

> *I walked about three miles to Lincoln School. My teacher was a colored woman, very strict. Her name was Mrs. Jackson. That's where I got the rest of my schooling, went up through the sixth grade. I never went to school a full term in my life. Times were tough, and every year cotton opened up in September and school started about the same time, but we went out to the cotton fields, my mother and all us kids, and we picked cotton to get the winter supply. We'd pick till about the last of October and then we'd come in and start school.*

In his annual message to the legislature, January 4, 1887, Governor Foraker "struck a responsive chord in the South" by insisting that the same care given the Ohio graves of Union soldiers should be extended to those of Confederate dead buried in his native state. Six months later, Secretary of War William C. Endicott came up with what he and Adjutant General Richard C. Drum regarded as a gracious gesture toward sectional reconciliation. The Union and Confederate battle flags gathering dust in a bureaucratic basement for twenty years would be returned to their home states. No one in the Administration was prepared for the response of patriots and demagogues to Cleveland's executive order.[15]

The governor of Kansas considered the proposal "an insult to the heroic dead and an outrage on their surviving comrades." Senator James S.

Governor J. B. Foraker, 1886–90

Hawley of Connecticut favored burning the flags of "our misguided brothers and wicked conspirators." Lucius Fairchild, the national commander of the Grand Army of the Republic, a Gettysburg survivor, thundered: "May God palsy the hand that wrote that order. May God palsy the brain that conceived it, and may God palsy the tongue that dictated it."[16]

From the shower of angry communications raining down on the governor's office, Foraker plucked a telegram from a veteran he knew well, Captain Erskine Carson of Hillsboro, who had been severely wounded in the second battle of Bull Run: "The old soldiers of Hillsboro hope you will not give up any captured rebel flags in the state house at Columbus. Intense feeling here among the boys who wore the blue."

"No rebel flags will be returned while I am governor," Foraker replied, and was astonished next morning when both telegrams "found a conspicuous place on the front page of every newspaper in Ohio and practically all the newspapers of the United States."[17]

The boost the Ohio Governor got from this flag-waving on the eve of another national election troubled Sherman Republicans who had never been quite certain of Foraker's loyalty to their candidate. When the party faithful gathered in Toledo on July 27 to nominate a candidate for governor to run that fall and, at the same time, prepare to do battle nationally with the Democrats in 1888, Foraker was escorted to his hotel by uniformed marching clubs. Delegates in the lobby were wearing badges proclaiming: "No rebel flags will be returned while I am governor." When the convention buckled down to business, Senator Sherman was endorsed unanimously, and the following day Foraker was nominated by acclamation for a second term as governor.[18]

He was reelected with a plurality of 23,732 and, for the first time, carried Hamilton County, thanks to the support of George Cox, "Boss of Cincinnati." In his first term, Foraker had offended Mark Hanna by not appointing his candidate for oil inspector, a desirable job because of the fees paid by oil refineries. The oil inspector also had the political advantages of choosing and controlling numerous deputies scattered across the state. In his second term, when a new oil inspector was to be chosen, Foraker again passed over Hanna's candidate and paid off a campaign debt by appointing his hometown political boss.[19]

"Foraker made a shrewd choice," Zane L. Miller points out. "Cox had grown up with the new city and received a liberal education in its ways."[20]

Cox, seven years younger than Foraker, had been on his own since the age of eight, shining shoes, selling newspapers, serving as lookout for a gambling joint, delivering groceries, and tending bar before acquiring his own saloon, from which sprang his political influence as a ward boss who could be counted on to flush out the vote. In 1884, as Blaine's Hamilton County campaign manager, he made the rounds of the city's polling places in the company of the affable supervisor of the election, William Howard Taft, and found no fraud. Blaine carried the county.[21]

The Plumed Knight was in Paris in early December, 1887, when he read newspaper accounts of an astonishing tariff message Cleveland had sent to Congress, indicting a protective system that in the last two years had seen the Treasury's surplus shoot up from $17,839,000 to $55,367,000. By the end of the fiscal year it would reach $140,000,000. Cleveland had become convinced that this "ruthless extortion" of the people's money invited "schemes of public plunder" and violated "the fundamental principles of a free government." Such a condition of affairs, he continued, "constrains our people to demand that by a revision of our revenue laws the receipts of the Government shall be reduced to the necessary expenses of its economical administration."

It was "an astute political move," Hal Williams points out, giving the party a chance to "expand its electoral base" by gathering "new recruits from eastern importers and merchants, southern and western farmers, and New England manufacturers who desired cheaper raw materials." Campaign orators could put the Republicans on the defensive by arguing "persuasively that high duties meant higher prices for consumers and that the tariff dampened economic growth by accumulating surplus funds in the Treasury."[22]

Blaine had ruled himself out as a presidential candidate, but, despite a typical Conkling putdown ("Blaine can be nominated by acclamation . . . and be defeated in the same manner"), the magnetic Man from Maine dominated the 1888 Republican National Convention when Foraker, pledged to Senator Sherman, arrived in Chicago in mid-June to preside over a restless Ohio delegation. Blaine diehards, refusing to take their candidate's decision as final, continued to cherish the hope that if he were offered the nomination, he would accept it.[23]

On Wednesday, June 20, when Foraker was called on to entertain the delegates while they waited for the report of the credentials committee, his extemporaneous remarks gave the visiting politicians a demonstration of the contrast between the warm, witty young Ohio governor and the dull, colorless, elderly "Ohio Icicle" to whom he and Congressman McKinley were committed.[24]

When he took the platform the following day to second Senator Sherman's nomination, Foraker was taken aback to find a huge floral piece placed at the speaker's stand. Red flowers on a white background spelled out "No rebel flags will be returned while I am governor."[25] The floral tribute, he learned later, was a gift from two well-meaning Chicago ladies whose brother he had pardoned a year before at the request of ex-Governor Foster.[26]

Despite his initial embarrassment, Foraker came through with a magnetic speech "that wrought the vast throng to the highest pitch of enthusiasm." If the Democrats, representing American labor, had chosen the red bandanna for their banner, he proclaimed, then the Republicans would carry the American flag. "Thousands of American flags were thrown into the air, men jumped on tables and chairs, and everyone cheered and screamed." The ten-minute demonstration ended with the old soldier's theme song, "Marching through Georgia."[27]

"Foraker is the pet and darling of this convention," the *New York Sun* reported. "The appearance of his face, the mention of his name, the sound of his voice, electrify the delegates and the spectators." Some Sherman loyalists were convinced that Foraker, "wild with ambition," was bent on becoming a candidate himself, as Garfield had done.[28]

The friendly *Cincinnati Commercial-Gazette* was confident the governor would "support Sherman and cover his mendacious enemies with confusion and shame." Blaine felt the same way. "The talk of Foraker's scheming for himself is nonsense and malice," he said when interviewed before the convention. "Foraker is a young man and has a great future before him. He may go to the Senate and be President later on."[29]

On the first ballot, Sherman received only 299 ballots, mostly from southern Negro delegates who had sold their votes to Hanna. Sherman had no support from New York, New Jersey, or New England. On the second ballot, Benjamin Harrison, whose family name was writ large in Indiana history, ended up with ninety-one votes. His great-grandfather had been a signer of the Declaration of Independence, and in 1841 his father, hero of the battle of Tippecanoe, had been president for the last month of his life. Like Foraker and McKinley, the present-day Harrison had a splendid war record and believed in tariff protection, but, unlike Foraker and McKinley, he was "a stranger to the art of popularizing himself." He could charm a crowd of twenty thousand, it was said, and then, with a handshake, make them all his enemies.[30]

On the fourth ballot, Saturday morning, June 23, Sherman's vote dropped to 235 and Harrison's shot up to 216. That afternoon Foraker made a surprise announcement. He had "been faithful and true to Mr. Sherman," he said, and had "stood by him until I feel the case is hopeless." But now, he believed, "I have honorably been absolved and I am for Blaine henceforth." On Sunday, after his defection to Blaine had been interpreted as a bid for a place on the national ticket, he denied having made the statement. Eight months later he acknowledged it.[31]

On Sunday, Blaine cabled the Maine delegation, withdrawing his name. At two o'clock Monday morning, as the Forakers told the story, they were awakened by a knock on the door. Charles Kurtz, the governor's secretary, said some Blaine men were outside in the hall and wanted to hold an immediate conference. Julia liked to tell what happened next.[32]

"Well, the only place to receive them was in that bedroom, the only thing for me to do was to leave, and the only place for me to go was the bathroom. So there I hid. The Blaine men crowded into the bedroom, led, I was to learn, by Senator Stephen B. Elkins of West Virginia and the Honorable Samuel Fessenden of Connecticut.

"The murmur of voices went on for some time. The bathroom was cold and I was very sleepy. At last I heard the meeting break up; I could go back to my room."

The delegation, her husband explained, had "just come from a meeting of Blaine leaders where it was decided to throw the entire Blaine strength to me on Monday morning if I would accept the nomination for President. . . . I told them that I appreciated the honor and would have been glad to accept their support, but that I was completely committed to Mr. Sherman and couldn't and wouldn't accept the nomination unless Sherman asked me to accept it."

"Well, it's almost three o'clock," Julia said, and turned out the gas.

Her oft-told tale, which also appears in her husband's memoirs, is questioned by latter-day historians. Their doubts are strengthened by Morgan's account of a drive Senator Elkins took with Tom Platt that Sunday afternoon when Blaine had put an end to speculation about his availability. The time had come to convince the New York boss that with Benjamin Harrison's support coming from doubtful states where Republicans would prevail because of the tariff issue, he was the man to beat Grover Cleveland.[33]

On the Saturday evening before the Elkins-Platt accord, Senator Sherman recalled, "I was telegraphed by different persons that I would certainly be nominated on Monday. That was the confident belief in Washington." The next day, while his West Virginia colleague was nailing down the New York vote for Harrison, Sherman read a newspaper story which expressed his feelings that day—although he couldn't remember talking to the reporter: "Senator Sherman says he does not believe that Foraker, or any other Ohio man will desert him."[34]

Some years later, after dipping into Senator Sherman's *Recollections* (1895), a United Press reporter got in touch with Blaine's "devoted friend," Samuel Fessenden, the Connecticut member of the Republican National Committee. Fessenden verified the Forakers' story of the 2:00 A.M. meeting. He and Senator Elkins had accompanied Ohio Delegate Charles L. Kurtz to the Forakers' hotel room, he said, and sat on the bed beside the governor.

> *We made it very clear to him that if he would consent to become a candidate he could be nominated without fail, and without difficulty, on the first or second ballot Monday. We assured Governor Foraker that we desired no pledges from him respecting policies or patronage, and that we only wanted him to agree not to get up and decline the nomination after the Convention had made him its candidate. Mr. Foraker, without hesitation, said firmly and emphatically:*
>
> *"I thank you, gentlemen, with all my heart, but I could not accept the nomination if it came to me unless Mr. Sherman first withdrew and asked me to become a candidate. I feel sure he will not do that. I came here to try and nominate him, and cannot consider the proposition to become a candidate. I will stand by him."*[35]

Foraker's biographer finds it "difficult to see how if Foraker had accepted the Blaine support he could have been nominated." When the senator's enemies continued to blame him for Sherman's defeat, his friend Murat Halstead reviewed the proceedings for the *Commercial Gazette* and reminded his readers that Harrison apparently had the nomination sewed up from the moment the convention assembled.[36]

Chapter Four

*"Slavery must be the greatest of crimes. Here we are,
all these years after it has been abolished, and
we are still paying the penalty for it."*

—*James B. Weaver, Populist presidential
candidate, 1892. Polled more than one million popular
and twenty-two electoral votes*

Harrison got news of the election outcome on the telegraph wires installed
at his Spiegel Grove estate in Indianapolis, but the results were so close he
was not certain of the outcome until three mornings later when he heard a
newsboy yelling, "All about the election of General Harrison." In 1841 the
seven-year-old future president-elect had seen his legendary grandfather,
William Henry Harrison, set out for Washington to become the country's
ninth president.[1] Thirty-one days after taking the oath of office, the hero of
Tippecanoe died of pneumonia.

In the last winter days of 1889, when Benjamin and Caroline Harrison
were on their way to Washington, the Forakers boarded their private car at
Piqua, Ohio, as the Harrisons were finishing dinner. They were invited to
join the family for ice cream and coffee. Afterward, when the president-
elect and the Ohio governor repaired to the far end of the car for a quiet

talk, Mrs. Harrison deposited "Tippecanoe's" infant great-grandson in her husband's lap, and, Julia recalled in her memoirs, he spent the rest of the trip with the baby "clawing at his hair [and] untying his cravat" as he "discoursed upon the newly-admitted Western states and the Indian troubles."[2]

He took the oath of office protected from the damp chill of an early spring day by "a complete armor of chamois leather under his suit." His grandfather still holds the presidential record for the shortest stay in the White House and the longest inaugural address. The grandson, reading from a text half the length of Old Tip's, pointed out that in the nation's second century the center of its population had moved from a point east of Baltimore to one near Cincinnati and that the population of the Territory of Dakota exceeded that of each of the original states except the Commonwealth of Virginia.[3]

"Shall the prejudices and paralysis of slavery continue to hang upon the skirts of progress?" he asked rhetorically, and then raised the possibility that "the farmers and the promoters of the great mining and manufacturing enterprises which have recently been established in the South may yet find that the free ballot of the workingman, without distinction of race, is needed for their defense as well as for his own."[4]

He had won the Executive Mansion by the narrowest of margins after a campaign in which money was tossed about "with a profusion never before known on American soil." But, he complained, he had no power because his party managers "had taken it all to themselves. I could not name my own Cabinet. They sold out every place to pay the election expenditures."[5]

He returned Blaine to the State Department and delivered the Post Office into the capable hands of John Wanamaker, the Philadelphia dry-goods magnate. Foraker was rumored to be under consideration for attorney general or secretary of war, but he had his eye on a Senate seat. If Sherman left the Senate to join Harrison's cabinet as secretary of the treasury, the governor planned to resign and have his successor appoint him to the vacancy. Sherman, however, opted to remain in the Senate, and on Christmas Eve, Foraker announced he had no claim on or desire for a Cabinet post.[6]

Lodge, who had been reelected to the House of Representatives, was eager to find a place for Roosevelt in the new administration. The New Yorker's name popped up two weeks after Harrison's inauguration, when Lodge's captivating wife, Nannie, received a letter from Blaine, a flirtatious admirer, who was casting about for a young assistant secretary of state.[7]

"Do you happen to know a young gentleman—gentleman strongly accented," he wrote, "not over forty-five, well educated, speaking French well, preferably German also (with an accomplished wife thoroughly accustomed to society) and able to spend ten to fifteen thousand—twenty still better, beyond the salary he might receive?"[8]

When Roosevelt's name was tossed into play, Blaine replied with a candid assessment of his old adversary: "I do somehow feel that my sleep at Augusta or Bar Harbor would not be quite so easy and refreshing if so brilliant and aggressive a man had hold of the helm."[9]

Blaine invited Cabot and Nannie to his Bar Harbor home in the summer of 1889 to help him "in taking care of the great 'White Elephant,' as he referred to his principal guest, the president. Lodge took advantage of his opportunity to put in a good word for Roosevelt and came away with the belief "he had convinced the politically minded President of the importance of reform."[10]

Six weeks after Roosevelt accepted the offer of a $3,500-a-year job as a member of the civil service commission, he expressed the belief that he had "strengthened the administration by showing, in striking contrast to the facts under Cleveland, that there is no humbug in the law now." Two years later he was not so certain that Harrison favored rigorous enforcement of existing laws, and privately the president was complaining that his opinionated Civil Service commissioner "wanted to put an end to all the evil in the world between sunrise and sunset."[11]

Election fraud had become a national issue, Harrison wrote Whitelaw Reid, editor of the *New York Tribune*, a few weeks before the off-year elections, pointing out that "these vile southern methods are spreading their contagion, like the yellow fever, into our northern states." The issue, he said, could not be ducked.[12]

"We will attempt to enact at this session of Congress a law which shall in some degree, if enforced, remedy the evils, in their relation to elections," Wisconsin's Senator John Coit Spooner wrote a politician back home, February 4, 1890.[13]

Some weeks later, on March 15, Lodge, allied in the Senate with Spooner and George F. Hoar of Massachusetts, introduced a House bill, H.R. 8242, "to regulate elections of Representatives in Congress." The proposed law touched off "the hottest sectional conflict in Congress since the end of Reconstruction." One outraged southern editor detected in every line "the gleam of a half-concealed bayonet."

"It is a dark blow at the freedom of the ballot," Cleveland said, beating a hasty retreat from reality.[14]

Black leaders packed the House galleries on July 2 as H.R. 8242 was approved by a vote of 155 to 149. It went to the Senate, where it ran afoul of a bold tariff measure crafted in the House by Major McKinley, chairman of the Ways and Means Committee. Senator Matthew S. Quay of Pennsylvania, who was also head of the Republican National Committee, insisted it would be impossible to move both the tariff and the election bills through Congress in the twelve weeks before the off-year elections.

Quay made his move on August 12 "in the midst of desultory Senate debate over the tariff," Hal Williams writes. "He proposed a bargain to Democrats to end their logjam. The Republicans would agree to postpone the election bill until the second session, which would meet in December. In return, the Democrats would stop their obstruction and allow the tariff bill to reach a vote in August or September."[15]

Thus ended the last serious effort of the Republican party to outlaw disfranchisement of southern Negroes. Redress finally came when a Texas Democrat signed the Civil Rights Act of 1964. "I think we have just delivered the South to the Republican party for a long time to come," Lyndon Johnson remarked at the time.[16]

On the eve of Ohio's Republican State Convention, in late June, 1889, Foraker agreed to go along with Boss Cox, who had urged him to put aside his senatorial ambitions for the good of the party. Reluctantly the governor announced he would run for a third term. It would be "the most bitterly contested fight I have ever had," he predicted, and he must have been pleased to find among his congratulatory letters one from Superior Court Judge Will Taft expressing "a sincere and grateful interest in seeing you win a fight where the risk is great, but the ultimate stake is very large."[17]

The governor's campaign got off to an ill-timed start when a law-and-order association in Cincinnati prevailed on the mayor to enforce the state's statute prohibiting the sale of strong drink on the Sabbath. Foraker, who, as governor, could hardly have done otherwise, wrote a letter to the mayor assuring him that he should "not tolerate any defiance of law." Brewers, liquor dealers, and saloon keepers joined the city's thirsty Republicans, especially local beer-garden patrons of German descent, in a crusade to throw the rascals out. Done in by tipplers caught up in a saloon keepers' rebellion, Foraker lost by a plurality of 10,872 votes.[18]

Julia regarded her husband's defeat as "the best thing that could have happened to Foraker." They had scrimped through his first term as governor on an annual salary of $4,000. It had been doubled in the second term, but $8,000 "hardly amounted to dizzy affluence with a family of growing children." Julia was happy to go back to Cincinnati and "become just a woman bossing the architect of a new house," which "was to be at last our own."

Mrs. Joseph B. Foraker

She also reflected on the consequences of victory:

Had Governor Foraker been reelected in 1889, he would have been undeniably in McKinley's way, whether he wanted to be or not, and for the second time brushed by the wings of a presidential nomination. This was just twice too often for my wishes and ambitions for my husband or my children. McKinley and Foraker were about the same age; both had fine Civil War records. But McKinley, although not rich, had many rich friends who would devotedly have put their resources at his disposal; and he was childless. Foraker, oppositely, had a single-handed way to make and was rich only in children. For these and other excellent reasons I never completely yearned to live in the White House.[19]

Taft, who in private had referred to Foraker as "double-faced," wrote to say he was "very, very sorry for the defeat" and expressed his "gratitude for what you have done for me." The young jurist had graduated from Yale in 1878 and come home to Cincinnati to fall in love with Helen (Nellie) Herron and, while studying law, cover Judge Foraker's courtroom for the *Commercial*. Foraker took a liking to the hard-working lawyer-journalist and, when one of his former colleagues on the superior court of Cincinnati resigned in January 1887, filled the vacancy by appointing Alphonso Taft's huge, amiable, twenty-nine-year-old son.[20]

A year later, when Taft was elected to succeed himself, Foraker offered his congratulations along with a reminder: "Don't forget the advice I gave you to quit the bench at the end of the time for which you have now been elected. You will then be of mature age and experience, and so established in the confidence of the people that all other things will come naturally."[21]

While Foraker was stumbling to the well once too often in the summer of 1889, Judge Taft was casting his ambitious eye on the Supreme Court of the United States. Foraker, in a letter to President Harrison, pointed out that Judge Taft's "appointment would be satisfactory to an unusually high degree to the Republicans of this state, and no Democrat could justly criticize it." When offered the prestigious post of solicitor general, Taft was inclined to turn it down, but Nellie persuaded him to accept this opportunity to get out of Cincinnati and be "thrown with the bigwigs."[22]

"There was something a little touching about Foraker's boyish enthusiasm for young Will Taft, his ambition for him," Julia recalled many years later. "Foraker's early life had been a stern struggle; in Mr. Taft's background he saw all the brilliance and charm of association that for him had glamour, and that he had missed."[23]

Foraker, back in his Walnut Hills home in January, 1890, resumed his law practice with his son, Benson. He intended to stay out of politics until he put himself "into a more satisfactory condition financially," but despite Hanna's insistence that he was "dead as a factor in our politics," the forty-three-year-old former governor was more determined than ever to wangle a seat in the Senate.[24]

Paying his annual visit to Cincinnati in the summer of 1891, Senator Sherman called on the ex-governor, who, in reply to an inquiry from the *Commercial-Gazette*, had said he was a candidate for the Senate and that no one knew it better than the incumbent. "Governor Foraker and I have always been friends," Senator Sherman told an interviewer, and pointed out that "one man has just as much right to try as another."[25]

When Ohio legislators met to elect a senator in January, 1892, Foraker had the backing of the *Commercial-Gazette* ("It is time for a new deal"), and he thought he had the votes he needed, but after four defections on a key procedural matter, Sherman won another term.[26]

A few months later, Foraker again spoke up for Will Taft when Congress empowered the president to appoint judges to the newly created appeals court in each of the nine circuits. Taft faced a "legion" of candidates but got the appointment and moved back to Cincinnati to sit on an appellate bench just below the Supreme Court, the "safe harbor" where he hoped eventually to spend the last years of his life. Neither he nor Nellie, his biographer points out, would have credited a seer who informed them that eight years later "he would sail far into the east and find his destiny—find that and the work which may have been the most valuable in his long career—on remote islands of which he had barely heard."[27]

The presidential contest in 1892 was between two men who knew the office at first hand, the austere Benjamin Harrison, and his stubborn predecessor, Grover Cleveland, whose much-admired courage "also included ample doses of maladroitness. In handling such issues as free silver, tariff revision, and patronage, Cleveland committed blunder after blunder that drove the majority of Democrats away from him." Henry L. Stoddard summed it up: "As President he could not dominate, and he did not know how to persuade." Henry Adams regarded the two candidates as "singular persons, of whom it was the common saying that one of them had no friends; the other only enemies."[28]

When a third party candidate, James B. Weaver, a former Union general, came south with the Populist message of the People's Party, he came as a presidential candidate who had spilled Confederate blood. Macon Democrats greeted Weaver and his wife with rocks, tomatoes, and rotten eggs, prompting an observer to remark, "Mrs. Weaver was made a regular walking omelet by the southern chivalry of Georgia." Weaver cut short his southern tour.[29]

Southern Democrats who defected to Weaver often became outcasts. They were snubbed at church, denied credit at country stores, charged higher prices for what they bought, and paid lower prices for what they sold. They "symbolized threats to white rule in a society fearing the Negro more than depression or Republicanism. 'It is like cutting off the right hand or putting out the right eye,' a Virginian said of leaving the old party."[30]

When black politicians set out to organize black voters, they "risked virtually everything, including their lives." If they lost an election, "they seldom had a pleasant lawyer's office or mercantile establishment to retire to." They compromised and sacrificed "for some promised long-term good of a Republican party that frequently turned its back on black voters and officeholders."[31]

"There is but one issue in the South," Weaver once remarked to a friend. "That is competition to see who can most hate the Negro. The man that wins gets the nomination. The whole thing is a dead drag on the country. . . . Slavery must be the greatest of crimes. Here we are, all these years after it has been abolished, and we are still paying the penalty for it."[32]

"I sympathize with you in your aspirations for your race, and I join with you in the hope that the race problem will soon cease to cause any political or social misunderstanding," Ohio's Governor McKinley told a Negro newspaperman in 1894. In that same year, Matt Warren, a $70-a-month Southern Pacific repairman in Los Angeles, joined the American Railway Union, an industrial union open to the lowliest railroad workers as long as they were "born of white parents." Two years later *Plessy v. Ferguson* cleared up any "misunderstanding" about the South's "separate but equal" society.[33]

Called on to consider the Louisiana law that had caused the plaintiff—a man with "one eighth African blood"—to be shunted off to a Jim Crow railroad car, the court held that *Plessy* had erred in assuming that "the enforced separation of the two races stamps the colored race with a badge of inferiority. If this be so, it is not by reason of anything found in the act, but solely because the colored race chooses to put that construction upon it." Matt Warren's towheaded son Earl was five years old that year.[34]

Commissioner Roosevelt, preparing to surrender his office and go back to New York, would miss not only Cabot Lodge, now in line for a Senate seat, but also his learned Washington friends, Henry Adams, the disillusioned, self-appointed "stable-companion to statesmen," and John Hay, the witty, gregarious man of letters and temporarily out-of-work diplomat. Adams was repelled and fascinated by the bustling, bespectacled, self-assured young Harvard cowboy bounding about Washington denouncing the "white-livered weaklings" running the government. Throughout the next eleven years he waited for the inevitable moment when "Teddy's luck" would install him in the white wedding-cake mansion where Abigail Adams, Henry's great-grand-mother, had been disturbed by the view from her bedroom window of "slaves half fed and destitute of clothing" at work on the front lawn.[35]

Bracing himself for the pain of leaving the capital, Roosevelt expressed a "profound gratification in knowing that there is no man more bitterly disliked by many of the men in my own party. When I leave on March 5, I shall at least have the knowledge that I have certainly not flinched from trying to enforce the law during these four years, even if my progress has been at times a little disheartening."[36]

In a letter to his "Darling Bye," April 26, 1893, the commissioner reported, "I saw Cleavland [sic] the other day and he asked me to stay on for a year or two longer; I shall therefore probably stay at least a year." The lame-duck Republican secretary of the navy bade the Civil Service commissioner farewell with the remark: "Well, my boy, you've been a thorn in our side during four years. I earnestly hope you will remain a thorn in the side of the next administration."[37]

Roosevelt spent the summer months agonizing over an offer to run again for mayor of New York, a temptation Edith urged him to resist. He finally went along with her. When Bamie learned of the decision, she fired off a scorching letter to her sister-in-law and received a reply: "I cannot begin to describe how terribly I feel at having failed him at such an important time. It is just as I said to you he never should have married me, and then he would have been free to take his own course quite unbiased."[38]

Adrenalin surged through Roosevelt the following February when Cuban *insurrectos* rose up against their Spanish oppressors. He let New York's governor, Levi P. Morton, know that "in the very improbable event of a war with Spain," he was applying for service in any regiment the state sent out. "I must have a commission in the force that goes to Cuba."[39]

Meanwhile he was torn between his political instincts, which would have him stay put until the next national campaign, and his impulse to throw in his lot with William L. Strong, the Republican reformer who had become mayor of New York. Roosevelt intimated that if he were asked to serve on the city's new police board, he would accept. His appointment was confirmed on April 17, 1895.[40]

"His teeth are big and white, his eyes are small and piercing, his voice is rasping," the *World* reported, and went on to add, "His heart is full of reform."[41]

He reported for work on May 6 and, as had been prearranged, was elected president of the board. When the meeting adjourned, he whisked two newspaper reporters, his idolatrous friend Jacob Riis and a skeptical young man from the *Evening Sun*, Lincoln Steffens, into his office. "Now, then," Commissioner Roosevelt said, "what'll we do?" As they were leaving, Riis remarked to Steffens, "Of course, Teddy is bound for the presidency."[42]

In the spring of 1895, when the Republican state convention met in Zanesville, Foraker showed a renewed interest in politics after a two-year lull. He wanted the delegates' unqualified endorsement for United States senator the following year; Mark Hanna wanted their endorsement of Governor McKinley for president. Both men got what they wanted, but it was Foraker's convention from the first to the last pounding of the gavel.[43]

He then played a leading role in the campaign and had the party's backing for senator, but to cash in on his popularity, Republicans would have to end up with control of the legislature which, at that time, elected United States senators. On November 5 the entire Foraker ticket was swept into office. On January 14, 1896, the legislators made it official. Senator Foraker would take his seat in Washington on March 4, 1897.

"Whatever may be said of his partisan favor or his impetuosity," declared the *Chicago Times-Herald*, "it will be conceded that his advent to the Senate means an accession of brains and courage."[44]

On the day of Foraker's victory, McKinley, the outgoing governor, dropped by his hotel room to offer his congratulations and discuss his presidential prospects. When he asked the "Senator" to attend the national Republican convention in June as a delegate-at-large and work for his nomination, Foraker hedged. He wanted to help in every possible way, he said, but because of his unfortunate experience as a Sherman delegate, which had been marked by "charges of treachery and bad faith," he preferred to attend as a spectator.

"I very much desire that you should go," McKinley wrote when he got back to Canton. "I am sure this is the wish of the Republicans of the State, as it is most earnestly mine."[45]

By the end of February, Foraker had been won over. William McKinley is "our friend, our neighbor, our fellow-citizen, our fellow-Republican," he reminded the home folks. Two weeks later, despite warnings from some of his strategists, McKinley asked Foraker to place his name in nomination at the national convention. Again Foraker agreed, and by the time he arrived in St. Louis on June 13, six days before the convention was to open, McKinley had become the logical nominee.[46]

On the fourth day, when the nominating speeches were to be made and the balloting to begin, the front lawn of McKinley's home in Canton was brightened by flowers spilling over from two white urns and by circular beds of red geraniums. McKinley's invalid wife, Ida, and her mother sat in the parlor, surrounded by friends. They could hear the Postal Telegraph and Western Union instruments clicking away upstairs. In the library the major was seated near the telephone manned by his wife's cousin, Sam Saxton, who read off bulletins as they came in.[47]

"The applause following Foraker's presentation of McKinley continued twenty-four minutes," Charles G. Dawes, a Nebraska lawyer whose father had served with the major in Congress, recorded in his diary.[48]

When voices in St. Louis could again be heard in Canton, Foraker was trying to resume his speech. "'You seem to have heard the name of my candidate before,' Sam Saxton read out. 'Ah,' McKinley said, smiling, 'that is like him. He knows what he is doing . . .'"[49]

"He found the industries of this country paralyzed and prostrated," Foraker preached to the true believers; "he quickened them with a new life that has brought to the American people a prosperity unprecedented in all their history. He found the labor of the country everywhere idle; he has given it everywhere employment."[50]

For two years, Roosevelt had fretted over President Cleveland's "playing the part of a coward" and adopting a "thoroughly improper and un-American tone in foreign affairs." Early in his administration he had withdrawn from the Senate his predecessor's treaty of annexation of Hawaii, an action Roosevelt regarded as "a crime against white civilization."[51]

During Christmas week, 1895, the president's neutrality in the Cuban rebellion against Spain was overshadowed by the fear, expressed by New York's bellicose police commissioner, that England might be permitted to trample the Monroe Doctrine in settling a dispute with Venezuela over a British Guiana boundary. As he wrote Lodge two days after the Roosevelts had opened their family presents, "Personally I rather hope the fight will come soon. The clamor of the peace faction has convinced me that this country needs war."[52]

Robert ("Fergie") Ferguson, a British friend of the family, suggested that the "great & glorious war for which he yearns, might give effective outlet to his more natural & active inclinations." Fergie also expressed the wish that "Theodore could have a spell abroad to study foreign politics a bit." Americans should have a better idea "of the trouble that is ahead in turn for the U.S.A. just as much as for decaying European monarchies."[53]

At the start of the 1896 campaign, Roosevelt told one of his Civil War heroes, General James Harrison Wilson, "I want to drive the Spaniards out of Cuba," and to a friend he confided, "I should like to be assistant secretary of the navy." When Jacob Riis and Lincoln Steffens asked if he considered himself a presidential possibility, Roosevelt bounded out of his chair, flushed with rage. "Don't you dare ask me that!" he shouted, and went on to point out that it was not a question ever to be put to a man in public office. "It almost always kills him politically. He loses his nerve; he can't do his work; he gives up the very traits that are making him a possibility." But the thirty-seven-year-old police commissioner agreed he "must be wanting to be President. Every young man does. But I won't let myself think of it."[54]

Chapter Five

"No triumph of peace is quite so great
as the supreme triumphs of war."

—*Theodore Roosevelt, Naval War College,*

June 2, 1897

Once McKinley had been nominated, Foraker took a four-week leave from politics to make his first and only trip to Europe, where he joined his son, Benson, and his three daughters, who had been there since May. When he got back home he came to the aid of his party, poking fun at thirty-six-year-old William Jennings Bryan, who had gone to Chicago with $100 in his pocket, delivered "one of the great political addresses of all time," and left town with $40 and the Democratic nomination, won "by a perfect blend of oratorical brilliance, political finesse, and sheer luck." The "gigantic troubadour, speaking like a siege gun," took the convention hostage with a line he had perfected on the lecture circuit: "You shall not press down upon the brow of labor this crown of thorns; you shall not crucify mankind upon a cross of gold."[1]

Free coinage of silver had become a religious symbol, giving "moral and patriotic dimensions" to a "wide range of popular grievances" at a time of rising unemployment and plummeting farm prices. "The ratio of 16 to 1 pegged silver's value at 16 ounces of silver to 1 ounce of gold, a formulation based on the market prices of the two metals back in the 1830s," Hal Williams explains. "Silver had slipped badly in price since then, and the actual ratio was now closer to 32 to 1, but silverites argued that free coinage would boost the price and restore the old relationship. The silverites believed in a quantity theory of money: the amount of money in circulation determined the level of activity in the economy. A money shortage meant declining activity and depression. Silver meant prosperity."[2]

Bryan delivered his acceptance speech in New York on a mid-August night with thermometers registering 88 degrees. Some twelve thousand followers, crowded into Madison Square Garden, cooled themselves with "Bryan Silver Fans" and settled back for what they expected to be a profound emotional experience. Instead a tedious reading of a prepared text consumed an hour and forty minutes and drove away half the audience.[3]

Three nights later, speaking in Columbus, Ohio, Foraker said he had read Bryan's speech, which filled eight columns of close print in the *Cincinnati Enquirer*. It took him a day or two to do it, he explained, but "I read every word of it and when I got done with it, I didn't know much more about the money question, but I thought I knew why he was called 'the Boy Orator of the Platte.' Geography tells us that the Platte is a very peculiar river; that it is a thousand miles long and only six inches deep. As I closed the reading of that speech I had another thought about him. I thought, 'Mr. Bryan made himself by one speech, and he has unmade himself by one speech.'"[4]

McKinley, following tradition, conducted no national canvass. Instead he made himself available to out-of-town delegations swarming over his North Market Street lawn in Canton. Visitors left with the memory of a pleasant, clean-shaven man whose features, a British reporter noted, suggested "dominant will and energy rather than subtlety of mind or emotion."[5]

Free silver would lead to inflation, consuming weekly wages and life savings, he warned his visitors, and denounced the Democrats for seeking "to array labor against capital, employer against employed." Roosevelt concurred. Bryan's "bitter rancor towards the well-off" was having a deplorable effect on those "who, whether through misfortune or through misconduct, have failed in life." Such remarks prompted a friendly biographer to remark that Roosevelt "was congenitally unable to understand the poor. People who lacked wealth, even through 'misfortune,' had 'failed in life.'"[6]

In his inaugural address, McKinley made the obligatory denunciation of lynching ("courts, not mobs, must execute the penalties of the law") and rejoiced that "the North and South no longer divide on the old lines, but upon principles and policies." Jingoids took note of his declaration: "We want no wars of conquest; we must avoid the temptation of territorial aggression. War should never be entered upon until every agency of peace has failed; peace is preferable to war in almost every contingency."[7]

Next day the *Washington Post*, reflecting on economic unrest at home and turmoil abroad, reported that "no President since the time of Lincoln thirty-six years ago, has come into power under circumstances more important and in the face of possibilities more tremendous than those under which Mr. McKinley now assumes the reins of government."[8]

In this spring week of new beginnings, Foraker's biographer suggests, Ohio's new senator may well have pondered the past: "Only a few years before he had battled McKinley in the hurly-burly of Ohio politics—and had won the governorship of Ohio and leadership in the Republican party. But Hanna had stepped in to back McKinley, leaving Foraker to gain what honors he could. Indeed, Foraker may have speculated as to what would have happened had Hanna continued their early friendship. Would it have paved his way to the presidency?"[9]

Cartoonists caricatured the relationship between Hanna and McKinley, leaving the lingering notion "that Hanna made McKinley president when, in fact, the politician used the businessman to reach the White House. Hanna was not the swollen plutocrat that his enemies depicted; he was a capitalist who dreamed about harmony between employers and workers, and his position with McKinley was always that of a subordinate. McKinley needed the organizational skills and fund-raising ability that Hanna brought to politics."[10]

Foraker called on Hanna shortly after the election and was amazed to learn that he had rejected McKinley's offer of the postmaster generalship and was working on a plan to have Senator Sherman appointed secretary of state, which would enable Ohio's new Republican governor to name him as Sherman's successor. The day after McKinley's inauguration, Foraker— Ohio's senior senator by one day—escorted his old adversary to the bar of the Senate. He did it "with an air of distinction and comradeship."[11]

McKinley wanted to find a place for Roosevelt in his administration, he assured Lodge, but when another booster brought up the New Yorker's name, McKinley confessed: "I am told that your friend Theodore—whom I know only slightly—is always getting into rows with everybody. I am afraid he is too pugnacious."[12]

The police commissioner had his eye fixed on the office of assistant secretary of the navy, but first he would have to come to terms with Tom Platt, New York's "Easy Boss," so named for the patience and courtesy encasing his cold-blooded decisiveness. Lodge sounded him out on his friend's appointment and reported: "He did not feel ready to say that he would support you, if you intended to go into the Navy Department and make war on him—or, as he put it, on the organization."[13]

"I shall write Platt at once, to get an appointment to see him," Roosevelt replied.[14]

Their meeting was "exceedingly polite," but Roosevelt was left with a delicate problem. Platt, maneuvering for a Senate seat, was competing against Joseph H. Choate, a distinguished liberal Republican who had served as Roosevelt's surrogate father at Harvard and as his political confidant ever since his first campaign for the Assembly.

"I feel that I owe both my nomination and my election more to you than to any other man," Roosevelt had once told his old friend, but when Choate's aides asked him to speak for their candidate, he turned them down. At a gathering of organization leaders brought together to endorse the Easy Boss, Roosevelt was seated at the Platt table. He may have winced when the Reverend Charles H. Parkhurst, president of the Society for the Prevention of Crime, sneered at "those who consent, spaniel-like to lick the hand of their master."[15]

"I refused to speak at the Choate meeting," Roosevelt wrote Lodge; "of course if I have to declare, I shall be for Choate against Platt, for the feeling about Platt is ugly; but it is a futile and useless fight, and as I have my hands full of fights which are neither futile nor useless, I do not care to be dragged into this."[16]

In a March 20 letter to his "Darling Bye," Roosevelt seemed ready to throw in the towel. "I have no ardent backers from New York State, and the machine leaders hate me more than any other man; and even all dear Cabot's work can not offset this." By this time, however, it had occurred to the machine leaders that Roosevelt might be less harmful in Washington than in Manhattan.[17]

When his name was sent to the Senate, April 5, and promptly confirmed, the *Post* predicted he would "bring with him to Washington all that machinery of disturbance and upheaval which is as much a part of his entourage as the very air he breathes." On the other side of the Atlantic, Londoners read a warning in the *Times* of the "menacing" influence the new assistant secretary might have on American foreign policy. With Cuba and Hawaii ripe for colonial conquest, "what now seems ominous is his extreme jingoism." He brought to the Navy Department a mentality that, in the words of a McKinley biographer, "lay somewhere between that of a boy scout and the young Kaiser Wilhelm of Germany."[18]

The new assistant secretary dined at the Executive Mansion on September 17 and next day took a drive with the president. "I gave him a paper showing exactly where all our ships are," he wrote Lodge, "and I also sketched in outline what I thought ought to be done if things looked menacing about Spain, urging the necessity of taking an immediate and prompt initiative if we wished to avoid the chance of some serious trouble, and of the Japs chipping in."

The main fleet, he advised, should be on the Cuban coast within forty-eight hours after the declaration of war. An expeditionary force should be landed on the island as soon as possible, and the Asiatic squadron should blockade and, if possible, take Manila. He doubted "the war would last six weeks."[19]

On June 2, making his first public speech as the navy's assistant secretary, he called on Congress to build more and bigger ships and, in a Rooseveltian flight of rhetoric, declared: "No triumph of peace is quite so great as the supreme triumphs of war."[20]

Foraker, who had been appointed to the Foreign Relations Committee, stood side by side with Roosevelt in enforcing the Monroe Doctrine, building a large navy and merchant marine, and putting an end to Spanish "barbarism" in Cuba. In his first important Senate speech, May 19, 1897, he spoke out in favor of a joint resolution recognizing the Cuban freedom-fighters as "belligerents," and thus according them "belligerent rights."

In the absence of such recognition a Cuban insurgent was "but a traitor on land and a pirate on sea," to be shot "like a dog" or "hanged at the yardarm." Passage of the resolution would "not make war with Spain," he argued. It would simply say "we will have nothing more to do with your war; we will put the contest on the high plane of legitimate warfare, and there leave you to fight it out."[21]

The speech, coming late in the day, was "most important and excited the greatest interest," the *Washington Post* noted, and quoted its peroration: "The United States has not any right in a moral point of view to stand longer a quasi copartner with Spain in the conduct of this brutal and atrocious war. The time has come to put an end to it. It is another 'covenant with sin and league with hell,' and for my part, by no word or speech or act or vote of mine shall the unholy alliance longer continue than until this resolution comes to be voted upon by the Senate."[22]

When Senator Redfield Proctor of Vermont showed Roosevelt a letter from Foraker praising an article he had written on Hawaii, the assistant secretary of the navy dropped a line to Ohio's new senior senator "to say how glad I am you wrote him. It was a very kind and generous thing to do; and I don't think I have ever seen a man more pleased than Proctor was. It seemed to me his article was one of the best there has been on the subject. In fact he is a jingo! and it is rather a relief to see a man who can't be touched by the timid people of wealth, or the unscrupulous ones either. I am very anxious to see you and have a chat over foreign affairs."[23]

Always a thorough researcher, Foraker reviewed the correspondence of the State Department and the files of the Foreign Relations Committee, talked to elder statesmen, and had his staff check every reference to Cuba in the *Congressional Record*. He prepared a resolution calling for recognition of Cuban independence and then waited for a propitious moment to introduce it.[24]

William Randolph Hearst was also keeping an impatient eye on Cuba. The twenty-one-year-old *Harvard Lampoon* business manager, having evolved into the thirty-four-year-old editor and owner of the *New York Journal*, was challenging Pulitzer's *World* with dramatic stunts and inflammatory fictions designed to nourish popular support for war with Spain.

As 1897 drew to a close, the unpredictable young publisher came up with the idea of hosting a Hearstian party for greater New York's New Year's Day incorporation of Brooklyn, the Bronx, Staten Island, and sections of Queens. Overnight the city would expand from 39 to 320 square miles, with an increase in population from 2,000,000 to 3,388,000 (1,200,000 of whom lived in what was to become the Borough of Brooklyn). New York would begin the new year as the world's second most populous city, surpassed only by London.

The California carpetbagger ordered carloads of fireworks for his New Year's Eve party. Rain, turning at times to snow, filled the local saloons with thirsty celebrants and teetotallers taking shelter from the storm. When fireworks frightened horses drawing a float down Broadway, fifteen bystanders were injured and a tuba was flattened. At midnight a dozen choral societies in City Hall Plaza broke into "Auld Lang Syne," and a battery of field guns fired a hundred-gun salute, putting a deafening end to what the *Tribune* described as "the biggest, noisiest and most hilarious New Year's celebration that Manhattan Island has ever known."[25]

Six weeks later the USS *Maine*, paying Cuba what was billed as a "courtesy visit," blew up in Havana harbor, killing 266 Americans. Trumpeting the slogan, "Remember the *Maine!*" Hearst and Pulitzer attributed the disaster to Spanish saboteurs, although it was widely known that the steel, steam-powered ships carrying tons of explosives were, in the words of the chairman of the Senate Committee on Naval Affairs, "little less than a volcano." Modern research indicates an accidental internal explosion on a coal-burning ship with inadequately ventilated bunkers.[26]

Ten days after the sinking of the *Maine*, Roosevelt took advantage of Navy Secretary Long's absence from his office and, disobeying his instructions to take no "step affecting the policy of the administration without consulting the President or me," he telegraphed Commodore George Dewey: "In the event of declaration of war Spain, your duty will be to see that the Spanish squadron does not leave the Asiatic coast, and then offensive operations in Philippine Islands."[27]

Long was furious when he discovered what his belligerent subordinate had done, but he did not countermand the order. He may have been "relieved the decision had been made for him," Harbaugh suggests and makes it clear that Roosevelt's "tactical wisdom" in issuing the order should not be confused with his "unofficial war-mongering." He quotes a student of Roosevelt's foreign policies who concluded that the hero of San Juan Hill "came close to seeking war for its own sake." William James wrote that his former Harvard student regarded "one foe . . . as good as another," and "swamps everything together in one flood of abstract bellicose emotion."[28]

While a naval inquiry board was investigating the loss of the *Maine*, Edith Roosevelt was battling a fever that for a month had never dropped below 101 degrees. "We could not tell whether she would live or die," Roosevelt wrote Brooks Adams, March 21, 1898. "At last she was put under the knife; and now, very slowly, she is crawling back to life."[29]

Three days later the naval board's report on the *Maine*, attributing the explosion to an external cause, reached the president. His calm, dispassion-ate response to Congress fell on the legislators "like a wet blanket," the *New York Herald* reported March 29. It was "not warlike enough for them," Charles Dawes, comptroller of the currency, noted in his journal, and he reflected the thinking of his friend in the Executive Mansion when he added: "Foraker introduced a resolution recognizing Cuba's independence and a resolution declaring war was also introduced. We all want Cuban indepen-dence, but if we fight it must be for humanity's sake, not from other mo-tives. War is a hideous wrong when used to achieve ends possible by peace."[30]

"I am utterly disgusted," Roosevelt wrote his brother-in-law, William S. Cowles, and in a letter to a friend the following week, Foraker reported: "We are all waiting for the president to head the column going into war. I urged him strongly to come out for intervention and independence. He agreed to the intervention proposal but declined to consider independence."[31]

"Our battleships are seizing Spanish vessels," Dawes wrote in his jour-nal, April 22. Four days later he noted: "The President's message recom-mending a declaration of war went to Congress today." During that interim he recorded the resignation of McKinley's venerable Secretary of State: "The great career of John Sherman should have closed in some other way. But old age has impaired his mental faculties and to old age the strongest minds must come."[32]

The first troops called up were black soldiers of the 25th Infantry, whose ranks included Mingo Sanders. Back in the spring of 1881, while Theodore Roosevelt and his bride were crossing the Atlantic on the *Celtic* (it was Alice's first overseas trip), Sanders had signed up in Charleston, South Carolina, where he had once watched a military company on parade.

"I thought it was the prettiest sight I had ever seen," he recalled years later. "I made up my mind right then and there that I would be a soldier some day, if I lived."[33]

Assigned to Company B, he spent his first winter with the 25th as a soldier in Dakota Territory, protecting Northern Pacific Railway workers and settlers on the Keya Paha and Niobrara rivers. In November, 1882, his company was transferred to Fort Snelling, Minnesota, where he put in five of the "least eventful" years of the regiment's history.[34]

In May, 1888, the 25th set out for Fort Shaw in Montana Territory, where, in the words of its historian, the regiment played a minor role in the

Pine Ridge Campaign of 1890–91, "the last important Indian war in which United States troops were engaged." In the summer of 1894, when the Northern Pacific was having labor troubles, Company B was moved to Fort Missoula to guard the trains and the mail.[35]

"The prejudice against the colored soldiers seems to be without foundation for if the 25th Infantry is an example of the colored regiments there is no exaggeration in the statement that there are no better troops in the service," the *Anaconda Standard* observed.[36]

On April 10, 1898, two weeks before war with Spain was declared, Company B was ordered to Chattanooga, Tennessee, where a training camp was set up in Chickamauga National Park. "If there be war," the *Daily Missoulian* observed as Mingo Sanders was packing to leave Fort Missoula, "the fortunes of the 25th will be followed with intense interest by the people of Missoula, who are satisfied that though it is a dark regiment not a white feather will be shown."[37]

On the first of May, newspapers reported an astonishing victory in Manila Bay. Commodore George Dewey had destroyed Spain's Asiatic fleet without the loss of a single American sailor. He attributed his success to the Navy Department's "hard work and preparation." Roosevelt let him know immediately how pleased he was to think that "I had any share in getting you the opportunity that you have used so well." The commodore was hurriedly promoted to rear admiral, the rank he should have been given when he took command of the Asiatic Squadron.[38]

Benson Foraker, serving as secretary for his father's Senate committee, left for Georgia on May 29 to join General James F. Wade's staff at Camp Thomas, located on the grounds of the Chickamauga battleground. Julia was in Kirksville, Missouri, with her son, Arthur, a delicate child of six, when word came that Benson had been ordered to Havana. In a heat wave of "particular ferocity," she made the forty-four-hour trip to New York, riding backward the whole way, "my section overflowing with women, children, lunch-baskets, and bananas." In record-breaking heat that night, "ambulances clanged up and down Fifth Avenue, picking up prostrated people. The next day Benson sailed."

In late October, the day after Julia returned to Washington, she got word that Benson had yellow fever. A month after a thoughtful colonel cabled the parents: YOU NEED HAVE NO FURTHER UNEASINESS ABOUT BENSON, he was on a ship heading home. He resumed his work with the

Senate committee, where, in his mother's words, he "was a favorite with everyone from President McKinley down—his sweet temper, his bubbling spirits and amusing exploits!" He appeared to have fully recovered, but, it turned out, his illness had "laid the foundation of the trouble which so prematurely robbed him of his life. War is yellow fever for us."[39]

Roosevelt was offered command of a regiment "to be composed exclusively of frontiersmen possessing special qualifications as horsemen and marksmen," but he asked to serve under his more experienced friend, Colonel Leonard Wood, who had won the Congressional Medal of Honor fighting Geronimo. Roosevelt sent a telegram to Brooks Brothers ordering an ordinary cavalry lieutenant-colonel's uniform in blue Cravenette." He also ordered a dozen pairs of steel-rimmed spectacles, which were to be "stowed in all parts of his uniform, while several were fastened with light thread into the lining of his campaign hat."[40]

"Theodore Roosevelt, that *wilder werwegener,* has left the Navy Department where he had the chance of his life and has joined a cowboy regiment," John Hay reported to a friend. When word reached Henry Adams in Constantinople, he asked his friend Elizabeth Cameron: "Is his wife dead? Has he quarreled with everybody? Is he quite mad?"[41]

"For two years I have been urging that we put Spain out of Cuba," the lieutenant colonel wrote *New York Sun* editor Paul Dana, responding to a "kind editorial" suggesting that he might be more useful at his desk than in the field, "and if there ever was a righteous war it will be this; and if, owing to the unfortunate delay in beginning it, we see our men dying of yellow fever in Cuba, I should hate to be comfortably at home in Washington, although I have as much dislike of death as anyone could have, and take as keen enjoyment in life."[42]

On the eve of the assault on the San Juan Heights, Lodge came across a biographical sketch of Roosevelt in a Madrid paper and sent him a translation: "He was born at Harlaam and immigrated to America at an early age. He was educated at the town of Harvard where there is a commercial school, as there are no colleges or universities in the United States. He then became a policeman in New York and is now the commander of the American Navy."[43]

Chapter Six

". . . when the wolf rises in the heart."

—*Theodore Roosevelt*

It was the only war the Rough Riders' eupeptic colonel would ever fight, and he made the most of it, displaying magnificent courage under fire and earning the admiration and affection not only of his men but also of the correspondents whose dispatches would blaze his path to the White House. The Dutch Protestant moralist who criticized Tolstoy for having "preached against war . . . as against marriage," approached the field of battle like a bridegroom advancing toward the nuptial couch.[1]

"All men who feel any power of joy in battle," he once said of his Cuban honeymoon, "know what it is like when the wolf rises in the heart."[2]

Roosevelt's outfit was dubbed "The Rough Riders," a term used in dime novels and adopted by another showman of the period, Buffalo Bill Cody, whose "Congress of the Rough Riders of the West" had displayed their horsemanship at the Chicago World's Fair. Unfortunately for Colonel Roosevelt, who had spent weeks training his cowboys, bear hunters, bronco busters, and polo players, his Rough Riders went to war as foot soldiers. There was no room in the Cuban armada for their horses. Only senior officers would be mounted. One-third of the Rough Riders also had to be left behind, but accommodations were found for two Vitagraph motion-picture cameramen.[3]

Commanded by Brigadier General William Rufus Shafter, a blunt, gout-ridden, 300-pound target of cartoonists, V Corps included not only Roosevelt's dismounted cavalry superstars but four black regiments as well—the 9th and 10th Cavalry (also without horses) and the 24th and 25th Infantry. The black outfits, along with some white troops, were assigned to six ships.

Aboard the *Leona* with the 10th Cavalry was Black Jack (originally "Nigger Jack") Pershing, whose pejorative nickname had been given him by West Point cadets because of his frontier service with Negro troopers before returning to the Academy for a tour of duty as instructor in tactics. On the *Concho* the 25th Infantry was given the lowest decks, where there was almost no light and one toilet to serve 1,256 men.[4]

"When they are all below with the dead lights and ports closed it is awful down there," Second Lieutenant Samuel P. Lyon of Company F wrote his wife, Mary. Sergeant Major Frank W. Pullen agreed that "it was neither fit for man nor beast."[5]

The 25th shared the *Concho* with a white regiment the black infantry-men had come to know in Montana when both outfits were patrolling the mines. They were on the best of terms, but once the ship was under way, on June 14, 1898, they were ordered by their brigade commander not to "in-termingle." The Negro soldiers were assigned the starboard side of the ship, their old friends the port.

"Still greater," Pullen continued, "was the surprise of everyone when another order was issued from the same source directing that the white regiment should make coffee first, all the time, and detailing a guard to see that the order was carried out. All of these things were done seemingly to humiliate us and without a word of protest from our officers."[6]

Thus they set off together to take up what Rudyard Kipling would label "the White Man's burden." As Roosevelt saw it, the world was to be "won," as the American West had been won, "by the power of the mighty civilized races which have not lost the fighting instinct, and which by their expan-sion are gradually bringing peace into the red wastes where the barbarian peoples of the world hold sway."[7]

William Randolph Hearst, having given the Navy, "without any condi-tions whatever," his 138-foot yacht, *Buccaneer*, chartered a steamship, *Sylvia*, to take him to the front with his staff and a lightweight printing press. He intended to publish a paper for the troops, the *Journal-Examiner.* He also planned to serve as a war correspondent, and like Roosevelt he made room for a "biograph expert," who would take motion pictures of his war. Historians were left to marvel that one small island could contain two such world-class egos.[8]

In the early morning hours of June 19 the officers and men of the 25th got their first view of the mountains of Santiago de Cuba. For the next two days the *Concho* was tossed about by rough seas. On the evening of the twenty-first the seasick men were ordered to prepare to disembark the following morning.

Unlike most of the officers and war correspondents describing the landing, Sergeant-Major Pullen took note of the ragged *insurrectos* waiting to welcome their deliverers. "The greater portion of those poor fellows were both coatless and shoeless, many of them being almost nude. They were by no means careful about their uniform. The thing every one seemed careful about was his munitions of war, for each man had his gun, ammunition and machete. Be it remembered that this portion of the Cuban army was almost entirely composed of black Cubans."[9]

The invaders landed at Daiquiri, a squalid coastal village of sun-baked houses thatched with palm trees. When they began their eighteen-mile march toward Santiago, the 25th led the way. The men had been ordered to come ashore with full field equipment, which included blankets and a shelter tent. The officers, as Lieutenant Lyon would remember so well, had been "directed to take nothing but their side arms and a raincoat, their bedding to be unloaded from the ship later. This never happened." Lyon was left to fight the war without blankets or a change of uniform.[10]

"Wood's Weary Walkers," as Colonel Wood's dismounted Rough Riders now referred to themselves, spent their first day on enemy soil tidying up their campsite, only to be ordered out on a seven-mile march to Siboney. It was ten o'clock when they came within view of the campfires warming troops already settled down in the abandoned village.

On either side, black overhanging ridges stood between the invaders and the port city of Santiago, where a Spanish squadron lay at anchor. If the Spaniards could pin down the *norteamericanos* for a few weeks, the lucky ones who survived the relentless shower of Mauser bullets from rifle pits and blockhouses would be laid low by yellow fever and dysentery. The key to glorious victory or humiliating defeat lay in scaling the heavily fortified heights of San Juan.[11]

On June 24, the day after Wood's Weary Walkers had made camp at Siboney, where Hearst had set up his printing press for the *Journal-Examiner*, they came under enemy fire for the first time on a jungle trail at a place called Las Guasimas. Roosevelt and Edward Marshall, a Hearst reporter, were discussing an Astor House luncheon with Marshall's employer. Roosevelt was dressed in the uniform he wore throughout the campaign, a coarse blue-flannel shirt, brown canvas trousers and leggings, and a broad-brimmed felt hat holding in place a blue polka-dot handkerchief that hung down over the nape of his neck. When the near-sighted Dakota rancher removed his hat to fan the stagnant air, he squinted more closely at some barbed wire lying across the trail where the 1st Volunteers had paused to reconnoiter.

"My God! This wire has been cut today," he said, and pointed out that the bright ends had a light rust from the morning dew.[12]

Suddenly the two men heard the blood-chilling whine of a Mauser bullet. The first soldier to fall was Sergeant Hamilton Fish, who died twenty minutes later, after giving "a small lady's hunting case watch from his belt to a messmate as a last souvenir." The aristocratic New York noncom was followed by Captain Allyn Capron, Jr., who took a bullet through the heart.[13]

Men of the 25th Infantry, ordered to reinforce the horseless cavalrymen, could have reached them in a couple of hours had their brigade commander, a white officer, not taken the wrong trail, "seemingly on purpose," Pullen noted, "and when we arrived at the place of battle twilight was fading into darkness."[14]

Correspondent Edward Marshall captured for his readers the historic moment when the first of the Rough Riders ran toward the opening the 10th Cavalry had cut through the barbed wire:

> *Perhaps a dozen of Roosevelt's men had passed into the thicket before he did. Then he stepped across the wire himself, and, from that instant, became the most magnificent soldier I have ever seen. It was as if that barbed wire strand had formed a dividing line in his life, and that when he stepped across it he left behind him in the bridle path all those unadmirable and conspicuous traits which have so often caused him to be justly criticized in civic life, and found on the other side of it, in that Cuban thicket, the coolness, the calm judgment, the towering heroism, which made him, perhaps, the most admired and best beloved of all Americans in Cuba.[15]*

Four days later the *New York Times* reported a coalition of independent Republicans intended to get him nominated for governor in September.

On the morning following the exchange of gunfire at Las Guasimas, the 25th ate a hearty breakfast and at one o'clock that afternoon broke camp and marched about six miles to Sevilla. At some point on this otherwise uneventful Saturday in late June, Colonel Roosevelt dropped by with his men.

"Can you give us some rations?" Sergeant Mingo Sanders remembered him asking, and eight years later, when he had been abruptly returned to civilian life, Sanders told Mary Church Terrell, president of the National Association of Colored Women: "I can see Colonel Roosevelt now just as plain as I saw him that day in Cuba. Our men had just received a fresh supply, so we all gladly divided our hard tack and bacon with the lieutenant-colonel of the Rough Riders, now President of the United States."[16]

When he got around to writing *The Rough Riders*, Roosevelt also re-called the day. "On the afternoon of the 25th we moved on a couple of miles, and camped in a marshy open spot close to a beautiful stream. Here we lay for several days." He made no reference to the hospitality recalled by Sergeant Sanders.[17]

While camped along the trail leading from Siboney to Santiago, the Americans scoured the woods for mangos and groused about the food and the high cost of a plug of tobacco (up from eight cents to two dollars). They could see Spaniards working on their trenches and parading through the streets of El Caney, the mountain village that would have to be taken in order to protect the troops assigned to storm the heights of San Juan.

No artillery was called on to "drop a shell among the busy men at work among the trenches or to interrupt the street parades in El Caney," Richard Harding Davis reported. "For four days before the American soldiers captured the same rifle-pits at El Caney and San Juan, with a loss of two thousand men, they watched their men diligently preparing for their coming, and wondered why there was no order to embarrass or to end these preparations."[18]

Among other oversights, the army had neglected to bring ice or ice-making machines to help reduce the fevers of the wounded. Hearst turned his supply over to the battlefield surgeons before boarding the *Sylvia* and heading for a Jamaican port, where his battlefield photographs could be handed over to a mail boat.[19]

On July 1, General Wood's promotion placed Roosevelt, now a full colonel, in command of the "Weary Walkers." The "great day" of his life began at 6:30 A.M., when Captain Capron, the father of the Rough Rider killed at Las Guasimas, directed artillery fire at El Caney. The 2nd Division was scheduled to capture the heavily fortified mountain village in an hour or so, then swing "to the left, cut off and take in the flank the Spaniards on San Juan hill, against which the main army was then to move in direct assault."[20]

Artillery support for the assault, essential to the success of such an operation, consisted of one battery of four outmoded black-powder guns emitting clouds of white smoke that defined their position for the Spaniards who responded with modern smokeless weapons. By 1:30 that afternoon, when the Americans were suffering heavy casualties as they crept forward, an order arrived from General Shafter to forget El Caney and move to assist the troops at San Juan. The order, Lodge noted in his history of the war, "must have seemed like a grim satire and was disregarded."[21]

The black infantrymen of the 25th were held in reserve in a mango grove that morning. Around noon, four companies (D, E, G, and H) were moved out to form a firing line, with Company C held in reserve. In marching to their position, Pullen recorded, they met some retreating companies of the 2nd Massachusetts Volunteers: "They were completely whipped, and took occasion to warn us, saying: 'Boys, there is no use to go up there, you cannot see a thing; they are slaughtering our men!'"[22]

The 25th, along with the 4th and 12th, was under fire for nine hours before El Caney fell.

From the heights of San Juan the Spaniards looked down on a stream and a grassy plain broken by hills, one of which would go down in history as Kettle Hill when the Rough Riders and the 9th Cavalry fought their way to its crest and found a large iron pot used in sugar refining. San Juan Hill, "the strongest of all the Spanish positions," was left to the black regulars of the 24th Infantry and the 10th Cavalry, fighting alongside the white infantrymen of the 13th and 21st regiments and the 1st New York Volunteers, who faced certain slaughter. Unlike the regulars and Roosevelt's volunteers, who were armed with the new smokeless Krag-Jorgensen rifles, the New Yorkers had been issued antiquated single-shot, black-powder Springfields. Each shot they fired sent a white smoke signal to enemy sharpshooters.[23]

Roosevelt, ordered to hold his men in reserve on Kettle Hill, kept sending messengers in search of some higher authority who could direct him to advance. Finally the order came and, as he recorded the moment, "I sprang on my horse and then my 'crowded hour' began."[24]

In the satirical version Finley Peter Dunne wrote for Mr. Dooley's admirers, the colonel told how he had "sint th' ar-rmy home an' attackted San Joon hill. 'Ar-rmed on'y with a small thirty-two which I used in th' West to shoot th' fleet prairie dog, I climbed that precipitous ascent in th' face iv th' most galling' fire I iver knew or heerd iv." He fired at the man nearest him "an' knew by th' expression iv his face that th' trusty bullet wint home. It passed through his frame, he fell, an' wan little home in far-off Catalonia was made happy be th' thought that their riprisintive had been kilt be th' future governor iv New York."[25]

Stephen Crane gave a novelist's eyewitness account: "No doubt when history begins to grind out her story we will find that many a thundering, fine, grand order was given for that day's work; but after all there will be no harm in contending that the fighting line, the men and their regimental officers, took the hill chiefly because they knew they could take it, some having no orders and others disobeying whatever orders they had. In civil life the newspapers would have called it a grand popular movement."[26]

Describing the battle portrayed in *The Rough Riders* (the irreverent Mr. Dooley renamed the book, *Alone in Cubia*), Roosevelt praised the colored troops of the 9th and 10th Cavalry, who had done "as well as any soldiers could possibly do," but he offended Negro readers of *The Rough Riders* by remarking that colored soldiers "are, of course, peculiarly dependent upon their white officers. Occasionally they produce noncommissioned officers who can take the initiative and accept responsibility precisely like the best class of whites; but this cannot be expected normally, nor is it fair to expect it."

He singled out "a score of so of colored infantrymen" who, he said, had drifted to the rear "either helping wounded men, or saying that they wished to find their own regiments. . . . This I could not allow, as it was depleting my line, so I jumped up, and walking a few yards to the rear, drew my revolver, halted the retreating soldiers, and called out to them that I appreciated the gallantry with which they had fought and would be sorry to hurt them, but that I should shoot the first man who, on any pretense whatever, went to the rear."[27]

In the *New York Age*, Sergeant Preston Holliday, a black cavalryman, responded to Roosevelt's charges. The alleged shirkers were not infantrymen, Holliday contended; they were members of the 10th Cavalry who had been ordered by one of their officers, Lieutenant Fleming, to carry wounded to the rear. "Colonel Roosevelt, seeing the men but not knowing their orders, drew his revolver as he said. But Lieutenant Fleming later assured him that the men were acting under his orders." Roosevelt returned the following day to apologize to the cavalrymen, Holliday wrote. "He had seen his mistake and found them far different from what he supposed."[28]

"I had no more trouble with them," Roosevelt wrote; "they seeming to accept me as one of their own officers. The colored cavalrymen had already so accepted me; in return, the Rough Riders, although for the most part Southwesterners, who have a strong color prejudice, grew to accept them with hearty good will as comrades, and were willing, in their own phrase, 'to drink out of the same canteen.'"[29]

In a self-effacing talk Lieutenant John Pershing gave in Chicago at a Thanksgiving service in his parents' church, he expressed his admiration for the courage of the black troopers as they crossed the San Juan River to reach the southern slopes of San Juan Hill: "The men took cover only when ordered to do so and exposed themselves fearlessly in crossing the open spaces." When Lieutenant Jules Ord, who led the charge across the river, was shot down, Pershing's biographer writes, Corporal John Walker, "in a frenzy of anger . . . killed the man who killed Ord, and in his quest for vengeance became probably the first American to reach the top of San Juan Hill."[30]

By the time the fighting ended, the 10th Cavalry had lost 10 percent of its officers and 20 percent of its enlisted men. "We officers of the 10th Cavalry could have taken our black heroes into our arms," Pershing said. "They had again fought their way into our affections." He remembered seeing "a colored trooper stop at a trench filled with Spanish dead and wounded, gently raise the head of a wounded Spanish lieutenant, and give him the last drop of water from his canteen."[31]

As the 25th Infantry was preparing to leave Cuba, Lieutenant Colonel A. S. Daggett paid tribute to his fallen men. "Being of a race which only thirty-five years ago emerged through a long and bloody war, from a condition of servitude, they in turn engaged in a war which was officially announced to be in the interest of humanity and gave all they had—their lives—that the oppressed might be free."[32]

"The brightest hours of your lives," he reminded the living, "were on the afternoon of July 1st. Formed in battle array, you advanced to the stone fort against volleys therefrom and rifle-pits in front, and against a galling fire from blockhouses, the church tower and the village on your left. You continued to advance, skillfully and bravely directed by the officers in immediate command, halting and delivering such a cool and well-directed fire that the enemy was compelled to wave the white flag in token of surrender."

A Spanish officer recalled:

> *I have never seen anything to equal the courage and dash of those Americans, who, stripped to the waist, offered their naked breasts to our murderous fire, and literally threw themselves on our trenches, on the very muzzles of our guns. We had the advantage of our position and mowed them down by the hundreds, but they never retreated or fell back an inch. As one man fell shot through the heart, another would take his place, with grim determination and unflinching devotion to duty in every line of his face. Their gallantry was heroic. We wondered at these men, who fought like lions and fell like men.[33]*

Colonel Daggett sent the regiment home with the reminder: "You may well return to the United States proud of your accomplishments; and if any one asks you what you have done, point him to El Caney."[34]

"When the war began," Ambassador John Hay wrote Colonel Roosevelt from the London embassy: "I was like the rest; I deplored your place in the Navy where you were so useful and so acceptable. But I knew it was idle to preach to a young man. You obeyed your own daemon, and I imagine we older fellows will all have to confess that you were in the right. As Sir Walter wrote:

> *One crowded hour of glorious life*
> *Is worth an age without a name.*

"You have written your name on several pages of your country's history, and they are all honorable to you and comfortable to your friends."[35]

Chapter Seven

*"There's only one life between this madman
and the White House."*

—*Mark Hanna,*

Republican National Convention,

Philadelphia, 1900

When Colonel Roosevelt made his triumphant return from Cuba in the summer of 1898, Senator Tom Platt invited Chauncey Depew, a wealthy Republican spellbinder and a generous campaign contributor, to meet him in Manhattan to discuss the distasteful possibility of running the hero of San Juan Heights for governor of New York to replace Frank Black, the Republican incumbent whose administration had been discredited when a million dollars appropriated for Erie Canal improvements were found to have been stolen or wasted.

Depew, who could be counted on to put both his oratorical powers and his purse at the service of his party in the coming campaign, pointed out that once he took to the hustings to plump for the reelection of Governor Black, hecklers would break in to ask embarrassing questions about "the Canal steal." If Roosevelt were the candidate, he could remind his audience that "we have nominated for governor a man who has demonstrated in public office and on the battlefield that he is a fighter for the right, and always victorious." After making assurances that every stolen dollar would be returned to the public till, Depew would then trot out the colonel and his Rough Riders while the band played the "Star-Spangled Banner."

"Roosevelt will be nominated," Boss Platt sighed.[1]

His emissary, Lemuel Quigg, a former *Tribune* reporter, asked the colonel for a "plain statement" that he would accept the nomination and would not "make war" on Platt and his organization. Roosevelt said he would, indeed, accept the nomination and also would "try to get on well with the organization," but "I should have to act finally as my own judgment and conscience dictated."[2]

"I have played it in bull luck this summer," the governor wrote his London friend Cecil Arthur Spring-Rice after slipping into office with a majority of 17,794 votes. "First, to get into the war; and then to get out of it; then to get elected. . . . I am more than contented to be Governor of New York, and shall not care if I never hold another office."[3]

One of the hundreds of bills Roosevelt signed, Harbaugh notes,

> *banned race discrimination and repealed a previous authorization of separate schools for Negroes on a local-option basis. In common with most white Americans of the period, the Governor did not regard Negroes in general as the equals of whites. But he did believe that many individual Negroes were superior to individual whites, and he felt deeply that they should have full opportunity to prove their merit. "My children sit in the same school with colored children," he righteously remarked when the bill came up.*[4]

On his way to Las Vegas, New Mexico, in late June to celebrate the first anniversary of the Rough Riders' arrival in Cuba, Governor Roosevelt reminisced with a reporter in Chicago: "It's about 3 o'clock now, isn't it? Well, one year ago today, almost to the moment, I was standing on the beach delivering a mental panegyric over my best nag, which was being drowned before my eyes. The poor fellow missed a whole lot of hardship and sport by kicking the quicksand that day."

"According to a dispatch in an afternoon paper," the reporter pointed out, "Mark Hanna is satisfied that your Presidential aspirations for 1900 have gone glimmering."

"You are the first to tell me that," Roosevelt replied, "or at least to infer that I had any aspirations of that character. Poor Mark! He's probably saved me a great deal of trouble and worry. And to think that he scooped the convention. Wonderful!"[5]

Roosevelt came home from the western trip excited by his reception at every whistle-stop. "I was received by dense throngs exactly as if I had been a presidential candidate," he wrote Lodge, but for the time being, he confided, "of all the work I would like to undertake, that of Secretary of War appeals to me most."[6]

In that office he would not only control the army but also define the country's new colonial policy. The Cabinet post, however, was offered to Elihu Root, a conservative New York corporation lawyer of uncommon ability who proceeded to reorganize the discredited and demoralized department, suppress a Philippine insurrection and, working closely with Senator Foraker, iron out the details of the country's colonial system in Porto Rico.[7]

On the day of Roosevelt's stopover in Chicago, Foraker happened to be in New York, where a *Times* reporter caught up with him at the Waldorf-Astoria and asked about the political situation in Ohio. "I have no doubt of Republican success," he replied, and the interview turned inevitably to the jungle war in the Philippines. Foraker voiced his suspicion that the press was not getting sufficient information from the War Department. "If more men and money are wanted, Congress will provide the means," he said, even though "the war is not popular."[8]

It was particularly unpopular among Negroes whose husbands, brothers, lovers, and sons had gone off to the war against Spain expecting "nothing but good" for people of color in Cuba and at home. After fighting "for the honor of our country," they had come back to the same old southern "mixture of local bigotry, harassment, and occasional violence." They waited in vain for the president to make good on his inaugural pledge, "Lynchings must not be tolerated," but, as Gould notes, "such an action on McKinley's part would have run counter to his zeal for sectional reconciliation and a Republican reluctance to return to the unfashionable tactics of Reconstruction."[9]

When eleven Negroes were killed in an outbreak of violence in Wilmington, North Carolina, in November, 1898, McKinley was urged by black leaders and northern sympathizers to denounce the bloodshed in his annual message. It went unmentioned. "A man of jelly who would turn us all loose to the mob and not say a word," grumbled T. Thomas Fortune, the black editor whose *New York Globe* had given fifteen-year-old Willie Du Bois his start in journalism.[10]

As discontent deepened in the summer of 1899, a black correspondent urged McKinley to "be President of the whole people, and act as he would if Indians were killing white men, as white men are killing Negroes." The president took a different course. He directed the War Department to recruit black volunteers, who were thought to be less susceptible to malaria and yellow fever, and commission black field officers. Two regiments reached the Philippines in January, 1900. This symbolic gesture was as far as he could go.[11]

In January, 1900, while Governor Roosevelt was seated at his desk in Albany assuring his friends he had no desire to run as McKinley's vice president that fall, he confided to Lodge that "the thing I should really like to do would be to be the first civil Governor General of the Philippines."[12]

Later that month, McKinley summoned Judge Taft to the Executive Mansion. Taft left Cincinnati on a night train, wondering what the president had in mind. There was no known vacancy on the Supreme Court. When he was ushered into McKinley's office, he found the president waiting with the secretaries of war and the navy, Elihu Root and John D. Long. To Taft's astonishment he was asked to serve on a new commission to the Philippine Islands and, possibly, be its president.

"He might as well have told me that he wanted me to take a flying machine," Taft later recalled.

Root, who had given up a lucrative corporate law practice to enter public service, bluntly reminded Judge Taft that he had enjoyed "an easy time of it holding office since you were twenty-one." Now, at forty-two, he had come to a crossroads. "You may go on holding the job you have in a humdrum, mediocre way. But here is something that will test you; something in the way of effort and struggle, and the question is, will you take the harder or the easier task?"[13]

Taft asked for a week to think it over. He went back home to discuss it with Nellie, who urged him to accept the appointment. His brother Horace concurred. Taft agreed on condition he head the commission, so that "I shall be really responsible for success or failure."[14]

Before settling on Taft for the Philippine assignment McKinley had turned to Foraker for advice. The senator gave his "hearty approval," which produced a grateful letter from his hometown protégé: "I shall always have a feeling that the course of my life has been largely due to you who gave me the opportunity and first honor from which all that I have had since has easily flowed," Taft wrote, and went on to add: "The work now to be undertaken is of the most perplexing and original character and I gravely fear that I am not qualified. But the die is cast—I must attempt it."[15]

Taft and his four fellow commissioners reached Manila aboard the USS *Hancock* on a sultry day in early June, but they detected a "certain frigidity" in the air. It emanated from the office of General Arthur MacArthur, who had spent the last two years in the islands serving as military governor while his son Douglas was leading his class (1903) at West Point. The general and his staff "were utterly cynical regarding their brown brothers—cynical and convinced that civilization could be brought to the Philippines by the Krag [rifle] and the bayonet alone." The five commissioners waited in the ship's cabin for the military governor's courtesy call. He didn't show up.

The general, Taft reported to Root, "looks at his task as one of conquering eight millions of recalcitrant, treacherous and sullen people." Taft's policy was based on the premise that "we hold the Philippines for the benefit of the Filipinos and we are not to pass a single act or to approve a single measure that has not that as its chief purpose."[16]

Foraker, as chairman of the Senate Committee on the Pacific Islands and Porto Rico, had familiarized himself with Luzon and the seven thousand surrounding islands to such an extent that he was a frequent witness before the Philippines Committee. He sent Taft a copy of his Porto Rico bill, which, its author recalled with pride in his memoirs, "proved to be the first organic law ever enacted for the government of territory belonging to the United States, and yet not a part of the United States."[17]

The Foraker Act, signed by President McKinley on April 12, 1900, gave Porto Rico a government drawn up along the lines of a British crown colony, dominated by Congress and the president, who appointed the governor and the executive council. Foraker, opposed to racial disfranchisement whether it cropped up at home or abroad, had done his best to give the natives citizenship, but Congress went along with the administration's refusal to grant the island territorial status, which would have offered it the prospect of eventual statehood, an offensive prospect for legislators who agreed with Root that the mainland electorate should not be "diluted" by island voters of color.[18]

When the Foraker Act was upheld by the Supreme Court (May 27, 1901), its author regarded the decision as "a complete vindication of the position held by the Republican Party with respect to the power of Congress to legislate for Porto Rico and the Philippines, and settles it 'once and for all' that the United States is the equal in sovereign power of any other independent Government."

The Senator's identification with the court's settlement of the Insular Cases, the *New York Times* reported, had political gossips in the capital suggesting that he was now the "'logical' candidate for President to succeed Mr. McKinley" when his second term ended in 1905. The senator, like the president, was from Ohio, a presidential breeding ground, and had a splendid war record, and, unlike McKinley, he could be counted on to attract voters with his "political audacity."[19]

In the 1800s, America's new industrial plant, moving more goods to more people than ever before, was also stifling competition by creating more "trusts." The "robber barons" flourished in a tax-free "artificial paradise" because of "a stable government dedicated to the preservation of private property and devoted to an ambiguous concept of laissez-faire. Through political alliances, principally with the Republican party, the big businessman consolidated his economic triumphs."[20]

America in the Gilded Age, reported James Bryce, the perceptive British historian and diplomat, had more millionaires than any other country. (John D. Rockefeller was a couple of hundred thousand dollars shy of being a *billionaire*.) If invective against their vast fortunes by labor's "more extreme sections" should result in "legislative attacks upon the accumulated wealth," Bryce predicted, "such attacks will be directed (at least in the first instance), not against individual rich men, but against incorporated companies, since it is through corporations that wealth has made itself obnoxious."[21]

Corporations were given "a constitutional rationale to undergird the developing laissez-faire of the age" when the Supreme Court declared that, under the due-process and equal-protection clauses of the Fourteenth Amendment, corporations were to be regarded as "persons." Former Senator Roscoe Conkling, representing a California railroad in two cases in the 1880s and speaking as one of the 1866 legislators who framed the text of the

Reconstruction amendment, insisted that the word "person" had been used when referring to property rights and "citizen" when referring to political rights.

Conking's "insinuation" has been rejected by "most historians," Bernard Schwartz writes, but points out that the matter was settled in 1886 when Chief Justice Morrison R. Waite, before hearing oral arguments in *Santa Clara v. Southern Pacific Railroad Company,* announced that the Fourteenth Amendment did, indeed, apply equal protection to corporations and that no argument would be heard on the matter. The corporate device had been "recognized as an indispensable adjunct to the nation's growth."[22]

As the nineteenth century drew to a close, the nation's industries were caught up in a merging frenzy that led, in 1890, to passage of the Sherman Antitrust Act, outlawing "every combination in restraint of trade." At the same time, however, states (New Jersey and Delaware, for example) were attracting new industries by framing incorporation laws permitting one corporation to hold stock in others, which then were free to operate in several states. Cartels, giving way to combinations, were placing an onerous burden on the federal courts.[23]

When the subject cropped up at one of Mark Hanna's celebrated Washington breakfasts in the late spring, as Republicans were preparing to gather in Philadelphia for the 1900 National Convention, Hanna turned to Foraker and asked him to draft the party's platform plank on trusts. The text the senator scribbled on a sheet of paper and handed to his host was later adopted with a few minor changes:

> *While recognizing the necessity and legitimacy of aggregations of capital to maintain and extend our rapidly increasing foreign trade, we condemn all conspiracies and combinations intended to restrict trade, limit production and affect prices, and favor such legislation as will effectively restrain and prevent all such abuses and protect and promote competition and secure the rights of producers, laborers, and all who are engaged in industry and commerce.*[24]

Hanna, the party's national chairman, descended on Philadelphia a few days before Foraker was able to leave Washington and announced that the speech nominating the president for a second term would be made by Senator Allison of Iowa. Foraker was furious. McKinley had asked him to place his name in nomination, and he had, of course, agreed. He called the Executive

Mansion and made an appointment with the president, who "very emphatically said with some indication of irritation, that he had not changed his mind."

As the senator was taking his leave, McKinley "rather abruptly and energetically said, 'I hope you will not allow the convention to be stampeded to Roosevelt for Vice President.'" Foraker said he was sorry to hear how the president felt about this matter and pointed out: "I thought the indications were that Roosevelt would be nominated, and that I thought he was the strongest man who could be put on the ticket with him, but that in addition I regarded myself as committed to his support and that I could not honorably do otherwise than support him if he should be a candidate. . . . He said it was all right for me to support Governor Roosevelt, and that he would understand that my action in doing so was not unfriendly to him."[25]

Foraker's "cordial" relations with Roosevelt had "become still more cordial" during the McKinley administration "because of our accord as to the Cuban questions, both before and after the Spanish-American War." Shortly before the convention, when Governor Roosevelt was on Capitol Hill buttonholing key Republican senators, he looked in on Foraker. "He wanted me to favor him by cooperating with Senator Lodge and other friends of his to prevent his nomination as Vice President." Foraker demurred, pointing out that "there was a strong sentiment throughout the country in favor of his nomination . . . and if the disposition to nominate him should continue he ought to yield to the demand."[26]

Hanna had called the convention to order at midday June 19 and was about to buckle down to the business at hand when Roosevelt made a star's entrance, sporting the wide-brimmed black hat he had affected in his campaign for governor as a reminder of his "crowded hour" on the heights of San Juan. Applause swept the hall during the two minutes it took for him to make his way to his seat. "He froze into military immobility, the hat against his heart, as the band struck up the national anthem. But on the platform a smile on the round face of Mark Hanna faded."

"Gentlemen," Wayne MacVeagh, Garfield's attorney-general, whispered to his neighbors, "that's an Acceptance Hat."[27]

Boss Matt Quay of Pennsylvania was promoting Roosevelt's candidacy in order to strike back at Hanna for having blocked his admission to the Senate. Quay was supported by New York's Senator Platt, who wanted to get Roosevelt out of the governor's office before he wrecked the Easy Boss's patronage system. On the second day of the convention, Quay outmaneu-vered Hanna by introducing a rule change that would have stripped him of his southern delegates. "Hanna, cornered and angry, taunted the bosses: 'Don't any of you realize that there's only one life between this madman and the White House?'"[28]

Chapter Eight

"He laughed with glee at the power and
place that had come to him.

—Lincoln Steffens, recalls an evening
with the new president, 1901

The new century began on the first day of January, 1901, not 1900, but with the end of the 1800s and with a presidential election coming up in the fall (a McKinley-Bryan rematch), 1900 was looked upon as a year of transition. A newly industrialized agrarian people had gone to war with Spain to liberate oppressed dark-skinned neighbors in Cuba and ended up with thousands of American soldiers, many of them black, stalking dark-skinned insurgents in Philippine jungles seven thousand miles away. Republicans called it "expansionism"; Democrats called it "imperialism."

New York's Democratic boss, Richard Croker, defined anti-imperialism as "opposition to the fashion of shooting everybody who doesn't speak English." Roosevelt's friend, William Allen White, assured readers of his *Emporia (Kansas) Gazette* that "only Anglo-Saxons can govern themselves." Rudyard Kipling, referring to the British Empire's war in South Africa as well as to the American post-Cuban quagmire in the Philippines, had made "the White Man's burden" an instant global cliché. A parodist presented the point of view of the burden:

Take up the White Man's burden;
Send forth your sturdy sons,
And load them down with whiskey
And Testaments and guns.
Throw in a few diseases
To spread in tropic climes,
For there the healthy niggers
Are quite behind the times.
And don't forget the factories!
On those benighted shores. . . .
They never work twelve hours a day,
And live in strange content.[1]

"We will not renounce our part in the mission of our race, trustees, under God, of the civilization of the world," Albert J. Beveridge, a thirty-seven-year-old Indiana Republican, proclaimed in his first Senate speech. He was on such cozy terms with his Creator that he could pass along the message: "He has marked us as His chosen people, henceforth to lead in the regeneration of the world."[2]

"Just a line to say how delighted I was with your speech," Roosevelt wired from Albany.[3]

Conquest of the Philippine Islands, the governor fervently believed, would place the United States among the world's "great fighting races." He had no patience with those "who cant about 'liberty' and the 'consent of the governed,' in order to excuse themselves for their unwillingness to play the part of men." Proponents of such doctrines, he said, "would leave the Apaches to work out their own salvation in Arizona" and would "condemn your forefathers and mine for ever having settled in these United States."[4]

Letters and newspaper clippings from back home kept black regulars in the Philippines informed of race riots and lynchings that, year after year, averaged one per week. The violence "reflected not only the racial prejudice that divided the poor of both races, but a systematic campaign to disenfranchise southern blacks, stripping them of rights they had clung to since Reconstruction." North Carolina sent four blacks to Congress in the years between the death of Abraham Lincoln and the reelection of William McKinley. North Carolinians sent their fifth black representative, Eva Clayton, to Washington with William Jefferson Clinton in 1992.[5]

On the first day of the new century, when the war in the Philippines was about to enter its third year, a *New York Times* editorial writer, who had "not a spark of sympathy with the reckless anti-imperialistic enemies of the Administration," raised the question, "How long?" and pointed out: "We have killed a good many Tagals, and they have killed or captured a good many of our troops. We have not conquered them, we have not restored peace and order to the Island of Luzon, nor inspired the natives with respect for our authority. . . . The American people are plainly tired of this Philippine war. . . . They find it hard to exclude from their minds the suspicion that somewhere incompetence is deferring the restoration of order and putting off the day when the civilizing work of building up can begin."

"This is New Year's Eve, dear one—tomorrow, only a few hours from now, we start a new year and a new century," Lieutenant Samuel P. Lyon wrote his wife, Mary, from the Philippines on December 31, 1900. He was one of the white officers attached to Company A, 25th Infantry, the Negro outfit that had shared its rations with the Rough Riders in Cuba. "I feel quite cheerful over the prospect. This next year must bring us together—that wonderful day when we see each other again must be one of these coming 365 so I am glad to see 1901 come and I am sure you are too."[6]

> *"My dear, dear wife," he wrote two weeks later.*
>
> *Just as I was about to begin my letter to you last night—information came to me that Dias, a muchly wanted insurrecto captain was staying in a house about five miles and a half from Santa Cruz—I took ten men and went after him—I surrounded the house without waking anyone—had the corporal break the door in and nailed the captain with three men before they were fairly awake. They had left their guns in the mountains, and only had two daggers—one of which I confiscated for the future adornment of our hall and gave the other to the man who discovered it. Got home about half past twelve. Today I had the captain over, and with the help of the water cure (which by the way don't talk about) and by looking as if I wanted to eat him—and explaining in detail how he was shortly to be hung if he didn't tell me all he knew, he confessed to knowing the whereabouts of six rifles— these I am going after tonight.*

About twenty men, absent from Lyon's roster, were still back in the States, being held as witnesses and prisoners in connection with some trouble they had been involved with in El Paso, Texas, while stationed at Fort Bliss. From company records and from conversations with the officer who had commanded the company at Fort Bliss, as Lyon would later testify at his court-martial, "it appeared to me that the disorders were almost entirely due to a relentless persecution of the men by the police and others of El Paso, on account of their color."[7]

On May 22, Lieutenant Lyon received a telegram ordering him to join the 27th Infantry at Plattsburg Barracks, New York. "I am stunned with joy," he wrote Mary, but on June 10, their fifth anniversary ("We are old married people now, dear"), his orders were changed. He felt "pretty blue." It was also his son Stuart's birthday. Two weeks later (June 24) he sent word: "I am ordered home at last."

At the start of the new century, Dorsie Willis, a restless sixth-grader, dropped out of school, wandered away from Oklahoma, and drifted for a while before ending up in a Kansas City, Missouri, packing plant. On his first payday in the new year, 1902, he held in his hand a ten-dollar bill redeemable in gold from the United States Treasury. It was, he thought, "about the prettiest thing I'd ever seen." He put it in a letter and sent it to his mother.

"Afterwards," he once told a friend, "I heard her say possibly a hundred times that she was 'broke.' What she meant was she'd gotten down to that ten-dollar gold certificate. She kept it as long as I can remember in a rag, and if you saw that rag out on the street, you wouldn't pick it up, it was so dirty."[8]

In his old age, shining shoes in a downtown Minneapolis bank building, Dorsie would shake his head and hold onto his money when the other men in the barber shop tossed a dollar bill into a jackpot on the morning of a big fight or a World Series game.

"Willis, you're tight," they used to say.

"Not tight, just careful," Dorsie insisted. "When I spend a dollar, I want to get something in a paper sack I can carry home."

In looking back over his life, he attributed his frugality to the example set by his mother.

She had a hard time. If there had been any such thing as relief, my father would never have got off of it. He died when he was forty-four, and my mother raised her family, six girls and three boys. She washed and ironed for a dollar a day, and then she'd come home and wash clothes for her kids. She couldn't buy us new clothes, so she'd darn and patch the ones we already had.

I was her first child and she could read me better than any of the others. I don't remember ever telling her a lie. She would of known, like when I'd get up in the morning, she'd say, "Dorsie, did you wash your face?" and I'd say, "Yes, Mamma," and she'd look at me. "Dorsie," she'd say, "when did you wash your face?" and I'd tell her, "Yesterday morning."

After I got big enough to go uptown by myself at night, I'd always come home at a certain time, just when the rest of the boys was getting started good. My mother never went to bed until I come in the house. Any time I was out she'd be sitting by the porch door, waiting. At the time I thought I was being mistreated, but all of those fellows I come up with like that, they're dead, so I figure I had a pretty smart mother.[9]

Throughout his life, Dorsie was haunted by the memory of bill collectors coming to the door, dunning his mother for payments she couldn't meet. "She'd send us kids to the door to tell 'em she wasn't home, so I decided that if I ever got married and had a family, my wife would never have to send anybody to the door to tell people she wasn't home, and I've never had that to happen. As far as I can remember I've never had a bill come due that I couldn't pay, and most times I paid before it was due. That's my way of life."

Dorsie's thoughts turned to marriage when, at eighteen, he was back in Oklahoma, living at home and calling on a slender black reed of a girl in Kingfisher, a few miles west of Guthrie. "She weighed a hundred and ten pounds," he used to say, "and that was when she was fat." Lucille Jordan, a minister's daughter, had attended Langston University, a Negro school in the town of the same name founded by Negroes at a time when there was talk of establishing a Negro community—perhaps a Negro state—in Oklahoma Territory.

"Every time I got hold of enough money to go see Lucille, it turned out she was in Fort Reno," Dorsie said.

Fort Reno, named for a Civil War casualty, Major General Jesse Lee Reno, was established in the 1870s to protect government agents from Cheyenne attacks. After the opening of Oklahoma Territory, the garrison's black soldiers had been put to work guarding the borders separating homesteaders and Indians. Lucille's sister was married to the First Sergeant of Company F, 25th Infantry.

"I figured Lucille must like soldiers," Dorsie later recalled, "so I decided, 'Well, I guess I'll have to join the army.'"[10]

He signed up for a three-year hitch on January 5, 1905, giving his occupation as "laborer." He had no dependents, drank intoxicating liquors "moderately," and had never been hurt upon the head or convicted of a felony. He wrote English "well," the recruiting officer noted, and his character and intelligence were both "good."

Five days later he was assigned to the 25th Infantry, but instead of heading for a rendezvous with Lucille in Fort Reno, where the 2nd Battalion was stationed, Dorsie was bundled off to Fort Niobrara, Nebraska, to join the regiment's 1st Battalion.

"I was disheartened about that, but I wrote to Lucille and told her what had happened and she said, 'Well, all right, I won't marry until you get out of the army.'"

Dorsie settled down to what he expected to be three routine years of close-order drill, white-glove inspections, practice marches, and fatigue duty. He had been assigned to Company D, commanded by Captain Samuel P. Lyon.[11]

Six months into his second term, President McKinley visited the Pan-American Exposition in Buffalo, where, on the morning of September 6, guarded by three Secret Service agents, he took his place in the receiving line at the Temple of Music. Leon Czolgosz, whose sanity strained the murky limits of its legal definition, was waiting for him, using his handkerchief to conceal a short-barreled, 32-caliber Iver-Johnson revolver.[12]

"Don't let them hurt him," the mortally wounded president murmured as he was being assisted to a chair, and when George Cortelyou, his secretary, bent over him, McKinley whispered, "My wife,—be careful, Cortelyou, how you tell her, oh, be careful."[13]

"I went to Buffalo at once," Roosevelt wrote in his autobiography. "The President's condition seemed to be improving, and after a day or two we were told that he was practically out of danger. I then joined my family, who were in the Adirondacks, near the foot of Mount Tahawus."[14]

A week after the shooting, gangrene had set in, and around six o'clock in the evening of September 13, telegraphers in the press tent began to send out the news that the president was dying. The following afternoon, Saturday, Roosevelt reached the Buffalo mansion of John G. Milburn, president of the Exposition, where the McKinleys were guests. The president's body had not been removed when Secretary of War Root greeted his successor and suggested he take the oath of office without delay. Roosevelt agreed, expressing his desire to "show the people at once that the administration of the government will not falter in spite of the terrible blow."[15]

Later that day the new president found time to write to Booker T. Washington, expressing regret at not being able to make his planned visit to the black educator's trade school at Tuskegee, Alabama. He urged Dr. Washington to come to the White House "as soon as possible" to discuss "the question of possible future appointments in the South exactly on the lines of our last conversation together."[16]

One evening during the period of national mourning, before moving into the president's house, Roosevelt relaxed in the company of two old newspaper friends, Lincoln Steffens and William Allen White. He "allowed his gladness to explode," Steffens later recalled. "With his feet, his fists, his face and with free words he laughed at his luck. He laughed at the rage of Boss Platt and at the tragic disappointment of Mark Hanna; these two had not only lost their President McKinley but had been given as a substitute the man they had thought to bury in the vice presidency. T. R. yelped at their downfall, and he laughed with glee at the power and place that had come to him."[17]

He moved into 1600 Pennsylvania Avenue on a Sunday. Edith was busy at Sagamore, so he asked his two sisters, Anna Cowles and Corinne Robinson, and his brothers-in-law, Lieutenant Commander William S. Cowles and Douglas Robinson, to join him for his first dinner in the White House.

"As we sat around the table," Mrs. Cowles remembered, "he turned and said: 'Do you realize that this is the birthday of our father, September 22? I have realized it as I signed various papers all day long, and I feel that it is a good omen that I begin my duties in this house on this day. I feel as if my father's hand were on my shoulder, and as if there were a special blessing over the life I am to lead here.'"[18]

The young President was in his twelfth year the day his father came home with Abraham Lincoln's thirty-year-old former secretary and announced, "This is Mr. John Hay, and I wish the children to shake hands with him." Mr. John Hay was now Teedie's secretary of state.[19]

"I think you know Mr. Roosevelt, our new President," Hay wrote a friend in England. "He is an old and intimate friend of mine: a young fellow of infinite dash and originality. He has gone to Canton to lay our dear McKinley to rest, and asked me to stay here on the avowed ground that, as I am the next heir to the Presidency, he did not want too many eggs in the same Pullman car."[20]

To his friend and neighbor, Henry Adams, Hay wrote more candidly: "Well, he is here in the saddle again. That is, he is in Canton and will have his first Cabinet meeting in the White House tomorrow. He came down from Buffalo Monday night—and in the station, without waiting an instant, told me I must stay with him—that I could not decline nor even consider. I saw, of course, it was best for him to start off that way, and so I said I would stay, forever, of course, for it would be worse to say I would stay a while than it would be to go out at once. I can still go at any moment he gets tired of me, or when I collapse."[21]

In *The Education of Henry Adams*, the sixty-three-year-old self-styled "Conservative Christian Anarchist" of Lafayette Square brooded over the power suddenly invested in his new forty-two-year-old neighbor: "Power when wielded by abnormal energy is the most serious of facts, and all Roosevelt's friends know that his restless and combative energy was more than abnormal. Roosevelt, more than any other man living within the range of notoriety, showed the singular primitive quality that belongs to ultimate matter—the quality that mediæval theology assigned to God—he was pure act."[22]

Chapter Nine

"Prof. Booker T. Washington was in the city yesterday,
and dined with the President last night."

—Washington Evening Star,

October 17, 1901

Less than a month after the Roosevelts moved their books, children, dogs, cats, ponies, guns, and trophies into the White House, Booker T. Washington came through the capital on his way to Yale's bicentennial celebration. When he reached the home of his host, a black Republican real estate dealer, he found an invitation to dine with the president at 7:30 that evening, October 16. The Tuskegee Institute president and a Republican politician from Colorado shared the family table with the president, his wife, his teenage daughter Alice, and his three sons, Ted, Kermit, and Archie.

"Prof. Booker T. Washington was in the city yesterday," the *Washington Evening Star* reported, October 17, 1901, "and dined with the President last night."

"The most damnable outrage ever perpetrated by a citizen of the United States," roared the *Memphis Scimitar.* In Richmond, Virginia, the *Times* interpreted the invitation to mean that "the President is willing that negroes shall mingle freely with whites in the social circle—that white women may receive attentions from negro men." "The action of President Roosevelt in entertaining that nigger will necessitate our killing a thousand niggers in the South before they will learn their place again," thundered South Carolina's Senator Benjamin ("Pitchfork Ben") Tillman, a pronouncement that prompted the editors of *Life* to suggest that he be jailed for "inciting murder."[1]

William Monroe Trotter, Harvard's first black Phi Beta Kappa (Class of '95), now editor of the *Boston Guardian*, denounced Washington as a hypocrite for accepting the invitation after embracing segregation in the South in his famous Atlanta speech assuring his white neighbors that members of the two races could remain "as separate as the fingers, yet as the hand in all things essential to mutual progress."[2]

The *Tuskegee News*, however, pointed out that for the last ten years the Associated Press had been routinely sending out stories of Dr. Washington "speaking and dining at some banquet in the North with governors etc." When news of the White House dinner hit the front pages in Ohio, where Foraker was campaigning, he was called on for some remarks following a glee club serenade at his hotel. "The Democrats now want the Republican administration at Washington turned out of power not because of Imperialism, the Spanish-American war, or anything done in Cuba, Porto Rico or the Philippines, or because of our opposition to the free and unlimited coinage of silver," he extemporized, "but because the new incumbent of the White House had courage enough and patriotism enough and a strong enough sense of equity and justice to know that the White House was the White House of the whole American people, of the American Negro as well as of the American white man."[3]

"Needless to say, everyone here is with you heart and soul on the Booker T. Washington matter," Lodge wrote from Massachusetts, and Roosevelt replied, "If these creatures had any sense they would understand they can't bluff me." He insisted he would not forfeit his self-respect "by fearing to have a man like Booker T. Washington to dinner if it cost me every political friend I have got."[4]

In the seven and one-half years he remained in the White House, however, he never again broke bread with an African-American guest. When Dr. Washington called on his friend in the White House, he came between meals.

The first time the Forakers dined at the Roosevelt White House, Julia recalled in her memoirs, "the great bubble and hum in the air" contrasted sharply with the strain imposed on guests "when the McKinleys were hosts; Mrs. McKinley, so physically unequal to the thing she bravely was attempting to do, and the president, masking his tender concern about his wife under a deferential solicitude for his guests that went to our hearts." Mrs. Roosevelt, "loveliest and wisest of hostesses," managed to "keep table talk off the rocks in spite of our monologistic, aggressive, brilliant host; helping each of her guests quietly to shine or, rather, making him feel that he shone, which, after all, is the art of it."[5]

Roosevelt was a stickler for ceremony at social functions, Julia discovered after dinner, when the gentlemen retired with the president and his wife shepherded the ladies to the East Room. "There were no chairs, only a bench or two against the wall. Mrs. Hanna, limping from an accident, and frail Mrs. Jessup sank down on a bench. Mrs. Roosevelt and all the rest of us remained standing, waiting for the President and the other gentlemen to join us. . . . Ladies stood whenever the President was on his feet."[6]

Whitelaw Reid, who presided over the American embassy in London, was Julia's escort on what proved to be for her the most memorable of the Roosevelts' small dinners. She sat on the president's left that night. At one point he turned to her and said: "I regard your husband as a very remarkable man, Mrs. Foraker. I am counting on him to become my administration Senator."[7]

"Tonight while I was preparing to dictate a message to Congress concerning the boiling caldron on the Isthmus of Panama, which has now begun to bubble over, up came the ushers with a telegram from you and Ted about the football match," Roosevelt wrote his son Kermit on November 4, 1903, the day rebels broke away from "the little wildcat republic of Columbia" and proclaimed the Republic of Panama. "Instantly I bolted into the next room to read it aloud to mother and sister, and we all cheered in unison."[8]

Roosevelt looked forward to the building of the isthmian canal ("the great bit of work of my administration") and directed Secretary of State Hay "to take personal direction" of talks with Columbia. The young president had no intention of permitting "the Bogota lot of jack rabbits" to "bar one of the future highways of civilization." On November 18 a treaty was signed with the victorious rebels, providing for an immediate payment of $10 million to Panama rather than Colombia.[9]

Most Americans, regardless of party, supported the canal, but "there was pervasive disagreement about how Roosevelt and his administration had used presidential authority and military muscle to accomplish the objectives of the United States." To the *New York Post* "this mad plunge of ours is simply and solely a vulgar and mercenary venture, without a rag to cover its sordidness and shame."[10]

Senator George Hoar, venerable founding father of the Republican Party in Massachusetts, took the floor of the Senate to castigate the president in what Foraker regarded as "a rather ill-natured speech," which in effect "very plainly charged him with responsibility for the secession of Panama from the Republic of Colombia." Hoar supported the building of the canal "at once" but insisted it be done "without taint or suspicion of national dishonor."[11]

As Hoar spoke, Connecticut's Senator Orville H. Platt sidled over to Foraker's seat and suggested that a rebuttal should be made immediately, so that both points of view would go out to the press that night. In impromptu remarks that fill three pages of small print in his memoirs, Foraker defended the administration: "Panama was acting in her own interest. She was exercising her right to object to the action of her Government, and her Government persisting in wronging her, she had a right, if she saw fit, to go into rebellion. . . . We do not have to wait until there is actual war."[12]

A dozen years later, recalling the scene in his memoirs, Foraker still felt "that neither our Government nor President Roosevelt did anything in that whole matter that was the subject of legitimate criticism." Ironically, as he dictated his recollections of the incident, Columbia was again pressing its claim for a $10 million indemnity.[13]

In the summer of 1901, a few weeks before McKinley set out for Buffalo, Taft received a letter from Roosevelt's friend and later his designated biographer, Joseph Bucklin Bishop, reporting on a conversation with the then vice president, who had expressed a desire to nominate him for president at the national convention in 1904. ("What a glorious candidate he would make!") On July 15 a letter dealing with the same subject was dispatched from Oyster Bay to Malacanan Palace in Manila.[14]

"Of course I should like to be president, and feel I could do the work well," Roosevelt wrote, and went on to express the belief that the "Machine and the mugwumps" in New York would make his nomination impossible. If empowered to name either a president or a chief justice, he continued, "I should feel in honor bound to name you." The vice president's letter placed in nomination the only person ever to hold both offices.[15]

The first weeks of Roosevelt's presidency turned out to be the worst in Taft's tenure as civil governor of the Philippines. Fifty American infantrymen had been killed in an ambush on the island of Samar, filling the Army & Navy Club "with rumors of insurrection in the most peaceful provinces." Then, in late October, when Nellie was touring China with friends, Taft was felled by dengue fever.[16]

Four days later he was rushed to the hospital for surgery that led to the discovery of an abscess in the perineum. Thanksgiving Day he was back in the operating room, and on Christmas Eve he and Nellie bundled the three children aboard the transport *Grant* bound for home. He had been away almost nineteen months.

In Washington, testifying before the Senate Committee on the Philippines, he said the insurrection was "now at an end" except for three mountain provinces. He was depressed by the hearings and longed to get out of the country to avoid further questioning, which, he confided to Nellie, "shows my unfitness for public life."[17]

Twice in October, 1902, Roosevelt offered him a seat on the Supreme Court, and twice Taft passed up his long-sought judicial sanctuary rather than abandon the people of the Philippines. Roosevelt was determined to have "men of my type" on the court, who pondered what the president and the Congress said and then decided what they had "really thought."[18]

Roosevelt's first appointment went to Oliver Wendell Holmes, chief justice of Massachusetts. When the second vacancy was offered to Taft, he began to wonder whether Roosevelt was dissatisfied with his performance in the Philippines, in which case, he wrote Root, "I could not accept a position on the Supreme bench. I shouldn't enjoy being kicked upstairs."[19]

On January 6, 1903, Taft received a firm, friendly letter from the White House informing him that he was to be brought home and benched. "I am very sorry. I have the greatest confidence in your judgment; but after all, old fellow, if you will permit me to say so, I am President and see the whole field."[20]

"Recognize soldier's duty to obey orders," Taft replied.[21]

Once word of the exchange of cables got out, the Tafts awakened to find Malacanan Palace besieged by some six thousand smiling, cheering Filipinos waving flags and banners, *¡Queremos Taft!* ("We Want Taft!") The chief justice of the Supreme Court solemnly affirmed that feelings of the Philippine people "would be deeply hurt by departure of Taft." A radical labor leader hailed the viceroy as "a saint," and an insurgent spokesman ranked the calamity of his departure with earthquakes, typhoons, and plagues.[22]

"All right," Roosevelt cabled the viceroy, "you shall stay where you are."[23]

Then, on March 27, 1903, Taft opened a "Dear Will" letter from the president: "The worst calamity that could happen to me personally and officially is impending, because Root tells me that he will have to leave me next fall. . . . I want to ask you whether if I can persuade Root to stay until a year hence, you cannot come back and take his place." Taft was won over by a reminder that "as Secretary of War you would still have ultimate control of the Philippine situation, and whatever was done would be under your immediate supervision."[24]

At a January 29, 1904, reception for Taft when he took over his new duties at the War Department, Root toasted him in verse. The last two lines caused it to be reprinted by the *Washington Post* five years later on the day after Taft's inauguration:

> *It needs no prophet's eye to read his fate,*
> *His time will surely come to head the state.*

On his way to Chillicothe to take part in the May 19–20, 1903, ceremonies celebrating the centennial anniversary of Ohio's admission to the Union, Foraker read interviews in which Senator Hanna's private secretary and "two of his most pronounced and dependable followers" were quoted as saying the president was not only unpopular with Ohio Republicans but also not as well equipped as Hanna to hold the office he had acquired by accident.

"If I am not very much mistaken," Foraker replied when newspaper reporters asked him to comment on the statements, "the Republicans of Ohio are in favor of the nomination of Theodore Roosevelt as our candidate in 1904, and . . . they will be very much disappointed if we do not so declare at our State convention."[25]

Hanna denied the statements but balked at the prospect of making a Roosevelt endorsement at this time. The 1903 convention, he contended, had no right to bind the state's 1904 delegates, although Foraker had cited two precedents, Sherman in 1888 and, as Hanna knew at first-hand, McKinley in 1895.[26]

"If Mr. Hanna is for me there could be no possible objection to his saying so," Roosevelt wrote Postmaster-General Henry Clay Payne on

May 23, and went on to add: "Of course he has a perfect right to be against me, but if such is the case his action should be based explicitly on that ground, and not on grounds that are foolish."[27]

The issue had been "forced" on him, Hanna explained in a telegram to the president, which ended with the assurance, "When you know all the facts I am sure you will approve my course."

"I have not asked any man for his support," the president replied, and closed by saying that "those who favor my administration and my nomination will favor indorsing both, and those who do not will oppose."[28]

Foraker, as his biographer points out, had seen "political implications for himself in Hanna's dilemma." Endorsement of Roosevelt would not only eliminate Ohio's junior senator as a presidential candidate, it would also enhance the senior senator's position in the administration, increasing his chances for the presidency in 1908."[29]

"Hanna and the trusts are smoked out," Foraker gleefully commented when his colleague made a grudging announcement of support. Roosevelt and Foraker, a reporter speculated, "had worked out an agreement whereby Foraker would lead the Roosevelt bandwagon for 1904 if Roosevelt would recommend him for 1908."[30]

Throughout the summer and fall, word spread that Roosevelt was fighting with Hanna and his Wall Street conspirators. "Don't these fools in New York know I'm sixty-six years old?" Hanna grumbled, and agreed there was, indeed, a conspiracy: "To kill me."[31]

Early in the new year, Roosevelt's suspicions of Hanna's scheming to replace him in the White House cropped up again. Writing his son Ted on January 29, 1904 (and warning him "not to let any of these letters in which I speak of political subjects lie about where they can be seen by anyone"), Roosevelt reported that Senator Hanna had become "intoxicated by the thought that perhaps he could be nominated himself, or at least dictate the nomination."[32]

Two weeks later, Hanna lay on his deathbed, brought down by typhoid fever. When Roosevelt learned of his illness, he dropped by and left a note, "May you soon be with us again, old fellow, as strong and vigorous as ever."[33]

"You touched a tender spot, old man, when you called personally this A.M.," Hanna replied, and added that "such 'drops' of kindness are good for a fellow."[34]

In a letter to Root written February 16, the day after Hanna's death, Roosevelt described him as "a big man in every way" and recalled that "after I came into office, under circumstances which were very hard for him, he resolutely declined to be drawn into the position which a smaller man of meaner cast would inevitably have taken; that is, the position of antagonizing public policies if I was identified with them."[35]

"He is mourned by all his countrymen," Foraker said in making the formal announcement to the Senate of their colleague's death. Political associates would mourn "their organizing leader who repeatedly led them to victory" and political opponents would remember "a bold and fearless foeman who commanded their respect and excited their admiration."[36]

In her memoirs twenty-six years later, Julia delivered a more personal eulogy based on the report her twelve-year-old son, Benson, brought back from a visit to the Hanna lakefront home in Cleveland:

> *There was a grind organ man and a monkey and Mr. Hanna took a lot of nickels and dimes out of his pocket and gave Benson a lot and they gave it to the monkey and the monkey took the money to the man and came right back for more and Mr. Hanna said the monkey could keep that up longer than he could . . . and a man with his collar turned up came along and Mr. Hanna said how is the baby and the man said the baby isn't any better and Mr. Hanna gave him a funny yellow-back dollar and said he'd seen some pretty sick kids pull through and the man just looked at the dollar and looked at it and didn't say anything.*[37]

"Am elected by overwhelming majority, about as great as that of McKinley four years ago," Roosevelt wired Kermit November 8.[38]

When he met with reporters in his office next door in the State, War, and Navy Building, he read a prepared statement thanking the American people for their support and, with a finality he would come to regret in 1908 and breach in 1912, he said: "The wise custom which limits the President to two terms regards the substance not the form. Under no circumstances will I be a candidate for or accept another nomination."[39]

When Foraker called at the White House a few days after the election, Roosevelt thanked him for his work in the campaign and, referring to himself as "His Excellency, not His Accidency," said he now felt at liberty to pursue his own policies rather than remain "under obligation to continue the policies of McKinley." Years later, retired from public life, Foraker looked back on the conversation and thought, "I might well have taken some alarm as to the future. But I did not."[40]

Foraker might also have profited from reading a letter Mark Twain had written a friend three weeks before the president-elect's inauguration:

> *Every time, in twenty-five years, that I have met Roosevelt the man, a wave of welcome has streaked through me with the hand-grip; but whenever (as a rule) I meet Roosevelt the statesman and politician, I find him destitute of morals and not respectworthy. It is plain that where his political self and his party self are concerned he has nothing resembling a conscience; that under those inspirations he is naively indifferent to the restraints of duty and even unaware of them; ready to kick the Constitution into the backyard whenever it gets in the way.*[41]

On Friday, March 3, 1905, the eve of Roosevelt's inauguration, John Hay wrote a "Dear Theodore" note accompanying a lock of Lincoln's hair given him by the son of the doctor who attended the President on his deathbed. "Please wear it tomorrow," Hay wrote; "you are one of the men who most thoroughly understand and appreciate Lincoln."[42]

Speaking of Negroes in a Lincoln Day address three weeks earlier, Roosevelt had advocated training for "the backward race," so that "it may enter into the possession of true freedom, while the forward race is enabled to preserve unharmed the high civilization wrought out by its forefathers." Thoughtful men of both races, he insisted, agreed that race purity must be maintained.[43]

The president who shares Mount Rushmore with Lincoln and two slave owners "accepted the racial mores of his time," as did McKinley, Taft, and Wilson, Gould notes. To have done otherwise would have "required a high order of political courage and would probably have impeded his effectiveness as president. Since Roosevelt wished to be judged by the highest standards for presidential conduct, it must be said that he failed to believe in and work for a future when racial equality and justice would be possible in the United States."[44]

In his inaugural address he described modern life as "both complex and intense," due to "the tremendous changes wrought by the extraordinary industrial development of the last half century," and pointed out that "never before have men tried so vast and formidable an experiment as that of administering the affairs of a continent under the forms of a Democratic republic." No mention was made of the color line that Du Bois had singled out as "the problem of the twentieth century."[45]

Sixty years before black Americans began hanging photographs of Martin Luther King, Jr., alongside reprints of *I Have A Dream*, Du Bois's nine-paragraph *Credo* published in scroll form looked down on rooms where black families ate, talked, prayed, and slept. It began: "I believe in God who made of one blood all races that dwell on earth. I believe that all men, black and brown, and white, are brothers, varying, through Time and Opportunity, in form and gift and feature, but differing in no essential particular, and alike in soul and in the possibility of infinite development."

He believed especially "in the Negro Race; in the beauty of its genius, the sweetness of its soul, and its strength in that meekness which shall inherit this turbulent earth." He believed as well "in Liberty for all men; the space to stretch their arms and their souls; the right to breathe and the right to vote; the freedom to choose their friends, enjoy the sunshine and ride on the railroads, uncursed by color."[46]

Roosevelt's first administration, as Woodward notes, "happened to coincide with the climax of southern racism and propaganda that accompanied and followed disfranchisement." The no longer "accidental President" set out to charm the South he had alienated in dining with Dr. Washington.[47]

In "His Excellency's" first spring he won over Texas with some thirty speeches. In the fall, when he captured Richmond, gossip had the Democrats nominating him for president in 1908. At Roswell, the ancestral Georgia home he knew so well from his mother's anecdotes, he posed for a photograph with two former slaves, "Aunt Grace," his mother's maid, and "Daddy William," who had helped decorate the mansion for his young mistress's wedding.

"I can hardly bear to leave here," the president murmured to his wife as they drove away.[48]

Thomas Nelson Page, the Old South's sentimental writer-diplomat, concluded that the president was now "more a Democrat than a Republican." Black Americans outside the Tuskegee orbit were inclined to agree. Of the fifty prominent Negroes asked by *The Voice of the Negro* for their opinion of the president's course, only ten were favorable.[49]

On July 10, 1905, Du Bois was one of the twenty-nine black men who crossed the international boundary into Canada to create "a new epoch." The architects of this first meeting of the Niagara Movement had invited no black sisters, a mistake they corrected the following year. Ironically the meeting was held fewer than a hundred miles from Seneca Falls, New York, where fifty-seven years earlier, Frederick Douglass had met with Elizabeth Cady Stanton and Lucretia Mott to demand equal rights for women.[50]

The Niagara Movement, Du Bois explained in *The Voice of the Negro*, was at present an organization composed of fifty-four men ("ministers, lawyers, editors, businessmen and teachers") who had been brought together in eighteen states by "common aspirations" in a critical time. "The staggering days of emancipation, of childhood, are gone."[51]

Chapter Ten

*"Regret to report serious shooting in
Brownsville last evening. . . ."*

—*Major Charles W. Penrose,
August 14, 1906*

Governor Roosevelt had seen the need for the state to protect "honest" corporations and "to discriminate sharply against those organized in a spirit of mere greed, for improper speculative purposes." The young president-elect was aware of the nation's "right of supervision and control as regards the great corporations that are its creatures."[1]

He was, however, wary of the new "literature of exposure," an outcropping of investigative journalism by, among others, Lincoln Steffens (boss rule of cities), Ida Tarbell (Standard Oil), Upton Sinclair (meat packing, oil) and Ray Stannard Baker, the only one to take a lively interest in race relations.[2]

"The soul of every scoundrel is gladdened whenever an honest man is assailed," Roosevelt said when called on to dedicate a new Capitol Hill office building in the spring of 1906. The assailants were "muckrakers," men and women who are often "indispensable to the well-being of society; but only if they know when to stop raking the muck, and to look upward to the celestial crown above them, to the crown of worthy endeavor."[3]

When Governor Bob La Follette came to the Senate after "restoring representative government in Wisconsin," as Steffens put it, he presented the newcomer to the president as the first of a breed of Republican reformers who would, he hoped, someday take over the Congress.[4]

The meeting of the two egoists was "comic," the muckraking matchmaker reported. "They began to back away from each other before they met; their hands touched, but their bodies, their feet walked away." Roosevelt dismissed the Westerner as "a shifty self-seeker" whose "real motives seemed to be not to get something good and efficient done but to make a personal reputation for himself by screaming for something he knew perfectly well could not be had."[5]

The president took an even harsher view of William Randolph Hearst, who for years—as a publisher, a two-term member of Congress (1903–1907), and now as the Democratic candidate for governor of New York—had preached "the gospel of envy, hatred and unrest." He had come to represent "the accumulation of years of discontent," Roosevelt wrote Lodge that fall when the publisher and absentee lawmaker took to the hustings. "There is a deep-seated unrest and dissatisfaction with corporate wealth and the use and abuse of it by men who have hitherto stood highest in the public eye. Hearst represents the chance to get even."[6]

Hearst, like Roosevelt, favored a large navy and advocated control of the trusts and legislation to give the Interstate Commerce Commission power to fix railroad rates. He was also carrying on an editorial campaign for a Constitutional amendment that, he contended, would make the Senate less subservient to big business by taking the election of its members away from state house politicians and giving it to registered voters.[7]

When one of his editors proposed a series of articles "on the fact that strictly speaking we had no Senate; we had only a chamber of butlers for industrialists and financiers," Hearst persuaded David Graham Phillips, a dapper, well-read, thirty-nine-year-old novelist, to prepare the articles for his new magazine, *Cosmopolitan*. The series appeared in nine monthly installments, from March through November, 1906, under the title "The Treason of the Senate."[8]

"Treason is a strong word," Phillips wrote in the first article, "but not too strong, rather too weak, to characterize the situation in which the Senate is the eager, resourceful, indefatigable agent of interests as hostile to the American people as any invading army could be, and vastly more dangerous."[9]

The series began with the pillorying of New York's gregarious Senator Chauncey M. Depew, a multimillionaire railroad lawyer whose two terms in "the best club in the world" were among the happiest years of the forty spent in the service of Commodore Vanderbilt and his family. They owned him, "mentally and morally," Phillips wrote, and mentioned the wife of a young Vanderbilt who had refused to seat the senator at her table. "I do not let my butler sit down with me," she explained to her husband. "Why should I let yours."[10]

On March 4, 1906, the day her father began his second year as an elected president, Alice Lee Roosevelt returned to Washington with her bridegroom, Nick Longworth, a freshman member of the House of Representatives from Cincinnati. He was, of course, a Republican and at Harvard had been a Porcellian. Alice was twenty-two, fourteen years younger than her bridegroom, a charming, bald-headed aristocrat who would become one of Capitol Hill's legendary womanizers. William ("Fishbait") Miller, the House's doorkeeper for nearly twenty-five years, relished the story of a visitor who, while waiting for the congressman in his office, opened a small box on his desk and selected what he took to be a cigarette. "Oh, I don't think you are going to like that cigarette," Longworth's secretary said with a straight face. It turned out to be a condom in disguise.[11]

Foraker had grown up in a rural Ohio ambience quite different from the splendid urban world of the Longworths and the Tafts, but as politicians the three men accommodated one another. Longworth certainly would want the senator's support in Cincinnati when he came up for reelection in the fall. As for Taft, when he returned from the Philippines to serve as Roosevelt's secretary of war, the Forakers had invited "several hundred guests" to meet him at a reception in their stately Sixteenth Street home, which also served as the senator's office.[12]

In early January, 1906, the Tafts were visiting friends in New Jersey when Roosevelt called to say there was another Supreme Court vacancy. It was not the center chair, but Will was inclined to accept it, especially when the president assured him he would be elevated to chief justice if—as there was reason to believe—such an opening should occur. Nellie vetoed the offer. In two years, Will should be running for president. The court could be saved for his old age.[13]

He stayed on as secretary of war, and Roosevelt agreed to delay the court appointment until after the off-year elections. As for his White House successor, the president insisted in a letter to William Allen White that he was "not going to try to nominate any man. Personally you know how highly I think of Secretary Taft, but I am not going to take a hand in his nomination for it is none of my business."[14]

No one, least of all the politically sophisticated Kansas editor, was likely to believe that Theodore Roosevelt would take no part in determining who would inherit responsibility for carrying out his policies. Roosevelt's letter that summer was written three months after his secretary of war had reported to his wife on a fateful White House conversation: "He thinks I am the one to take his mantle and that now I would be nominated."[15]

Senator Foraker was also thinking of himself as a possible presidential candidate in 1908. He had not been ready for the nomination in 1888, when his wife hid in a hotel bathroom while Blaine men were said to have offered their support to her husband. His qualifications at that time included an impressive record as soldier, judge, and governor but no political experience outside Ohio. His years in Washington had convinced him that congressional service made a man better prepared to take over the duties of chief executive.[16]

As Ohio's senior senator he had not only written his party's trust-busting plank in McKinley's 1900 platform, he had also played a leading role three years later in the passage of the Elkins Antirebate Act, which, to the mounting anger of farmers and shippers, had failed to put an end to the railroads' discriminatory practices. Their bookkeepers had come up with ways to get around the Interstate Commerce Commission. Roosevelt and Foraker found themselves in agreement on the necessity of railroad reform, but the conservative Cincinnati lawyer drew the line at the Hepburn Act, incorporating the Administration's plan to confer rate-making power upon the Interstate Commerce Commission.[17]

He balked at this "new kind of federal executive power to control the complex processes of an industrialized state," denouncing the rate bill as an unconstitutional delegation of the legislative, executive, and judicial powers of government to a politically appointed board. Control of rates, he argued, should come under the jurisdiction of the courts. When the final vote on the bill came on May 18, Foraker was surrounded by a pride of Republican senators who agreed with him but saw no point in squandering their political capital on a lost cause. They gritted their teeth and voted "Aye," while the Democrats, with the exception of two Alabama holdouts, joined their colleagues on the other side of the aisle in approving the Hepburn Bill 77 to 3. Foraker, the Senate's lone Republican dissenter, voted his convictions.[18]

"It is far pleasanter to go with the tide of public sentiment," he said, and, his biographer points out, he bucked the tide "knowing that his opposition probably would shatter his chances for the presidency in 1908." He had no idea at the time that Congressman Hearst had bought (but neglected to share with the author of his *Treason* series) a cache of letters stolen from the files of Standard Oil's pious, wire-pulling vice president, John D. Archbold. Hearst was saving the letters for 1908, when Senator Foraker would be coming up for reelection and might even be running against him for the presidency.[19]

In the spring of 1906, Dorsie Willis worked with oil-soaked rags to clean the protective coating of cosmoline from the working parts of the 25th Infantry's new rifle, the Springfield Model 1903. While Captain Lyon saw to it that his men in Company D were learning how to handle the weapon, Company A was dispatched to Wyoming, where part of the Washakie Reservation had been thrown open to settlers.[20]

Meanwhile the War Department, having decided to abandon Fort Niobrara's crumbling adobe buildings, was transferring the three remaining companies—B, C, and D—to Fort Brown, sprawled on the banks of the Rio Grande, separated from Mexico by the Rio Grande and from Brownsville, Texas, by a narrow dirt road.

When the townspeople learned that Negroes were to replace the white soldiers at the old Mexican War garrison, there was talk in the Elizabeth Street saloons of forming a posse to meet the train and keep the men from disembarking. An outraged businessman fired off a letter to Senator C. A. Culberson, who passed it to Secretary of War Taft. The senator received a prompt reply: "The fact is that a certain amount of race prejudice between white and black seems to have become almost universal throughout the country, and no matter where colored troops are sent there are always some who make objections to their coming. It is a fact, however, as shown by our records, that colored troops are quite as well disciplined and behaved as the average of other troops, and it does not seem logical to anticipate any greater trouble from them than from the rest."[21]

The three companies of black soldiers, commanded by five white officers, scrambled off the train in Brownsville on July 28, 1906, formed ranks, and marched from the depot to their new quarters. Watching their arrival, a white sergeant stationed at the Fort Brown hospital was astonished to discover they had brought no prisoners with them. He had never seen an outfit show up at a new post without having somebody under arrest.

"It was a good showing for the battalion," he later testified.[22]

During their four years in Nebraska, no color line had been drawn against the soldiers in local saloons. When they set out to slake their thirst in Texas, they found they could drink freely in the town's six Mexican beer joints but not at the three bars on Elizabeth Street. John Tillman installed a Jim Crow bar at the rear of his Ruby Saloon, but the soldiers boycotted it. They were refused service of any sort by H. H. Weller and the Crixell brothers.

On Friday, August 10, the day before the men were to be paid, two enterprising soldiers of B Company opened a beer joint at Sixteenth and Monroe, diagonally across the street from the garrison's northeast corner. The saloon was financed by Private John Hollomon, the battalion's money-lender, and operated by Private Ernest Allison, who was about to be honorably discharged and had decided not to reenlist.

On payday the place was packed, but there were no drunken fights, no police incidents. The next evening, Sunday, August 12, Major Charles W. Penrose had a friendly chat with Mayor Frederick J. Combe, the post's attending surgeon. Dr. Combe, who had once served as medical officer for a black cavalry unit, commented on how well the major's men had behaved the day before. He had grown up in Brownsville, he said, and had never experienced a quieter payday.[23]

Next morning, Mayor Combe was told of an attack on a white woman by a man she described as a Negro in army uniform. He called on Major Penrose, and they agreed the men should be confined to the post that night by an eight o'clock curfew. Around midnight, when the first shots rang out, the soldiers assumed they were under attack because of the white woman's accusation that had closed their new drinking place shortly before eight o'clock.[24]

"It was the only time in my life I ever heard the call to arms," Dorsie Willis recalled sixty-odd years later. "If you'd heard it, you'd know it was something different from all the other calls we'd heard. When that call went out, the noncommissioned officer in charge of quarters woke up everybody and opened the gun racks. The gun racks sat in the middle of the barracks and they were locked every night. He opened the gun racks and we got our guns and fell out in front of the barracks."[25]

Roll calls of the three companies began before the ten- to twenty-minute assault ended. Every man was present or accounted for. Every rifle was inspected, and none showed evidence of having been recently fired. Not until they were confronted by empty shells left behind by the raiders did the battalion's five white officers agree that some of their men were lying when they signed sworn statements denying any knowledge of who had done the shooting. The shells could have been fired only by the army's new Springfield rifles.[26]

Major Penrose drafted a telegram to the Military Secretary, Department of Texas, San Antonio: "Regret to report serious shooting in Brownsville last evening, in which one civilian was killed and chief of police so seriously wounded that right arm will have to be amputated. Brownsville officials claim shooting was done by enlisted men of this command, and are borne out in their opinion by empty shells and clips picked up in the streets."[27]

Roosevelt was at Sagamore Hill that day entertaining Owen Wister, author of *The Virginian*, the prototypical Western fable of the knight-errant cowboy. The novelist and the president, to whom the book was dedicated, had "hunted and ridden over the same trails," the *Washington Post* reported. "They will have many a camp-fire yarn to exchange."[28]

Dan, as Roosevelt addressed his friend from Harvard days, may have found himself caught up in a discussion of *Lady Baltimore*, Wister's new Charleston, South Carolina, novel, which Roosevelt regarded, at least in part, as "a tract of the times," favoring the South against the North in its portrayal of race relations. He entirely agreed that, as a race and in the mass, Negroes "are altogether inferior to the whites." However, as he had written Wister that spring, he had no sympathy for Charleston aristocrats who "shriek in public about miscegenation, but . . . leer as they talk to me privately of the colored mistresses and colored children of white men whom they know."[29]

In Indianola, Mississippi, Roosevelt had reappointed Mrs. Minnie M. Cox, "a quiet, sophisticated Negro woman," with a teacher's certificate from Fisk University, as postmaster. She and her husband, Wayne W. Cox, a railway mail-service employee, were prosperous landowners, and both were loyal Republicans. When a Negro doctor came to town and began taking Negro patients away from white doctors, a mob formed to drive him away, along with the "negro wench" running the local post office.

The town's "best citizens," Roosevelt reminded Wister, had done "what your Charleston friends have invariably and at all times done in such emergencies; that is they 'deprecated' the conduct of the mob and said it was 'not representative of the real southern feeling;' and then added that to save trouble the woman must go! She went. The mayor and the sheriff notified her and me that they could not protect her if she came back."

The Coxes later resettled in Indianola and organized the Delta Penny Savings Bank. When Roosevelt dropped in on them in the spring of 1905, they were living "in one of the best resident houses in Indianola." They also owned a large plantation nearby worth $35,000 to $40,000.

"Now the fantastic fools and moral cowards who encouraged or permitted the mob to turn her out are depositing their funds in the husband's bank," Roosevelt wrote Dan Wister two months before he turned up at the White House on the day the "best citizens" of Brownsville, Texas, began looking into "the nigger raid," as they had called it from the moment the first shots rang out.[30]

In the absence of Secretary Taft (who was vacationing in Canada), the War Department's military secretary, Major General F. C. Ainsworth, had to break the Sabbath on August 19 to draft two telegrams dealing with the midnight raid. One went to Oyster Bay, advising the president to remove the Brownsville soldiers; the other went to Major Penrose at Fort Brown: "Have you any doubt as to your ability to restrain troops from further violence?"

As indicated by his reference to "further violence," General Ainsworth had already affirmed the soldiers' guilt. The only question in his mind, and also in the minds of the town's "best citizens," that weekend was not whether the black infantrymen had shot up the town but whether their officers could keep them from doing it again.

"Have no doubt of my ability to restrain troops," Major Penrose replied. "Everything quiet in city, but very bitter feeling exists in both city and surrounding country."

Major Augustus P. Blocksom of the Inspector General's Department had reached Brownsville on a night train Saturday, August 18, and telegraphed the War Department: "Causes of disturbance are racial. People did not desire colored troops here and showed they thought them inferior socially by certain slights and denial of privileges at public bars, etc. Soldiers resented this."[31]

The attack was carried out by nine to fifteen soldiers, who fired seventy-five to a hundred and fifty rounds in a period of from eight to ten minutes, Major Blocksom reported. In passing, he mentioned a rumor circulating in the lower part of town that neither he nor any of the community's leaders took seriously: "Claim made that citizens fired first, but I believe without foundation."[32]

The government never investigated this rumor, leaving a pertinent question unanswered: If soldiers had made the attack, why did they fire their first shots just outside Fort Brown and then retreat to the center of town, which by the time the attack ended, was swarming with armed and angry white townspeople while, back at the fort, the soldiers were answering roll call?[33]

Heavily armed special deputies took turns standing watch on the town side of Garrison Road. On the army side, separated from the townspeople by a waist-high brick wall, the deputies counted sixty-five soldiers on guard. Armed sentries had been stationed at ten-foot intervals, and with each sentry stood three unarmed men from different companies.

"At present all is quiet, and it is considered quite probable by those in authority that no further outbreak is likely," the *Brownsville Daily Herald* reported in its news columns, but editorially it denounced the governor and the adjutant general for dismissing the attack as a "drunken riot or spree." Quite the contrary, insisted the editorial writer, "it was a premeditated plot to massacre the families of certain citizens."[34]

Blocksom's final report, August 29, ended with the gratuitous observation: "It must be confessed the colored soldier is much more aggressive in his attitude on the social equality question than he used to be." The sentence may have received a thoughtful second reading from his commander-in-chief, who now had reclaimed some of the southern ground lost by breaking bread with Dr. Washington, hospitality he had come to regard as perhaps "unwise."[35]

Chapter Eleven

"It is important to protect Cubans in Cuba, but it
is even more important to protect Americans in America."

—*Joseph Benson Foraker*

Chattanooga Daily Times, *October 16, 1906*

Relations between Foraker and Roosevelt had continued to deteriorate following the senator's lonely stand on the railroad rate bill. In late September, 1906, six weeks after what appeared to have been a minor outbreak of violence on a hot summer night in a Texas border town, Cuba's President Palma was facing a revolt that within a few days could cause an American property loss Taft estimated at $200 million. When Roosevelt dispatched troops to preserve order, Foraker responded with a telegram reminding him that, under the Platt Amendment (1901), Congress, not the president, was empowered to intervene in the island's domestic affairs.[1]

"I thank you for your very kind telegram of September 27th," Roosevelt replied from Oyster Bay the following day, and explained: "I am sure you will agree with me that it would not have been wise to summon Congress to consider the situation in Cuba, which was changing from week to week and almost from day to day. . . . I realized then and realize now, as a matter of course, that anything I do must be of a tentative nature, and that as soon as Congress comes together it must decide as to what policy we shall permanently follow."[2]

In a letter to Lodge, Roosevelt wrote more candidly of his reaction to Foraker's telegram:

> *I do not know whether he was speaking purely from foolish convictions, or whether, as was much more probable, with the deliberate desire to be mischievous. . . . He is a very powerful and very vindictive man, and he is one of the most unblushing servers and beneficiaries of corporate wealth within or without office that I have ever met. It is possible that he has grown to feel so angry over my course, that is over my having helped rescue the Republican party and therefore the country from the ruin into which, if he had had his way, it would have been thrown by the party being made to appear as simply an appanage to Wall Street—that he intends hereafter to fight me on every point, good or bad.*[3]

Taft, in the meantime, had been sent to Havana to deal with the uprising against President Palma. "A good deal of an old ass," the White House trouble-shooter wrote Nellie, and in a moment of despair during a "great thunderstorm," he found himself "looking out on Havana harbor and were it not for you and the children and others near and dear, I should not regret it if one of the bolts now flashing and resounding struck me."[4]

Gloom soon gave way to his abundant good humor, and making use of the Platt Amendment, he set up shop as provisional governor of "the Republic of Cuba under the Provisional Administration of the United States." He ran the troubled island "as a receiver carries on the business of a corporation, or a trustee the business of his ward."

Once they realized their young republic was not going to be gobbled up by the *norteamericanos*, the Cubans "succumbed to the earnest and patent sincerity of the large man who had arrived from the United States." Taft's successor, Charles E. Magoon, took over the receivership on October 13.[5]

Three days later, while the Brownsville soldiers were being interrogated about what the War Department and the president had come to regard as a "conspiracy of silence" to shield a pack of midnight assassins in their ranks, Foraker returned to Chattanooga and to a time in Tennessee when, as a teenage lieutenant, he had stormed Missionary Ridge.

"Colonel" Foraker, the *Daily Times* reported Tuesday, October 16, was due to arrive with his wife and two sons at 6:30 A.M. Next day, in a sidebar accompanying the text of the senator's speech, he was described as "one of the leading orators of America," who was also "one of the few men of his party who is now considered seriously as a presidential possibility."

On October 18 the *Daily Times* reported that the senator's "notable address on the political and racial situation" had been heard by fifteen hundred people and that his audience would have more than doubled if the gathering of Union veterans had not conflicted with such other attractions as Barnum & Bailey's circus, the state grand lodge meeting of the IOOF, and the carnival week diversions of the Knights of Pythias. The senator was introduced as "a political hero" and given an ovation.

What began as a history lesson ("the war was not fought to destroy the south, but to save it; not because we hated and despised our foes, but because we loved them too much to allow them to leave us") reached a moving climax in the description of Appomattox, where "our conquering hero turned the whole country, conquerors and conquered alike, from thoughts of war and struggle and blood and violence to the paths and pursuits of peace by quietly directing General Lee to have his men 'keep their horses and take them home with them, for they would need them to do the spring planting with.' Never in all human history were grander words uttered on such an occasion. Their simplicity made them sublime."

As the old Union soldier spoke in Chattanooga, Southerners were mourning the death of Varina Davis, the widow of their Confederate president. Now, forty-one years after he fled Richmond—where Varina would be buried beside him on a bluff overlooking the James River—the flag of the United States had forty-five stars instead of twenty-nine he had known and flew over a country with a population of eighty million instead of thirty-one million.

Foraker's words would seem prophetic when read two generations later: "Man's capacity for self-government, as demonstrated by us, has spread the spirit of democracy among all the nations. . . . Nearly every civilized country has either a written constitution or a struggle in progress such as they have in Russia, that will not end until they have one."

As he approached the climax of his talk, Foraker took up the plight of the Negro: "All attempts by lynching or other forms of violence to reduce him to a servile condition will be found, if persisted in, just as odious to the American people of this day as was slavery to the American people of 1861–65."

In a single generation since Emancipation, he pointed out, people of color had acquired property worth more than half a billion dollars, and "where probably not one man in a thousand could then read or write, today less than half of them are illiterate. We have seen them establishing schools and colleges and universities of their own and successfully conducting them." The black man's situation must be remedied, he continued, and the remedy "must be one consistent with his manhood and his just rights as a citizen. . . . It is important to protect Cubans in Cuba, but it is even more important to protect Americans in America."[6]

On October 30, less than two weeks after Foraker's Chattanooga speech, Roosevelt invited Booker T. Washington to the White House for a private talk. The subject, Dr. Washington guessed, would be the Brownsville shooting spree or the recent riot in Atlanta, birthplace of the 1895 compromise by which southern whites had left Tuskegee Institute's founder free to rule over his "empire of poverty in exchange for his assurance that he was not seeking social equality."[7]

In the new century the politically deft architect of accommodation and industrial training found himself under increasingly heavy attack from college-educated blacks, none more outspoken than William Monroe Trotter of Boston (Harvard B.A., *magna cum laude*, 1895). Week after week the editor of *The Guardian* ran editorials lambasting Washington and his wonderworking Tuskegee machine.

As Trotter's biographer points out, the two men "could scarcely have been more different."

> *Washington was born in slavery, never knew his father (some white man) or even the date of his birth, and was raised by his uneducated and overworked mother. Trotter was born in freedom and was raised in a stable household dominated by a remarkable patriarch. . . . Washington read history and found cause for hope: "merit, no matter under what skin found, is in the long run recognized and rewarded." Trotter read the same history and discerned a continuity in the Negro's treatment by white Americans: "a spirit of ruthless and rapacious domination of his interests by them from the foundation of the republic."*[8]

In his 1934 eulogy, Du Bois recalled their undergraduate years at Harvard, when Trotter "was even then forming his philosophy of life. Colored students must not herd together, just because they were colored. He had his white friends and companions, and they liked him. He was no hanger-on, but a leader among them. . . . Out of this rose his life-long philosophy: Intense hatred of all racial discrimination and segregation."[9]

At the start of the new century there were fewer than three thousand Negro college graduates in the United States and fewer than one thousand Negro college students. Seventy percent of the graduates had ended up teaching or preaching, not competing with white professionals, except for the few who had gone into law (4.7 percent) and medicine (6.3 percent), and most of them depended on black clients and patients.[10]

"The Negro race, like all races, is going to be saved by its exceptional men," Du Bois insisted. He looked to what he called "The Talented Tenth" to rise and pull "all that are worth saving up to their vantage ground." He believed in industrial training for black boys, but insisted that "the object of all true education is not to make men carpenters, it is to make carpenters men." This called for "the Negro college and college-bred men."[11]

But, he was fond of saying, education "is not simply a matter of schools; it is much more a matter of family and group life—the training of one's home, of one's daily companions, of one's social class." The teachers for a boy born into the black world of the South were "the physicians and clergymen, the trained fathers and mothers, the influential and forceful men about him of all kinds." The only alternative to "thoughtful men of trained leadership" was "a headless misguided rabble."[12]

"Men of America," he wrote in 1903, "the problem is plain before you. Here is a race transplanted through the criminal foolishness of your fathers. Whether you like it or not the millions are here, and here they will remain. If you do not lift them up, they will pull you down."[13]

Du Bois met Booker T. Washington for the first time in 1902, when he was invited to leave Atlanta University and join the Tuskegee faculty. Negotiations cooled the following year when Tuskegeeans read his criticism of Washington in *The Souls of Black Folks*.[14]

Du Bois remained in Atlanta, where on the night of September 22, less than six weeks after the Brownsville Affray, "ten thousand white people (most of them under 20) had beaten every black person they found on the streets of the city. The post office, train station, and white-owned businesses had been pillaged whenever the marauding mob, ferreting out its prey like a huge bloodhound, sniffed terrified black employees in hiding." After five days and nights of violence, ten Negroes and one white person were dead.[15]

Five-year-old Margaret Mitchell, who much later said half-jokingly that she was ten before she discovered the South had lost the War Between the States, would never forget the night she crawled "out from under the bed where I had prudently taken refuge to see the militia tramp up Jackson Street and camp on our lawn and the street."[16]

Booker Washington was in New York at the time and, contrary to myth-makers, did not rush home. He returned to Atlanta on the 28th. Du Bois was at Calhoun School in Alabama. On the train heading home he composed his "Litany of Atlanta," in which he cried out to God, "Thy silence is white terror to our hearts!"[17]

He revered life, had never killed a bird, never shot a rabbit.

> *Nearly all my schoolmates in the South carried pistols. I never owned one. I could never conceive myself killing a human being. But in 1906 I rushed back from Alabama to Atlanta, where my wife and six-year-old child were living. A mob had raged for days killing Negroes. I bought a Winchester double-barrelled shotgun and two dozen rounds of shells filled with buckshot. If a white mob had stepped on the campus where I lived I would without hesitation have sprayed their guts over the grass. They did not come. They went to south Atlanta where the police let them steal and kill. My gun was fired but once and then by error into a row of* Congressional Records *which lined the lower shelf of my library.*[18]

Roosevelt was about to take off for Panama in late October, when he asked Dr. Washington to drop by for a talk. Brownsville, not Atlanta, was on the president's mind. He confided that he was about to discharge without honor the 167 black infantrymen who, he was convinced, had conspired to shield the men responsible for the midnight assault.

"A great blunder," Washington thought, and later wrote to the president urging him to hold off "until after your return from Panama. There is some information which I must put before you before you take final action."[19]

"You can not have any information to give me privately to which I could pay heed, my dear Mr. Washington," Roosevelt replied, "because the information on which I act came out of the investigation itself."[20]

The president's letter was written on Monday, November 5, the eve of the off-year elections. Next day the dismissal order lay on Roosevelt's White House desk while he hunted wild turkey in the woods surrounding his Pine Knot, Virginia, retreat.

The order was held up until Republican voters had gone to the polls in New York and chosen Charles Evans Hughes instead of Wiliam Randolph Hearst to be their governor. In Ohio they had given Alice Roosevelt's husband another two years in Congress. The Cincinnati constituency Longworth shared with Senator Foraker included some 3,200 black voters, enough to have defeated the nation's First Son-in-Law if only half of them had defected because of the Brownsville decree.[21]

"The picture of a President whose chief merit is supposed to lie in his fearless bravery dodging an issue like this one, until after the votes are counted, is not pleasant to look upon, even though it stamps him as a clever politician," the editor of the *Waterville (Maine) Sentinel* declared, and Dr. Washington agreed: the delay made the president's action "all the more regrettable."[22]

To make it more palatable, the dismissal order was coupled with a demand for the investigation and possible court-martial of a white officer quoted as having made remarks denigrating all Negroes in uniform. ("For the life of me I cannot see why the United States should try to make soldiers out of them.")[23]

If it turned out that Colonel William L. Pitcher, 27th Infantry, had been quoted correctly, he would be brought up on specific charges and, with the assistance of counsel, face his accusers in a public place. He would, in short, have his day in court. Not one of the Brownsville soldiers, each of whom had sworn to his innocence, would ever be charged, tried, and convicted.

"They appear to stand together in a determination to resist the detection of the guilty; therefore they should stand together when the penalty falls," the president had decided, as though the *appearance* of guilt could replace all reasonable doubt. The administration's position, a *New York Times* editorial writer pointed "is in flat contravention of that provision of the Constitution which declares that no person shall be deprived of life, liberty or property 'without due process of law.'"[24]

On Thursday, November 8, Roosevelt was still exulting over the Republican triumph. By defeating Hearst, he wrote Will Taft, Hughes had won a "fight for civilization." While the president selected reading matter for a voyage to Panama ("Milton's prose works, Tacitus and a German novel called Jorn Uhl"), Julia Foraker was preserving a newspaper report that Ohio's two senators had won not only the endorsement of their party, but the endorsement of their constituents as well.[25]

"It establishes their complete mastery of the Republican party in Ohio," the *Cincinnati Enquirer* pointed out, "and assures Senator Foraker, without serious opposition, endorsement in the next Republican state convention [1908] to succeed himself, and in addition thereto a solid delegation in the national convention for the Presidency, if he so desires."[26]

Next day, in Norfolk, Virginia, Roosevelt was piped aboard the USS *Louisiana*. Waving goodbye from the deck, he called out: "I am going down to see how the ditch is getting along." Taft was out on the hustings that day, winding up his successful political tour, and in Washington, General Ainsworth was dispatching a confidential telegram to the army's commanding general in Texas, advising him that "orders will be sent today directing discharge without honor of all enlisted men of Twenty-fifth Infantry present at Fort Brown at time of disturbance there."[27]

Roosevelt was posing for photographers on the banks of his "ditch," and six soldiers already had been discharged when Taft returned to his War Department office on Saturday, November 17. He had been warned, the *New York Times* reported, "that the negro vote in Ohio carries the balance of power, and every bit of it would be alienated from the Republicans by this order."[28]

On that same morning, Mrs. Mary Church Terrell, president of the National Association of Colored Women, discovered that her newly installed home telephone was in working order when it rang and she found herself talking to John Milholland in New York. The wealthy white founding father of the Constitution League asked her "to go see Secretary Taft right away to urge him to suspend the order till an investigation can be made."

She spent the rest of the day sitting outside the secretary's office, she wrote in *The Independent*. It was late afternoon when she was admitted to the company of this "honest generous-hearted man," who spared her "the flowery words of a politician."

"I do not wonder that you are proud of the record of your soldiers," Taft said after Mrs. Terrell had urged him to hold up the dismissal order. "They have served their country well."[29]

His confidential telegram to the president was transmitted at 7:15 that night: "New York Republican Club and many others appealing for a suspension of the order discharging colored troops until your return that you may have a rehearing. . . . Much agitation on the subject and it may be well to convince people of fairness of hearing by granting rehearing."[30]

"An order from a Cabinet officer suspending the operation of a previous one issued by his chief, the President of the United States, is an event probably without precedent," a *New York Times* Washington correspondent reported Tuesday, November 20, and took it as an indication that the secretary of war "has enlisted zealously in the cause of the discharged soldiers, and is determined to uphold them at any cost."

Roosevelt responded from Puerto Rico the following day: "Discharge is not to be suspended unless there are new facts of such importance as to warrant your cabling me. I care nothing whatever for the yelling of either the politicians or the sentimentalists."[31]

Taft was "too big a man to play the lackey," declared the *Minneapolis Daily Tribune.* The secretary of war, however, bowing to the ancient wisdom of his calling, rose above principle and ordered the military authorities to proceed with the discharge of the three companies.[32]

"I am not responsible for the Brownsville order, but I think it entirely justified," he wrote his brother Charles, leading a not unsympathetic biographer to suggest that in this instance the future chief justice of the United States had "permitted temporary atrophy of the judicial lobes of his brain."[33]

After examining the War Department documents on which the president had acted, the *New York Times* was astonished to find that "no evidence had been gathered to prove a conspiracy on the part of the members of the battalion. The whole proceeding in fact was based on the assumption of the officers who made the inquiry that those who did not take part in the riot at Brownsville 'must know' who did." In the one hundred and twelve pages of this "extraordinary document" was "not a particle of evidence . . . to prove that any enlisted man had a certain knowledge of the identity of any of the participants in the riot."[34]

When the last man of Company D received his discharge without honor, Captain Lyon turned to Gilchrist Stewart, the black lawyer who had made an independent investigation for the Constitution League. "Here goes the last of the best disciplined, best behaved, and best regulated battalion in the United States Army," Lyon said, with tears in his eyes.[35]

The last man on the battalion's roster was twenty-year-old Dorsie W. Willis, who had enlisted in the hope of making a favorable impression on the slender daughter of a Guthrie, Oklahoma, preacher. When Dorsie reached home that fall, Lucille Jordan was sitting on the front porch with his three older sisters, the ones who took care of the younger children while their mother worked. Dorsie and Lucille were married a few weeks later, and their son was born the following year. They named him Reginald.

Years later, Dorsie still enjoyed comparing his childhood with his son's: "My father never spent a dollar for anything for me to play with. Anything I played with I made it myself. So with Reginald, you see, it had to be different. Whatever he wanted, he got mostly. When he'd get tired of playing with something, he'd leave it out in the yard, and his mother was always after him to bring the stuff into the house. He'd say, 'Mama, I'm tired of that. Give it to some poor kid.' His mother and I used to say, 'He'll certainly be surprised when he grows up and finds out how poor he is.'"[36]

Execution of the dismissal order was completed by 9:30 A.M., November 26. Next morning, Roosevelt was back at his White House desk. Senator Foraker, his wife recalled, was in his office at home during those autumn weeks before Congress met again, "writing, wiring, sending men out to Texas to take sworn testimony, to secure exact details; spending hours and hours in a thickening jungle of newspapers, clippings, letters, and calf-bound books. I remember, as he read on and on, his unconscious ejaculation of dissent: 'No, that isn't true. . . . That doesn't follow at all. . . . No, no, there is nothing in that.' The thing was too much for Foraker's sense of justice, too much for his legal sense."[37]

"We must not fail to have a full set of affidavits in the Brownsville matter when Congress meets," Roosevelt reminded his secretary of war and, well aware of Foraker's skill in a floor debate, he emphatically added: *Very important.*"[38]

Chapter Twelve

"They ask no favors because they are Negroes,
but only for justice because they are men."

—*Joseph Benson Foraker, April 14, 1908*

When the second session of the Fifty-ninth Congress convened on Monday, December 3, 1906, Senator Boies Penrose of Pennsylvania took the floor to "submit a resolution asking for certain information." Vice President Charles W. Fairbanks reminded him that on opening day the usual practice was not "to consider miscellaneous business until after the message from the president has been received." Penrose obtained unanimous consent to offer his resolution, which called for the president to be "requested" to supply information regarding his order dismissing Companies B, C, and D, 25th Infantry.

Foraker, by chance, happened to have in his coat pocket a draft of a similar resolution he had dictated to his stenographer and intended to introduce the following day. He immediately offered it as a substitute. It "directed" the secretary of war to furnish the Senate with copies of "all official letters, telegrams, reports, orders, etc., filed in the War Department" along with the military records of each of the men involved and any rulings the War Department might have made in similar cases.[1]

When Taft responded by reminding the press that the president had statutory power to dismiss soldiers without honor, Foraker agreed, but pointed out that no such discharge could be granted when "punishment is inflicted as though it had been in pursuance of the sentence of a court-martial." In enacting the articles of war, he reminded the former appellate judge, Congress had been careful "to provide that there shall be no conviction of any enlisted man of any offense upon which a discharge can be predicated until he has had a trial before a court-martial or some other duly constituted tribunal." In short, "no man can be deprived of life, liberty, or property without due process of law."[2]

A blacker crime never "stained the annals of our Army," the president thundered in his response, December 19, and went on to add: "These soldiers were not schoolboys on a frolic. They were full grown men, in the uniform of the United States Army, armed with deadly weapons . . . and the crime they committed was murder."[3]

Roosevelt's reference to "schoolboys on a frolic" struck back at newspaper reports of a homely irony in his handling of the soldiers' alleged "conspiracy of silence." Shortly before the three infantry companies were dismissed, Ted Roosevelt and a fellow-student at Harvard were fleeing two policemen on the Boston Common when young Roosevelt's companion collided with one of the officers, broke the man's nose and escaped. Hauled off to the police station and asked to name his friend, Ted refused. When it was suggested that his father would advise him to identify the fugitive from justice, the youth replied: "I don't think he would."[4]

The president also took issue with Foraker's reminder that the statute establishing a "discharge without honor" was never to be used as punishment: "I deny emphatically that such is the case, because as punishment it is utterly inadequate. The punishment meet for mutineers and murderers such as those guilty of the Brownsville assault is death; and a punishment only less severe ought to be meted out to those who have aided and abetted mutiny and murder and treason by refusing to help in their detection."[5]

Senator Lodge, hurrying to the defense of his old friend in the White House, pointed out that during the last two years the army had discharged 352 men without honor. Foraker reminded him that "in no one of those cases was there any punishment involved, but simply a withholding of honor." He cited the typical case of a youngster who manages to enlist by lying about his age and some weeks or months later his mother claims he is her only source of support and asks to have him sent back home.[6]

Although Congress had carefully provided that no soldier "charged with an offense should be found guilty of it and be punished for it otherwise than by court-martial," Foraker continued, the 167 black infantrymen had been sent home "branded as participators in the commission of one of the most atrocious crimes that ever disgraced the United States Army."

"I have sought to secure for the colored people all their rights under the law," the president insisted in defense of his racial policies. He had also "condemned in unstinted terms the crime of lynching perpetrated by white men," he continued, "and I should take instant advantage of any opportunity whereby I could bring to justice a mob of lynchers. In precisely the same spirit I have now acted with reference to these colored men who have been guilty of a black and dastardly crime."[7]

The 167 men sent home in disgrace viewed themselves as the victims, not the perpetrators, of a lynching for which the president had supplied the rope.

The most virulent of the Senate's southern white supremacists was seated directly in front of the presiding officer. Pitchfork Ben Tillman of South Carolina, a rude, rumpled, one-eyed giant with "the fiercest face ever seen on a public man," practiced what he called "cornfield law" and boasted of having "imbibed my knowledge of jurisprudence and human liberty with my mother's milk." He was amused to find that Foraker, a colleague from the North whose radical and aggressive utterances had earned him the nickname "Fire Alarm Joe," should now find himself aligned with "that Senator from the South who is supposed to have a broiled negro for breakfast." Tillman insisted he wanted to be just to the negro if he knew how. "Probably I do not know how. But I would be sufficiently just not to lynch 167 of them because twenty-odd had been guilty of something. No southern mob has ever gone that far in taking life without due process of law."[8]

He called attention to the Administration's successful "conspiracy of silence" a couple of years earlier to protect fifty to seventy white artillerymen involved in the fatal shooting of a noncommissioned officer of the National Guard in Athens, Ohio. The soldiers had marched into the town in the early hours of a pleasant summer evening to liberate one of their men who had been jailed. When a corporal of the provost guard ordered them to halt, he was gunned down in a fusillade which wounded two other militiamen and one private citizen.[9]

Government officials, Ohio's Representative Charles H. Grosvenor complained in a letter to Taft, had moved into Athens, manipulated the preliminary examination of witnesses, denounced the prosecution, and left the townspeople powerless to punish the murderers of "a fine young man of Warren County, Ohio."

Taft reminded the congressman that "an enlisted man is more or less a ward of the Government," which prompted Tillman to ask, "Is the white enlisted man a ward of the government and the black enlisted man not?"[10]

Roosevelt had an articulate young champion at Groton, sixteen-year-old Frederick Lewis Allen, who would grow up to be a Harper's editor and write *Only Yesterday*, a graceful examination of the 1920s. In preparing for a debate in which young Allen would defend the dismissal of the Brownsville soldiers, his teammate Kermit Roosevelt wrote to his father asking for ammunition.[11]

"Mr. Loeb sent you the matter about the Brownsville incident for your debate, didn't he?" the president replied on January 19, five days after sending another message on the subject to Capitol Hill. "It is really not any of the Senate's business; but they have had a terrific fight over it and now they are nearly to the crisis. I do not know how it will come out. I hope those that support me will win; but if they do not, it will not make the slightest difference in my attitude."[12]

Kermit's team won the debate and a month or so later, when the president visited the school, Allen interviewed him for the *Weekly Groton*. "The first thing I noticed was his voice. It is very weak, and when he makes a joke, or gets off some particularly apt word, it rises to a squeaky falsetto. He'd say, I don't want you to be 'NICE BOYS'—the last two words in falsetto, with a grin on his face. And all through he had that remarkable tenseness, and terseness—he spoke as though he were so angry to get his words out, at first—snarling in a sort of nasal way, over each word."[13]

A few days after sending Kermit the Brownsville material, Roosevelt wrote a friend:

> *I have had a perfectly comic time with the Senate. They have been hopping about, insisting that they could not desert Foraker, because it would "split the party;" and I finally told the most active of the compromisers that if they split off Foraker they split off a splinter, but that if they split off me they would split the party neatly in two; and that I should state most unhesitatingly, and whenever it became necessary in*

public, that the opposition to me on Brownsville was simply a cloak to cover antagonism to my actions about trusts, swollen fortunes and the like.[14]

Foraker noted in his memoirs that, unlike many others who had criticized the president's decision, he had not attributed it to "any selfish purpose of any kind." Nor had he made "the slightest reference" connecting the dismissal of the black soldiers with the Booker T. Washington dinner, "although such connection was commonly made in ordinary conversation by those who privately criticized the action." He still hoped that once the truth had been established, "the President would in manly fashion undo the wrong he had done."[15]

Roosevelt could see nothing wrong in having rendered "substantial justice" to men he regarded as murderers and conspirators. If any doubts began to prick him, Pringle points out, they were blunted by the "conviction of righteousness that strengthened him in his moments of inner doubt." When the term "substantial justice" cropped up in a 1915 lawsuit, Roosevelt was asked how he could be sure "substantial justice" had been done.

"Because I did it," he replied.

"You mean to say that when you do a thing thereby substantial justice is done?"

"I do. When I do a thing, I do it so as to do substantial justice. I mean just that."[16]

While the Senate was squaring off for a fight on the dismissal of the Brownsville soldiers, Roosevelt was fretting over ethical problems posed by being named a Nobel Peace Laureate because of his involvement in bringing an end to the war between Japan and Russia.

"It appears that there is a large sum of money—they say about $40,000— that goes with it," he wrote Kermit (December 5, 1906).

> *Now, I hate to do anything foolish or quixotic and above all I hate to do anything that means the refusal of money which would ultimately come to you children. But Mother and I talked it over and came to the conclusion that while I was President at any rate, and perhaps anyhow, I could not accept money given to me for making peace between two nations, especially when I was able to make peace simply because I was President. To receive money for making peace would in any event be a*

little too much like being given money for rescuing a man from drowning, or for performing a daring feat in war.[17]

Roosevelt, holding center stage at the Gridiron Club dinner that December, flashed his trademark smile when the veteran minstrel man Lew Dockstader shuffled onto the stage in blackface and asked to see the president.

"I'se an old nigger from down Tuskegee way," he said. "I was up here and heard the President was here, so I came in here to see him. I'se surely interested in dat man. I had a boy in dem colored troops down at Brownsville, but I 'spect he's on his way home now."

The newspapermen also poked fun at the president's trip to Panama ("He sailed right in and turned around, then sailed right home again") and at his abortive campaign for simplified spelling ("Andru Karnagie had removed the letter C from the Gridiron Dikshunary"). Taft, portrayed as the president's heir apparent, was saluted in a song, "Waiting for Teddy's Shoes."[18]

Some weeks later, both the president and his crown prince were sitting at the club's head table when the subject of the Brownsville Affray again cropped up. This time it made headlines and history.

The Washington newspapermen who had banded together in 1885 to form the Gridiron Club adhered to two rules for their celebrated dinners: "Ladies are always present and reporters are never present." Actually, the affairs were for men only, and the banquet room swarmed with reporters; the traditional caveat barred stag party humor and assured guest speakers their remarks would not be reported. The second rule was shattered at their dinner on January 26, 1907. As for the meal itself, as Julia Foraker would always remember, it "never got beyond the quail."[19]

As he made his way through a Washington snowstorm to the Willard Hotel that Saturday night, Foraker had no idea he would be called upon to speak. He wasn't even sure Roosevelt would be present. When he entered the banquet room, he saw the club's most distinguished guests, including the president and Secretary Taft, seated at a table on a raised platform that ran the length of the room. Roosevelt sat to the right of the club president, Samuel G. Blythe of the *New York World*. On Blythe's left sat Vice President Fairbanks, a foreign minister, and J. P. Morgan.

Four other tables, running at right angles to the speaker's table, formed a gridiron. Foraker was seated at the first table on the left of Roosevelt's, with the president of the Associated Press and Champ Clark, Missouri's affable Democratic congressman.

When Roosevelt was introduced, everyone settled back for an amusing few minutes of banter. Instead, they were brought to the edge of their seats by a "battle royal" that could "not be ignored or silenced by club etiquette," the *Washington Post* reported in violation of the club's gag rule. Roosevelt preached "a sermon on the duty of everyone to see the light as he saw it." J. P. Morgan and Henry Rogers of Standard Oil glowered as he called Wall Street to repentance. If his railroad and corporate reforms had not been put through by conservative forces, he argued in his strident, high-pitched voice, the plutocracy would have been at the mercy of "the mob, the mob, the mob."

As for the Senate debate on the Brownsville affray, it was "academic," the president contended, because his power to issue the dismissal order was not subject to review. Indiana's Republican Senator Jim Watson clocked the speech at fifty-five minutes. Although Foraker's name was never mentioned, the *Post* described the president's diatribe "as a lecture to him as an individual and the Senate as a whole for stirring up the Brownsville mess."[20]

"Now is the time to bridge the bloody chasm," Blythe said, and set another precedent by announcing, "I have the pleasure of introducing Senator Foraker."[21]

The Ohio senator was "a very handsome man," Champ Clark recalled in his memoirs, "over six feet tall, weighing slightly over two hundred pounds, with as fine a shock of iron-gray hair as was ever seen on a man's head. When he arose to address the club his face was as white as a sheet." He began by responding to the president's remarks on railroads and corporations, explaining that he too "favored governmental supervision and regulation" and that "our only difference was not as to whether there should be such regulation, but as to the character of the legislation that should be enacted to secure it."[22]

Turning to the Brownsville debate, he reminded the president that in laying out his policy with respect to corporations, he had stated:

> that no man in this country was so high or so low that he would not punish him, if he could, for violating the law, and on the other hand, no man was either so high or so low that he would not give him the full protection of the law if innocent of the offence against the law. I said I

agreed with him entirely in that sentiment, but stated that I thought
he had failed to apply that principle in the Brownsville case, where,
according to his own statement of it, there were doubtless many men
with splendid records as soldiers, absolutely innocent, yet branded as
criminals, and dismissed without honor.

Foraker then denied newspaper speculation that he had taken up the case of the black soldiers in order to get votes. "I was not after votes," he said, "but I was seeking to provide for those men an opportunity to be heard in their own defense, to give them a chance to confront their accusers and cross-examine their witnesses, and establish the real facts in the case."

In closing he touched on his personal relationship with the president, pointing out that "there was a time, as the President well knew, when I loved him as though one of my own family and that there was nothing legitimate or honorable that I would not have striven to do for him; that while I had that affectionate regard for him, yet I did not feel that it stood in the way, or that I had any right to allow it to stand in the way of my differing from the President, when in my judgment, he was in error." He pointed out that their disagreements "had been in the open, and I thought the President himself would testify that I had fired no shots from ambush."[23]

"The very minute that Senator Foraker sat down the President jumped up like a 'jack-out-of-the-box,' and without waiting for anybody to introduce him, began his reply," Champ Clark wrote, and proceeded to quote Roosevelt's remarks on the Brownsville soldiers:

Some of these men were bloody butchers; they ought to be hung. The
only reason that I didn't have them hung was because I couldn't find
out which ones of them did the shooting. None of the battalion would
testify against them. . . . It is my business and the business of nobody
else. It is not the business of the Congress. . . . All the talk on that
subject is academic. If they pass a resolution to reinstate these men, I
will veto it; if they pass it over my veto, I will pay no attention to it. I
welcome impeachment![24]

It was two o'clock in the morning when Foraker got home, "white and fagged, but not defeated," Julia remembered for the rest of her long life. They were in the library when he told her what had happened and she urged him to write everything down for the children.

"The fire had gone out," she recalled in her memoirs; "we put on fresh logs; it was oddly symbolic. Everything afterwards served to add to the flame of discord between the Gridiron duelists, once friends."[25]

The Forakers had been in politics long enough to comprehend the remark Emerson once made to the young namesake of his Boston friend, Dr. Oliver Wendell Holmes: "When you strike at a king, you must kill him."[26]

In San Antonio, Texas, on Monday morning, February 4, 1907, a general court-martial assembled to consider the "neglect of duty" charge brought against Major Charles W. Penrose, commanding officer of the 1st Battalion, 25th Infantry (Colored). In Washington, D.C., that same morning, the Senate Military Affairs Committee began questioning the first black soldiers called to shed light on "the affray at Brownsville, Texas, on the night of August 13, 1906."[27]

The committee had been directed to ascertain all the facts "without questioning the legality or justice of any act of the President in relation thereto." That Monday night, when Secret Service agents assigned to the White House went home, the president clapped his broad-brimmed Rough Riders hat on his head, slipped out through a side entrance, and spent the next hour and a half coatless and alone with his thoughts, walking in a fast-driving snow.[28]

The Brownsville matter was now in the hands of a committee which, fortunately for the president, included Cabot Lodge and was presided over by an Administration loyalist, Francis Emroy Warren, whose charming, improvident daughter, Frankie, would no longer have to make do on a captain's pay. Her personable West Point husband, Jack Pershing, was now a brigadier general serving in Tokyo, where his wife had just given birth to a daughter. In mid-September, a month after the Texas incident, Roosevelt had sent the Pershing nomination to the Senate, carrying him "over the careers of 900 captains, majors, lieutenant colonels, and colonels," his father-in-law noted, along with "a tidy collection of almost instant enemies."[29]

The president, striding through the snow, could take comfort in the knowledge that Lodge would speak for him in the Senate hearings and that the committee chairman was not likely to buck the Administration responsible for so many of Wyoming's forts and public buildings as well as for the promotion of his son-in-law. Senator Warren was also apprehensive about the current investigations by Interior and Justice of charges that the Warren Live Stock Company had used violence to intimidate settlers casting a covetous eye on 46,000 acres of land the company was accused of having fenced illegally.[30]

"Attorneys were barred from the committee room, the negro soldiers under investigation having no representatives at the hearing other than members of the committee," the *Washington Post* reported Tuesday, February 5, and explained, "It is understood that Senator Foraker, author of the resolution of inquiry, will look after the interests of the men if they are placed in jeopardy."

Throughout the first day, Chairman Warren had to correct colleagues who kept referring to the proceedings as a "trial." Roosevelt had insisted that white officers and colored soldiers would be treated "in precisely the same way," but both Major Penrose, the battalion's commanding officer, and Captain Edgar A. Macklin, the officer of the day who had slept through the raid, were to be defended by counsel at a trial in which they would face specific charges. Their men, with no lawyers at their side, were making do with a "hearing."

Both officers were acquitted. In the case of Major Penrose the court found that, although there was no negligence on his part, certain men of his command "did assemble, armed with rifles, and did proceed to the town of Brownsville, Tex., and did then and there shoot and wound and kill certain citizens thereof." Their commanding officer, brought before a jury of his peers, had faced his accusers in a public place and, with the assistance of counsel, had been cleared of the charges brought against him. Some enlisted men who were not on trial had appeared as witnesses, without counsel and with no formal charges lodged against them. The same tribunals that left the two white officers free to resume their army careers had pronounced the black enlisted men guilty of armed assault and murder.[31]

By the time the five white officers serving at Fort Brown on the night of the raid arrived in Washington to testify before Senator Warren's committee, they were unanimous in agreement on the soldiers' innocence. Evidence brought out at the two courts-martial was confirmed and amplified by Senator Foraker's masterful presentation of fact and law, and by his cross-examination of hostile witnesses, notably Inspector General Ernest A. Garlington, who spoke with a South Carolina accent as he told how he reached the conclusion the men had formed a "conspiracy of silence."

"Do you think colored people, generally, are truthful?" Foraker asked.

"No, sir; I do not."

"You would not believe their testimony ordinarily, even under oath, would you?"

"Where their own interest, or some special interest, was concerned. It depends entirely upon the circumstances."

"You think a colored man might testify truthfully about the weather, but that he would not testify truthfully about a crime?"

"He might have some difficulty in testifying about the weather."[32]

In his report to the president, General Garlington had mentioned "a possible general understanding among the enlisted men" that they would take the position the town had been shot up by townspeople," but, he added, "I could find no evidence of such understanding." In reporting to the Congress, Roosevelt translated this to mean that it had now been "conclusively" proved that the men had not only shot up the town, but had also "stolidly and as one man broken their oaths of enlistment and refused to help discover the criminals."[33]

The Administration, still trying to bolster its rhetoric with factual evidence, suffered a damaging blow when the Senate committee received a report by army ballistic experts on their examination of thirty-three spent cartridges presumably left by the raiders. All had been fired by four Springfield rifles assigned to men of Company B. One of the men, Sergeant William Blaney, had never set foot in Brownsville. He was on leave the night of August 13, 1906, and his rifle (serial number 45683) was in an arms chest sealed by ten screws and locked in a storeroom.

Quartermaster Sergeant Walker McCurdy, a sixteen-year veteran with combat service in Cuba and the Philippines, cleared up the mystery of how shells fired in Nebraska had ended up in a back alley of a Texas town. After target practice at Fort Niobrara, spent shells were collected, decapped, and cleaned before being returned to an army arsenal. Company B had tried to make do with a Krag rifle decapper modified to accommodate Springfield cartridge cases, and when it finally broke down, some 1,500 to 1,600 shell casings, each in the same condition as when it was fired in Nebraska, were packed into a venerable foot locker and transported to Texas.

"The box was bursted," McCurdy explained, and his first sergeant, Mingo Sanders, corroborated the testimony.

For several days, while the storeroom was being tidied up, the open box sat on Company B's back porch, within reach of quick-fingered young scavengers, who hawked the shell casings around town as souvenirs. Thus, the evidence on which the five officers had based their belief in the soldiers' guilt had turned out to be a persuasive argument that they had been framed by local rednecks bent on having them removed and replaced by white soldiers, who would be free to spend their money in Elizabeth Street's Jim Crow saloons, shops, and eating establishments.[34]

The Military Affairs Committee wound up its investigation on March 10, 1908, and took a vote based on testimony that would fill three thousand pages. There were eight Republicans on the committee and, Foraker pointed out, "four of them joined with the [five] Democrats, all of whom were against the Negroes before a word of testimony was heard, and made the majority report." Conceived in a coupling of politics and prejudice, the report affirmed the soldier's guilt.

Three Republicans joined Foraker in his dissent, but they too were divided and filed two minority reports. Morgan G. Bulkeley (Connecticut), James A. Hemenway (Indiana), and Nathan B. Scott (West Virginia) agreed that the testimony of soldiers and townspeople was too contradictory and unreliable to sustain a charge of guilt. Foraker and Bulkeley went one step further. They flatly declared that "the weight of the testimony shows that none of the soldiers of the Twenty-fifth U.S. Infantry participated in the shooting affray."[35]

"The President and his friends have not the courage to confess their original error," the *New York Times* reported; "the endeavor to escape its consequences leaves them distinctly ridiculous."[36]

On March 11 of Roosevelt's last year in office, Vice President Fairbanks presented a message from the White House proposing a one-year extension of an expired law permitting the reinstatement of men who could succeed in doing what none of them had thus far managed to do, prove they were not "implicated" in the raid and had not "withheld any evidence" that might lead to the apprehension of its perpetrators. When Foraker asked if the men would be entitled to back pay, Chairman Warren suggested that "pay shall commence at the time of their reenlistment."

Foraker countered by introducing a bill (S. 5729) permitting a soldier to re-enlist, pick up his back pay, have his service record cleared, and regain his former rank once he had taken an oath attesting his innocence, as each of them had already done in affidavits gathered by Captain Lyon of Company D.[37]

Roosevelt, in a letter to Warren, expressed his outrage at this "proposal to condone murder and perjury in the past and put a premium on murder and perjury in the future by permitting any murderer or perjurer, who will again perjure himself, to be restored to the United States army, and again wear the uniform which he has already disgraced."[38]

Section 2 of Foraker's bill, however, specified that any soldier making such an oath would still be liable to prosecution if he had perjured himself. Roosevelt took the position that the men must prove their innocence. Foraker contended it was up to the government to prove their guilt.

On April 14, when Foraker was scheduled to deliver a major address on the Brownsville matter, Negroes began to gather outside the doors of the Senate's public galleries four hours before they opened. Step by step, for more than two hours, the Ohio Senator guided his spellbound audience through three official investigations, none of which had ever considered the possibility that someone other than the soldiers might have done the shooting. Now the condemned men must prove their innocence of "guilty knowledge" to the same judge who, after pronouncing their guilt and fixing their punishment, had declared that "very few, if any" of them could be ignorant of what had occurred.

"The vilest horse thief, the most dangerous burglar, or the bloodiest murderer would not be required either to prove his innocence or to submit to a trial before a judge who had in even the most casual way expressed the opinion that the defendant was guilty," Foraker said, and closed his defense of the black battalion by posing and answering the question: "Who are these men that it should be even suggested that they should be treated worse than common criminals? They are at once both citizens and soldiers of the Republic. . . . In every war in which we have permitted them to participate they have distinguished themselves for efficiency and valor. They have shed their blood and laid down their lives in the fierce shock of battle, side by side with their white comrades. . . . They ask no favors because they are Negroes, but only for justice because they are men."

So great was the hubbub when Foraker's peroration ended that the Senate reading clerk found it impossible to make himself heard. A presidential request for four new battleships was drowned out by cheering Negroes who hooted the vice president's threat to clear the galleries.[39]

The president now "turned against Foraker the full force of his dangerous enmity," Julia recalled some twenty-odd years later. The Forakers were no longer invited to White House dinners and, with Secret Service men keeping an eye on their front door, "people began to change their calling hours from daytime to evening." Foraker's mail was opened and resealed; his rec-ommendations for judicial appointments were rejected.[40]

At afternoon receptions the vice president's wife, Cornelia Cole Fair-banks, a friend of Julia's from their Ohio school days, would "retreat to a far corner, stand with her back to the wall so she could keep an eye on every-body, then signal me to come close to her and we would speak in whispers." Cornelia, who sat at the president's right at Cabinet dinners reported that he "couldn't keep off the subject of Foraker and his wicked interest in the black battalion. He would pound the table at a point. The glasses shivered."[41]

"Whatever may be the whole truth about the Brownsville case," Grover Cleveland wrote in *McClure's* (April, 1907), "it has been a display of genuine courage for a Republican Senator to take the position assumed by Mr. Foraker. It has been due to him that there has been a real discussion of the President's action in all its bearings."[42]

He was supported by the strongest newspapers in the North, Julia wrote, "but in the end, officially, Foraker came to press his fight for justice almost alone, to lead the forlornest of hopes. There was something gallant in this that touched the imagination. A man who would act thus would risk pulling his house about his head, could be moved only by the sincerest conviction that a great wrong was being done."[43]

Finally, "sadly badgered by the 'Brownsville nightmare,'" Roosevelt dis-patched an emissary to the Forakers' imposing yellow-brick showplace on the northwest corner of Sixteenth and P streets. Pennsylvania's powerful Senator Boies Penrose, Julia wrote, chose to arrive after dark with his mes-sage from the president.

"It was this: If Senator Foraker would drop the Brownsville fight Mr. Roosevelt was prepared to offer him any distinguished post which he might desire. An ambassadorship, perhaps. If so, which embassy would the Sena-tor prefer? This was quite comic, this idea of transporting, or rather, de-porting, the troubling Foraker to foreign shores. But it didn't make Foraker smile. He only stared at the Senator from Pennsylvania. . . . Brownsville would be fought to the finish."[44]

Chapter Thirteen

"The malice of politics would
make you miserable."

—*Louise Torrey Taft,*
to her son, Will,
January 21, 1907

"That scoundrel, Foraker, is doing all the damage he can with the negroes," Roosevelt wrote Nick Longworth, June 26, 1907, and went on to add, "A blacker wrong to the colored race than Foraker and his friends have committed it would not be possible to imagine." The subject was still festering in his thoughts next day when he wrote Lodge: "Taft, thank Heaven, is up to the point of making an aggressive fight against Foraker, and anything you think he ought to say on the subject of Brownsville you can confidentially send him." When Lodge advised against making any reference to Brownsville, Roosevelt disagreed, but sent his friend's note on to Taft with a dissenting opinion: "Foraker has attacked you, and it is to my mind not only proper but advisable that he should be met just as sharply as *we* know how." (emphasis added)[1]

"Rather than compromise with Foraker, I would give up all hope of the presidency," Taft wrote his campaign manager, Arthur I. Vorys, July 23, a week before the state central committee was to meet in Columbus. In a letter to Roosevelt, written the same day, he referred to Foraker as "the blackmailer in all Ohio politics." He also said that, if defeated for the presidency, he would go after Foraker's senate seat.[2]

"While under no circumstances would I have advised you to take the position you have taken in refusing to compromise with Foraker on the lines that the local politicians want," Roosevelt replied, "yet, now that you have taken it, I wish to say that I count it as just one of those fine and manly things which I would naturally expect from you. . . . If you are not to be President I should like to see you Chief Justice; but if the chance of being either does not come, then I should indeed like to see you Senator from Ohio; and should earnestly wish that we might meet as colleagues!"[3]

That summer, when Theodore Burton, a bookish, well-liked Ohio congressman, turned to the president for advice on whether he should forfeit his seat in the House and run for mayor of Cleveland, Roosevelt expressed regret for a loss of legislative leadership that "cannot be made up" but advised him to "make the fight." He took the advice and lost to the city's legendary Tom Johnson. To Mark Hanna the man was "a socialist-anarchist-nihilist," to Roosevelt a "ruffian," and to Lincoln Steffens "the best mayor of the best governed city in the United States."[4]

Burton was a lame-duck congressman when the Ohio Republican League met in Columbus on November 20, 1907, and adopted a resolution presented by former Lieutenant Governor Warren G. Harding pledging "loyal support" for Foraker's reelection to the Senate and also naming him as "our choice as Republican candidate for President of the United States in 1908." Two months later, on January 22, Harding's paper, the *Marion Star*, announced in a double-leaded editorial: "Foraker is defeated and Ohio is for Taft!"[5]

"My friends and I were both surprised and chagrined, but we accepted the situation with the best grace possible," Foraker wrote later, and expressed the thought that "under the peculiar circumstances I ought to be generous in judging friends, even those who did things that were injurious to my cause, for I recognized that it involved some sacrifice for them to stand by me with the National Administration and all its forces and influences arrayed against me in open and active hostility."[6]

Writing to Kermit a few days later, Roosevelt reported that "the campaign for Taft seems to be getting along well," and went on to add: "Of course the statements that I am trying to dictate his nomination are ludicrous falsehoods, and the statements that I am using the offices to force his nomination are wicked falsehoods." Taft had been on the hustings for only a few weeks when Roosevelt wrote to express his sympathy: "Of course, you are not enjoying the campaign. I wish you had some of my bad temper! It is at times a real aid to enjoyment."[7]

Nellie Taft, as her husband often remarked, was the "family politician." She was determined to maneuver him into the White House, but as early as 1902 he had told Roosevelt he preferred to occupy himself "with something more attractive than a presidential campaign or dodging office seekers in the White House." He was fond of saying, "There could hardly be a weaker candidate than I would be."[8]

When a reporter asked his eighty-year-old mother to name her candidate for the presidency, Louisa Torrey Taft replied "Elihu Root" and went on to explain that her son belonged on the Supreme Court rather than in the White House. "Roosevelt is a good fighter and enjoys it," she had written Will a few months earlier, "but the malice of politics would make you miserable."[9]

Taft also had leaned toward Root (Roosevelt's first choice) as well as New York's Governor Hughes, but his favorite candidate was still the incumbent, whose popularity would insure Hearst's defeat if, as seemed possible, the Democrats nominated "such a dealer in filth as this hideous product of yellow journalism." After Hughes had defeated him in the gubernatorial race, Hearst completed his term in the House of Representatives in March, 1907, and in the summer of the following year, respectably married and resettled on New York's Riverside Drive, he was taking an interest in the new Independence Party.[10]

He knew, of course, that its candidate, Thomas L. Hisgen, a Massachusetts businessman, could not prevail in 1908, but a strong race could put the party's 1912 candidate in contention for the presidency. Hearst planned "to go before the country with a flaming issue—his very own issue, his private property, and exclusive." A cache of letters stolen from Standard Oil files might help nominate and elect this silent, lonely man, who, wrote Ambrose Bierce, was loved only by God, "and God's love he values only in so far as he fancies that it may promote his amusing ambition to darken the door of the White House."[11]

Ben Tillman turned up in Ohio in the summer of 1907 calling for repeal of the Fourteenth and Fifteenth Amendments assuring all United States citizens "equal protection of the laws" and the right to vote regardless of "race, color, or previous condition of servitude." Foraker countered by asking why "the white men of the seceding states should have full representation for themselves and an additional representation equally as large for their colored population, and that they alone should do all the voting."[12]

Roosevelt disagreed, objecting strongly to a Republican platform proposal put forth by Foraker's Constitution League allies in the Brownsville debate, to adjust southern representation in Congress and the electoral college to accord with "the letter and spirit of the Fourteenth and Fifteenth Amendments." The president insisted that "the best colored men I know, like Booker Washington for instance, say that no good can come from such a movement."

If the proposal should be offered by "any one of the creatures, black or white, who have been doing so much to the detriment of both negro and white man by their wicked and silly agitation of the Brownsville matter, the proper course is to vote it down. These creatures have no place in the Republican party and are entitled to the scorn and abhorrence of every patriotic citizen. Foraker's desire is simply to scuttle the ship. He wants to do all the damage he can to the Republican party, and in order to achieve his purpose is willing to strike hands with Tillman or anyone else in order to do everything he possibly can to damage and discredit the nation and to impair the future well-being of decent colored men and decent white men alike . . . Tell the negro or white agitator who declaims about Brownsville that he is standing up for murder. . . ."[13]

By the time Republican delegates started packing lightweight summer wear for their week in Chicago, most Negroes were riding the bumpy road of the Taft bandwagon despite the trickery and fraud responsible for the South's lily-white delegations. "It is out of the question for the colored man to vote for Bryan," the *Dallas Express* explained. "The 'Jim Crow' laws of every Democratic state, the exclusion from the jury of almost every southern court, the mockery of a fair trial before every southern tribunal, all stand as brazen reminders of the eternal enmity of the Democracy toward the Negro."[14]

"If between the two parties who stand on identically the same platform you can prefer the party who perpetrated Brownsville, well and good!" Du Bois countered. "But I shall vote for Bryan."[15]

In response to the question whether President Bryan would put as many Negroes on the federal payroll as had President Roosevelt, Du Bois suggested that Negroes "should be voting not to secure jobs for the few, but to secure justice for all." It was, he admitted, a choice between two evils, and pointed out that "it took America forty years to get a chance to vote on slavery; it may take us a hundred years to get a chance to vote squarely on the color-line; but that chance will come and we will hasten the chance by voting intelligently and not blindly and ignorantly at every preliminary step."[16]

When Republican delegates gathered in the Chicago Coliseum in mid-June, Chairman Lodge touched off a demonstration ("Four, four, four years more!") by remarking, "The President is the most abused and most popular man in the United States today." When he finally succeeded in restoring order, Lodge declared that "no friend to Theodore Roosevelt" would impugn "both his sincerity and his good faith" by attempting "to use his name as a candidate for the presidency." Inevitably, the delegates confirmed their president's choice, but, as Nellie Taft would neither forget nor forgive, her husband's demonstration lasted only twenty-nine minutes—twenty less than Roosevelt's.[17]

"Although I fear it may be unwelcome and probably misunderstood," Foraker wired the nominee, "it is nevertheless my pleasure to avail myself of my privilege to send you heartiest congratulations and best wishes for success in November."

"I assure you that your kindly note of congratulations gave me the greatest pleasure and I thank you for it from the bottom of my heart," Taft replied. "I have never ceased to remember that I owe to you my first substantial start in public life, and that it came without solicitation."[18]

In August, however, when the state campaign was about to open in Youngstown, Taft went along with his supporters in a move to humiliate Foraker by excluding him from the speakers' platform, where he had been a star performer for twenty years. On September 2 the two men turned up in Toledo for a Grand Army parade. As Foraker's carriage passed the reviewing stand where Taft was seated, the senator hopped out, walked over to the candidate, and, after a pleasant greeting, sat beside him for the rest of the ceremony.[19]

When they appeared together that afternoon at a Lincoln Club reception, Taft spoke briefly but found time to recall again that Foraker had given him his start in public life. Foraker declared that Taft "would be his leader until the polls close." Next day the nationwide press carried pictures of the two men at what was portrayed as a "Love Feast." No deal had been made with Foraker, Taft assured Roosevelt and, in a letter to William Rockhill

Nelson, publisher of the *Kansas City Star*, he pointed out that the senator "can be useful with the colored vote and the Grand Army vote."[20]

Booker T. Washington's biographer regards Roosevelt's summary dismissal of the Brownsville soldiers as "the grossest single racial injustice of that so-called Progressive Era," but the Tuskegeean not only remained loyal to his "white boss," he also used the incident "to strengthen his machine, and become more than ever the black boss."[21]

In the summer of 1907, when Taft's campaign manager warned of Brownsville's "serious and far-reaching result," Washington assured him he was "doing some quiet and effective work with the colored newspapers." As the new owners of the *New York Age*, Washington and his private secretary, Emmett J. Scott, reversed the paper's editorial stand on Brownsville and attacked critics of the dismissal order as "ghouls" who had been bought off to "raise the black flag of Race Discrimination."[22]

Two months before the election the Niagara Movement, mortally wounded by the Tuskegee Machine but still angry and eloquent, met on Foraker's turf—Oberlin, Ohio—and delivered a bristling message to "the Negro haters of America," advising their black followers to "obey the law, defend no crime, conceal no criminal, seek no quarrel: but arm yourselves, and when the mob invades your home, shoot, and shoot to kill."

Negroes were also urged to register and vote "whenever and wherever you have the right . . . Remember that the conduct of the Republican party toward Negroes has been a disgraceful failure to keep just promises. The dominant Roosevelt faction has sinned in this respect beyond forgiveness. We therefore trust that every black voter will uphold men like Joseph Benson Foraker, and will leave no stone unturned to defeat William H. Taft. Remember Brownsville, and establish next November the principle of independence in voting, not only for punishing enemies, but for rebuking false friends."[23]

Midway in the 1908 campaign, Foraker and his older son, Benson, now practicing law in Cincinnati, dropped by Taft's hometown headquarters for what was reported to have been a pleasant chat. "All that talk about a peace pact is unfounded," Taft told reporters, "because there has been nothing but peace." Later that day, September 10, at the request of Taft's chief of staff, Foraker agreed to preside at a meeting to be held in Cincinnati's Music Hall on September 22, and in response to "the special desire of Mr. Taft," the senator also agreed to introduce the candidate." Then, "like a flash," Foraker wrote in his memoirs, "the whole situation was changed by a speech made by Mr. William R. Hearst, at Columbus, Ohio, on the evening of September 17, 1908."[24]

Julia awakened the following morning to "a day of rare beauty darkened suddenly by a poisonous fog." She opened the daily paper as usual that Friday, preparing to mark items that might be of interest to her husband, and found a "choice morsel" splashed across the front page at a time when "the most damaging thing that could be done to a public man was to link his name with the trusts." Hearst, campaigning for the Independence candidate, had built his speech around a series of letters he said had been given to him by a stranger who came to his hotel room in Columbus shortly before he left to make his speech. Actually, he had bought them in 1904 and 1905 from two thieves who had stolen them from John D. Archbold, a Methodist deacon who, on weekdays, worked at 26 Broadway as the corporate official who poured Standard Oil on troubled political waters.[25]

On February 16, 1900, Hearst revealed, Archbold wrote the Ohio senator: "Here is still another very objectionable bill. It is so outrageous as to be ridiculous, but it needs to be looked after, and I hope there will be no difficulty in killing it." A few weeks later, on March 26, Archbold sent Foraker a "certificate of deposit in your favor for $15,000." In other letters, written in 1902 and 1903, Archbold had urged the senator to support the reelection of a friendly state supreme court judge and to oppose a candidate for attorney general who had worked against Standard Oil in a case in Ohio.[26]

"Foraker met the accusation like a whirlwind," Julia recalled. "The afternoon papers of the same day carried his clear and complete setting forth of his association with Standard Oil from the beginning." It was "common knowledge" that he had been compensated for legal services performed for the oil company, Foraker pointed out, and explained, "That employment ended before my first term in the Senate expired. I have not represented the company since."[27]

That night, speaking in St. Louis, Hearst read a January 27, 1902, letter from Archbold expressing his pleasure in handing Foraker "forthwith a certificate of deposit, $50,000, in accordance with our understanding. Your letter states the condition correctly, and I trust that the transaction will be successfully consummated."[28]

"For the first, last, only time in my life I saw my husband at a loss," Julia recalled. "He couldn't remember ever having had such a letter. Couldn't remember ever having received such a sum from Mr. Archbold. (A lawyer's memory for a fifty-thousand-dollar retainer is usually excellent)."[29]

Later that Saturday morning, September 19, Julia walked in on her husband and Benson moments after they had managed to track down the complete correspondence, only half of which Hearst had read. A Republican friend had asked Foraker to help him raise $135,000 to buy the *Ohio State Journal*. Standard Oil's $50,000 certificate of deposit was a loan, not to Foraker, but to his friend. Hearst had neglected to read the letter Foraker wrote Archbold a month later returning the $50,000 draft because the newspaper deal had fallen through.[30]

Defending himself in his memoirs, Foraker pointed out that when he went to work for Standard Oil in December, 1898, "it was not foreseen by me, and probably not by anybody else, that it would become the object of Federal legislation or of Federal prosecution." The situation had changed by the spring of 1906, when Archbold wrote to ask: "In the possibility of an action against us in Ohio, are you in position to accept a retainer from us?"

Foraker turned down the offer "because of my relations to the public service." Two years later, in response to the Hearst charges, he issued statements to the press explaining that "instead of being an employment, as the former employment was, to aid the company in complying with the orders of the courts and the statutes of the State, it was to be an employment to resist suits and prosecutions instituted by the State."[31]

Foraker, as his biographer points out, was sent to the Senate by "a state legislature controlled by business interests and machine politicians." The $150,000 he spent on his Sixteenth Street mansion in Washington had come from fees paid by, among others, "railroads, a tobacco trust, a street railways syndicate, a telephone company, and several public utilities."[32]

The United States Senate, at the turn of the century, was composed mostly of men who "had devoted their adult years to politics," Rothman notes. They came to Washington "with a deeply ingrained respect for the machinery of organization, they appreciated the connections between ambition and party loyalty. They had no intentions of adopting the role of maverick."[33]

Foraker was no maverick, but, as his Ohio colleague, Senator Charles Dick, pointed out in the *North American Review:* "If political elimination should be the reward of his independent stand on any public issue, he would accept his martyrdom as philosophically as ever did any victim of persecution, and find regret only in the fact that he had but one life to give for a cause. He cannot be deterred from supporting any cause he deems right, simply because it may be unpopular."[34]

In his *Treason* series, Phillips characterized Foraker as an extravagant millionaire whose chief usefulness to "the interests and to his private fortunes has been his oratory. He is about the best stump speaker at the command of the backers of the merged political machines." But when political scientist George H. Haynes asked "five impartial observers of the Washington scene" to evaluate senators in the Fifty-eighth Congress (1903–1905), Foraker was one of eight listed under "Statesmanship."[35]

The $50,000 Standard Oil loan hit the front pages on a Saturday morning, three days before Foraker was to introduce Taft at the Music Hall. Later that day, while Benson was chatting with reporters, Julia joined her husband in another room where he was meeting with two of his colleagues, Charles Dick, Ohio's junior senator, and Winthrop Murray Crane of Massachusetts. Senator Crane handed Julia a letter her husband had just written Taft, advising him of his decision not to attend the Music Hall meeting on Tuesday evening, not because he deemed his explanation of the Archbold correspondence "insufficient, nor because of any lack of loyalty to your cause, but only because I do not wish to do anything that might injure the cause or embarrass you personally."

"I don't think that Mr. Taft will consent to such a thing," Senator Crane remarked, and then, as he picked up his hat, he asked Julia, "Do you?"[36]

"If the positions of the two men were reversed," she said, "if my husband were the presidential candidate and Mr. Taft the Senator, I know what would happen. My husband would refuse to believe the charge brought against an intimate old friend. He would recognize it as an election trick and denounce it. He would insist that the Senator appear on the platform with him—or he would not appear. But now—"

She began making points on the carpet with her parasol, unable to continue.[37]

Taft was on the phone talking to Roosevelt when Crane and Dick arrived with Foraker's letter. The candidate seemed "disturbed and embarrassed," they said when they returned to the senator's office and reported that "Mr. Taft desired to be excused from doing more than expressing to them the hope that I would be willing to confer with the committee with respect to the meeting and take such course as the committee might recommend."

Foraker interpreted this to mean that "Mr. Taft preferred I should not attend the meeting." He immediately canceled the engagement "and all my other engagements for speeches during the campaign." He was "both surprised and mortified by Mr. Taft's action for it seemed to give credence to Mr. Hearst's charges and to discredit thereby the answers I had published."[38]

Roosevelt not only talked to Taft by phone that Saturday, but also sent him a confidential telegram pointing out that if he were running for president, he would "in view of these disclosures decline to appear upon the platform with Foraker." It was essential, the president emphasized, "that we should show unmistakably how completely loose from us Mr. Foraker is." When reporters asked Taft to comment on Foraker's situation, he refused.[39]

"I will not strike a man when he is down," he said.[40]

Foraker remembered the words as "a cheerful and comforting observation that showed the quality and measure of the friendship and gratitude he had so frequently expressed." Julia lived the rest of her long life with the memory of Will Taft's silence as he watched "the wave engulf his old friend."[41]

In her analysis of the campaign results, Emma Lou Thornbrough notes that Taft's margin of victory in some northern states with impressive numbers of Negro voters (Ohio, Pennsylvania, Indiana, Illinois) was smaller than Roosevelt's in 1904, but, oddly enough, it was larger in New York and New Jersey.

Apparently, she concluded, "the Brownsville episode did not lead to a marked defection of Negroes from the Republican party, nor did Taft appear to have suffered personally because of his part in the affair. This does not mean, however, that the discharge of the colored soldiers had not created a real threat to the traditional loyalty of Negroes to the Republican party. There is abundant evidence that the members of the race were aroused over the treatment of the soldiers as they had not been aroused by the action of any other President."[42]

A Taft biographer, studying the same returns, ticked off some disquieting statistical evidence of "the unrest which was to increase during the coming four years." Taft's lead over Bryan (1,269,606) was less than half the lead Roosevelt had piled up in 1904. He had lost three states Roosevelt had carried (Colorado, Nebraska, and Nevada), and Oklahomans, voting in their first presidential election, had opted for Bryan. Democrats had won the state house not only in Ohio, home of the Tafts and the Longworths, but also in Indiana, Minnesota, North Dakota, and Montana. As in 1884 and 1892, "the tide was beginning to run against the Grand Old Party."[43]

"Without doubt more Negroes voted against Mr. Taft than ever before voted against a Republican candidate," Du Bois wrote, and suggested that "four years from today we should stand ready to make Mr. Taft give an account of his stewardship: to reelect him, if he has done well; to seek by all legitimate means to defeat him if he does ill."[44]

In an editorial, "Dividing the South," the *New York Times*, speculated on what might have happened if Roosevelt had run instead of Taft. "What keeps the South solid," the writer stipulated, "is the feeling in that section with regard to negroes. One element in Mr. Roosevelt's popularity, as compared with that of Mr. Taft, is the impression that the former is more sympathetic with, or less antipathetic to, that feeling, than the latter, and in this impression it is not to be denied that the Brownsville affair has much to do."[45]

"No man ever had a greater opportunity," La Follete telegraphed the president-elect. "The country confides in your constructive leadership *for the progressive legislation needed to serve equal opportunity for all in our industrial development.*"[46]

"It is a very different office from that of governor general of the Philippines, and I don't know that I shall rise to the occasion or not," Taft wrote in a private letter, and in addressing a New York audience, he recalled having "heard of the man who went into office with a majority and went out with unanimity."[47]

Shortly after his election, when arrangements were made for him to propose a liberal southern policy to the North Carolina Society of New York, he dutifully read the ingratiating words prepared for him, and then sent a chill down black spines with an offhand remark: "The best friend that the Southern Negro can have is the Southern white man."[48]

"They tell me Foraker is preparing a violent attack on me," Roosevelt wrote Kermit on November 22. "I can imagine nothing to which I should be more indifferent."[49]

When Congress convened on December 14, Foraker presented, as an amendment to an existing bill (S. 5729), the proposal that a commission of five retired generals be appointed to serve as a tribunal that would give the Brownsville soldiers an opportunity "to confront their accusers" and "if there be a guilty man in that battalion, no man should throw a straw in the way of having that guilt established."[50]

Roosevelt had never wavered in his insistence that there was not the "slightest doubt" about the soldiers' guilt, but the government's five investigations had failed to produce evidence on which charges could be brought against a single member of the three infantry companies. Two months before the Republican Convention, the president and his secretary of war had quietly tapped a military contingency fund for the first of their unauthorized $55,000 payments to a private detective, William G. Baldwin, and a Roanoke, Virginia journalist, Herbert J. Browne, who had assured them that the guilty men would be unmasked before the voters went to the polls in November.[51]

Their report, based on deceit, coercion, and manufactured evidence, had not been completed in time to be used in the campaign, but, unbeknownst to Foraker, it had been delivered to the Senate with a message from the White House the morning he was to propose the establishment of a court of inquiry. The Browne-Baldwin report, the president stated, "enables us to fix with *tolerable definiteness* at least some of the criminals who took the lead in the murderous shooting of private citizens at Brownsville." (emphasis added)

Roosevelt's message recommended passage of a law "allowing the Secretary of War, within a fixed period of time, say, a year, to reinstate any of these soldiers whom he, after careful examination, finds to have been innocent." Presumably, under the president's revised rules of evidence, the secretary of war could establish guilt by a standard new to American jurisprudence, "tolerable definiteness."[52]

In a rambling defense of the Administration, Senator Lodge delivered a glancing blow at "the growth of altruism," which had caused "revulsion" to get out of hand. "In some of our States and in many countries of Europe, the death penalty has been abolished, even in cases of murder," he pointed out, and went on to suggest: "Before the era of reform there was little or no public sympathy with the criminal. Today we seem almost to have reached the point where the sympathy is so strictly confined to the criminal that there is now none left for the victim of the crime."[53]

Throughout the month of December, Foraker continued to battle for his Senate seat. Despite the election of a Democratic governor, Republicans had held onto the Ohio legislature, which insured the election of a Republican senator. Burton, with Roosevelt in his corner, seemed the likely winner until Taft's wealthy half-brother Charles had embarrassed both the president and the president-elect by announcing his candidacy. Charlie Taft, owner of a string of newspapers and the Cincinnati Reds, had served an undistinguished term in the House of Representatives (1895–97). Now, counting on support from George Cox, he and his socially ambitious wife had begun to dream of life in Washington with one Taft in the White House, another in the Senate.[54]

In late December, when the senatorial candidates set up campaign offices in Columbus, Charles Taft backed a proposal to leave the decision to a Republican caucus he had reason to believe he could control. Foraker joined Burton in opposing such a move. On December 29, Warren Harding, sensing a deadlock, put himself forward as the "logical" candidate.[55]

On that same day, Roosevelt let it be known that to support Foraker's attempt to block the caucus would be an act of "treason" against the Republican party. Foraker, he was convinced, wanted to bypass the caucus and proceed with his rumored deal to get another term for himself from the legislators who, in 1911, would be free to replace Senator Dick with a Democrat.[56]

Two days later, on New Year's Eve, the anti-Burton forces collapsed. Charlie, to spare his brother further embarrassment, bowed out. Cox announced his support for Burton. Foraker withdrew. The end had been foreshadowed early that spring when he inadvertently addressed the colleague presiding over the Senate as "Your honor." Then, bowing and smiling, he remarked, "I suppose it will not be long before I must become accustomed to the phrase, 'May it please the court.'"[57]

On January 12, 1909, the day Ohio legislators formally agreed to replace him with Burton, Foraker took the Senate floor to question the legality of the funds the president and the president-elect had used to pay for the Browne-Baldwin investigation. In the course of the debate he demolished the report they had built around a shameless forgery, the so-called "confession" of Boyd Conyers, a young Company B recruit from Monroe, Georgia. When the Administration sleuths, with their threats, promises, and misrepresentations, failed to pry from Conyers anything they could use, Browne made up his own version of a Company B conspiracy and put it forth as a "confession" by this likeable, hard-working, happily married young Negro whom Foraker remembered as a Senate committee witness.[58]

"It would not require any word of argument or of testimony from anybody to show the utter wickedness of these charges against him," Foraker declared, recalling the youth's "frank, open, manly face and manner as he testified, manifestly anxious to tell the truth and the whole truth, and withholding nothing whatever."[59]

Sheriff E. C. Arnold, who had sat in on Browne's two interviews with Conyers, read the "confession" and pronounced it "the most absolutely false, the most willful misrepresentation of the truth, and the most shameful perversion of what really did take place between them that I have ever seen over the signature of any person." The *New York World* dismissed the president's new evidence as "too flimsy to deserve serious consideration."[60]

Foraker spent his last weeks of public service rounding up the votes he needed to get the Brownsville soldiers before a court of inquiry. On February 2 he was ready to set a date on which the matter would be brought to a vote. His colleagues agreed to make their decision on Senate bill 5729 on the afternoon of February 23 at four o'clock. It passed, supported by fifty-six Republicans and opposed by twenty-six Democrats.[61]

Four days later, when the bill came before the people's representatives in "the other body," it prevailed, 211 yeas to 102 nays, but not before men on both sides of the aisle had been deeply moved by a freshman Democrat from Alabama, Spanish-American War hero Richmond Pearson Hobson. A month before San Juan Hill, this young Naval Academy graduate (Class of '89) and seven volunteers for a seemingly suicidal mission had sealed off Admiral Cervera's fleet by sinking the collier *Merrimack* in Santiago Harbor.

"These three minutes will cost me a contest in my district, and may cost me my seat in Congress," Hobson began and pointed out that the court of inquiry should have been established immediately after the Brownsville crimes were committed. Now two and a half years later, the president had made justice impossible by scattering the men, guilty and innocent alike, to the four winds.

"Mr. Speaker," he continued:

I saw black men carrying our flag on San Juan Hill; I have seen them before Manila. A black man took my father, wounded, from the field of Chancellorsville. Black men remained on my grandfather's plantation after the proclamation of emancipation and took care of my mother and grandmother. The white man is supreme in this country; he will remain supreme. That makes it only the more sacred that he should give absolute justice to the black man who is in our midst. [Loud applause.] I submit it to the conscience of my colleagues. This ought not to be made a party measure. We are standing here on the field of eternal justice, where all men are the same. It is justice that links man to the divine. Whether the heavens fall or the earth melt away, while we live let us be just. [Loud applause.]"[62]

The Administration bill authorized the secretary of war to appoint a court of inquiry of five retired high-ranking officers to look into the "shooting affray" and deliver their final report within one year of their appointment. Any soldier the tribunal found to be qualified for reenlistment could then sign up and "be considered to have reenlisted immediately after his discharge."

Foraker was not happy with the bill, but he knew that once he left Washington no one in the Congress "would champion the cause in which I had so long labored," so he accepted the compromise. His bill would have stated specifically that every soldier not shown to be guilty as a principal or an accessory should be considered eligible to reenlist. He feared the creation of a tribunal "that could easily say, if the testimony fell short of an absolute demonstration, that they were not satisfied that the men were, in the language of the act, 'qualified for reenlistment,' and thereby, without making any affirmation of guilt, deny relief; and what I feared is exactly what afterward occurred."[63]

The soldiers were represented by Brigadier General A. S. Daggett, who had commanded the 25th Infantry in Cuba, and Napoleon B. Marshall, a Negro attorney with a law degree from Harvard, who had worked with Foraker in gathering the evidence on which his demand for a Senate investigation was based. After the court of inquiry had permitted eighty men to testify, the door was closed on more than seventy others awaiting their day in court.

Marshall, unable to determine whether the tribunal had proceeded as a court of inquiry or as a court-martial, declined to make a closing argument.

He simply recorded the fact that for three years he had "diligently and honestly striven to ferret out the persons engaged in this crime" and, after "close personal contact with nearly all the soldiers discharged," he had never found "one clue which might lead to the identification of a single soldier." His investigations had tended to indicate that the crime had been "committed by persons not in the military service."

The generals, called upon to choose between two commanders-in-chief and a parcel of black soldiers, found 14 men who, for reasons left unstated, were considered "qualified" for reenlistment. They closed the book on the other 153. Foraker recorded emphatically in his memoirs that "even THAT Court" was unable to name any man in the battalion who had participated in the shooting.[64]

"To be successful a farce should lead up to a grotesque climax," the *New York World* noted. "The Court of Inquiry has done all that could possibly be asked of it to make this Brownsville burlesque upon justice a triumph of absurdity."[65]

Chapter Fourteen

"He's weak. They'll get around him."

—President Roosevelt on President-elect Taft,

March 3, 1909

Roosevelt was living among packing boxes and safari gear, settling down to the serious business of assembling the armament he would need in attacking African wildlife for editors at *Scribner's* and taxidermists at the *Smithsonian*. His ship was to depart from Hoboken on March 23, less than three weeks after Taft's inauguration. Captain Archie Butt, the president's aide, felt sure he was "going to Africa as much for Taft as for himself. If he were anywhere near telegraph lines it would be hard for the public not to suspect that Taft was being managed by him." In Wall Street watering holes moneylenders toasted African wildlife, "May every lion do his duty."[1]

"Ha! Ha!" Roosevelt wrote the president-elect on New Year's Eve. "You are making up your Cabinet. I in a light-hearted way have spent the morning testing rifles for my African trip. Life has compensations."[2]

Roosevelt had beamed approval when, the day after his election, Taft indicated great interest in "the southern question" and expressed his willingness to consult with Dr. Washington. As president, however, he intended to take a different course in regard to federal appointments for southern Negroes. "I am not going to put into places of such prominence in the

South, where the race feeling is strong, Negroes whose appointment will only tend to increase that race feeling," he wrote *Kansas City Star* publisher William Rockhill Nelson, "but I shall look about and make appointments in the North and recognize the Negroes as often as I can."[3]

Taft cited the case of Dr. William D. Crum, the Negro whom Roosevelt had appointed collector of the port at Charleston, South Carolina. When southern senators succeeded in blocking confirmation of the appointment, Roosevelt kept it alive for two years before finally prevailing in 1905 after he had become an elected president. The Crum appointment, Washington's biographer notes, "symbolized all that was good about Rooseveltian race policy under Washington's advice, until Brownsville had blurred that image to obliteration. All that Taft saw in Dr. Crum was a political liability."[4]

"I am really delighted about Booker Washington's attitude and what he says Crum will do," Roosevelt said when told the controversial black office-holder had agreed to resign. "This is first-rate." Three days before the inauguration, Dr. Crum's letter of resignation lay on Roosevelt's desk. "No pressure" had been brought to bear on him, he said; he had resigned to save Mr. Taft "possible embarrassment as to his reappointment."[5]

As Washington's biographer points out:

> The scar of Brownsville was not on the Republican body but on the black soul. Even among blacks who were circumstantially Republican, who had no other place to go, Brownsville was an unforgettable shock. It erased any illusion about Roosevelt's benevolence created by the dinner at the White House and his vague promise of an open "door of hope." The end of Reconstruction, the persistent Republican refusal to challenge the white decision to make the black man voteless, had all led to Brownsville. Those who bolted the party got nothing for their pains, but Washington, now that he had a monopoly of the black patronage, was to find the patronage itself slipping through his fingers. Who needed a Wizard who could only change gold into dross?[6]

Roosevelt broke with precedent by inviting the Tafts to spend the night before the inauguration in the White House. It was his way, Nellie later recalled, of "bidding us a warm welcome to the post which he was about to vacate, and my husband accepted with grateful appreciation."[7]

"People have attempted to represent that you and I were in some way at odds during this last three months," Taft wrote in reply to Roosevelt's invitation; "whereas you and I know that there has not been the slightest difference between us, and I welcome the opportunity to stay the last night of your administration under the White House roof to make as emphatic as possible the refutation of any such suggestion."[8]

There had been differences, but each of the two old friends had done his best to make the transition as comfortable as possible. When Roosevelt asked Taft to appoint his secretary, Bill Loeb, to his Cabinet for a few months to give him prestige "which would then secure him in a good place of business," Taft bridled at the "manipulation of a Cabinet place for personal reasons" and resolved the problem by naming him collector of the port of New York, the job Roosevelt's father had been denied by Boss Conkling.[9]

Roosevelt, chatting with his aide, could find no fault with his successor who was, he insisted, "going about this thing just as I would do," but toward the end of his last full day in the White House, when Mark Sullivan, who covered the capital for *Collier's*, asked, "How do you really think Taft will make out?" Roosevelt replied: "He's all right, he means well and he'll do his best. But he's weak. They'll get around him."[10]

On the eve of her husband's inauguration, Nellie Taft awakened to a stormy day "filled with innumerable minor engagements and small incidents, with instructions and counter-instructions," but she and Will, dressed for dinner and managed to make their way to the White House before eight o'clock. Edith Roosevelt seemed depressed, not at the prospect of leaving Washington, Nellie thought, but at the long, possibly dangerous trip her husband and teen-age son were about to undertake. Roosevelt and Taft, along with family (Alice and her Aunty Bye) and the Lodges, did what they could to brighten the evening, "but their efforts was [*sic*] not entirely successful."[11]

"It went off without a hitch," Captain Butt reported, crediting the president who talked so "naturally and entertainingly" that "the salad course was reached before one had time to realize it."[12]

After dinner, Taft, the first president to own an automobile, was driven to the New Willard Hotel to join seven hundred Yale men at a "smoker." When he entered the tenth-floor ballroom he was greeted by the school yell: "Brek-kek-kek-kek-kek—Yale!" The first Yale president (George Bush would be the second, Bill Clinton the third) made a stab at humility, expressing his hope to "make good" and "to be able to stand just criticism and to profit by it, and not to care a dern for unjust criticism."[13]

Gifford Pinchot, the conservationist mentor to whom Roosevelt had expressed "a peculiar debt of obligation for a very large part of the achievement of this Administration," found Taft's talk "curiously full of hesitation and foreboding." Looking back later, he was unable to "remember a single confident note in the whole of it." The president-elect sounded to him "like a man whose job had got him down even before he tackled it. He had set the stage for his own defeat."[14]

During the forty-five minutes Taft was absent, the president's dinner party had narrowed down to the Roosevelts, Nellie Taft, and Archie Butt. The gracious hostess, in black silk and lace with a dark aigrette, "arose and said she would go to her room and advised Mrs. Taft to do the same." Nellie repaired to the Blue Bedroom in the southeast corner of the White House, where a bronze plate under the mantel against the side wall reminded visitors: "In this room Abraham Lincoln signed the Emancipation Proclamation of January 1, 1863, whereby four million slaves were given their freedom and slavery forever prohibited in these United States."[15]

On her first night in the home she had been mentally redecorating for years at Roosevelt's dinner parties, Nellie went to bed early, but her "mind was never more wide awake." When she finally fell asleep "in the early morning hours," it was with kind feelings for the chief of the weather bureau who had predicted fair weather for the inauguration. Next morning, looking out at the "ice-bound" capital, she was struck by the "ludicrous vision of a haughty, gold-laced parade sliding, rather than marching with measured precision, down Pennsylvania Avenue."[16]

Roosevelt had decided he would, of course, ride to the Capitol with his successor, but instead of returning to the White House with him, he would proceed directly from the Capitol to the Union Station, where Edith and the children would be waiting for him. Once Nellie Taft got wind of the plan, she decided to set another precedent. She would ride back to the White House in her husband's carriage. The inaugural committee phrased the news tactfully. Mrs. Taft had "consented" to the arrangement in response to the committee's "urgent request."[17]

On his last morning as president, to the astonishment of reporters covering the White House, Roosevelt signed a bill "providing for the Negro soldiers of the Twenty-fifth Infantry who were peremptorily discharged from the army without honor, to reenlist in the event they established innocence of any connection with the shooting up of Brownsville."

The new law was expected to "cause applications to flow into the War

Department from every member of the three companies," the *New York Times* reported, giving rise to the expectation that this wretched business would finally be settled, but, aside from the fourteen men the court of inquiry would eventually permit to reapply (eleven took advantage of the opportunity), none of the other one hundred and fifty-six infantrymen ever got back into uniform because of the bill Roosevelt signed that bleak late winter morning.[18]

The two presidents were to ride to the Capitol in a closed carriage. Roosevelt entered it a few minutes after ten o'clock. He was followed by Taft, who sat beside his old friend. Lodge sat facing Taft. Philander Knox, a wealthy corporation lawyer who had resigned from the Senate to serve as secretary of state in the new Administration, faced Roosevelt. Just before the carriage reached the White House gates a *Washington Post* reporter heard a "loud laugh," signifying that "all were in good spirits."[19]

The presidential carriage, trailed by Troop A, Ohio National Guard, moved slowly down the ice-covered avenue that linked the chief executive with the makers and the interpreters of the country's laws. The three Taft children, Robert, Helen, and Charlie, were in the gallery when their father was ushered into the Senate chamber. Eleven-year-old Charlie had a copy of *Treasure Island* in case he lost interest in what his father had to say in the presence of the Congress, the Supreme Court, the Diplomatic Corps, and official families.

The oath was administered, Taft read his address (Charlie never opened his book), and when Roosevelt shook Will's hand, Nellie heard him say something like "Bully speech, old man" before he hurried off to the Union Station. What he really said, Taft told her later, was, "God bless you, old man. It is a great state document."[20]

To Booker Washington's biographer, it was "the worst inaugural address since Reconstruction in reference to black political rights." The Brownsville affair, having "blighted the Roosevelt administration," would now serve as "the prelude to the downhill slide of the black politicos in the new administration." Having disposed of Dr. Crum, Taft intended to remove most black officeholders in the South and make a only a few token appointments in the North, while Dr. Washington "helplessly watched the collapse of the little black political empire he had built."[21]

The "only living ex-President," heading back to Oyster Bay in "a modest stateroom," had left his successor a deficit of $150 million for the current fiscal year, James Albertus Tawney, chairman of the House Appropriations Committee, reported to his colleagues. "A halt must be called on this extravagance," he warned, "or the country would be bankrupt." The federal budget had soared to one billion dollars.[22]

On the day before Taft's inauguration, the *Washington Post* reported that "the colored citizens of Washington" had arranged to give Senator Foraker a silver and gold loving cup "as a token of high esteem and in appreciation of his efforts in behalf of the discharged Brownsville battalion." The cup, resting on an ebony base, was nearly two feet high and weighed just under 100 ounces. The three handles around the bowl, labeled B, C and D, represented the three companies caught up in the Brownsville affair. Raised letters around the base spelled out "Twenty-fifth Infantry." The peroration of the senator's Black Battalion speech was inscribed in the gold lining: "They ask no favors because they are Negroes, but only for justice because they are men."

B Company's former first sergeant, Mingo Sanders, occupied "a conspicuous seat" at the Metropolitan A.M.E. Church that Saturday night when Foraker was introduced. He recalled a commencement address he had given at Wilberforce in June, 1907, when Senate hearings on Brownsville were underway and he had been warned that because of his defense of the soldiers he would be "eliminated from public life."

If that turned out to be true, he had assured the young black graduates and their families, he would return to private life with "the consoling satisfaction of feeling and knowing that I have been rebuked for an act that I shall never regret; but always esteem as creditable to my heart as a man, and to my sense of justice and duty as a public official."

Once the applause had died down, he took a dig at Roosevelt: "Now that I have been eliminated, those words are put to the test and truthfully I can say here tonight, I go back to my home carrying with me my own self respect. [Applause.] That is a great deal more than some other people can do. [Applause.]"

He paid tribute to two black lawyers, Napoleon B. Marshall and Gilchrist Stewart, who had helped him prepare his defense of the soldiers, and thanked Senator Morgan G. Bulkeley of Connecticut ("I love him like a brother"), who had stood with him in signing the minority report affirming the men's innocence.

He gave voice to the apprehension he felt when he read newspaper reports of the president-elect's speech to a colored audience in New Orleans on Lincoln's birthday. "The South," Taft had been reported as saying, "understood the race question better than anybody else, and that in consequence the North must stand aside and let them settle it." That speech, Foraker said, had awakened the fear that "I might be again compelled to differ with the President of the United States, which I would do, although disagreeable, rather than acquiesce in such a wrong."

Foraker closed with an appeal for support of his Ohio protégé, now president. "Everybody should help him who can. I can do but little, but you can do much. I exhort you, therefore, to help him, trust him, have confidence in him, and in every way you can, support him and uphold him."[23]

Bourke Cockran, Manhattan's charismatic Democratic congressman by way of County Sligo, joined the president on one of his morning rides and asked how he liked his new office. "I hardly know yet," Taft replied. "When I hear someone say Mr. President, I look around expecting to see Roosevelt." Nellie Taft was irritated a few nights later when her husband, at dinner, kept referring to Theodore as "the President."

"You mean ex-President, Will," she said.

"I suppose I do, dear," he replied, "but he will always be the President to me, and I can never think of him as anything else."[24]

Archie Butt suggested it would be politic for his new employer to send his predecessor a bon voyage message and gift. Taft agreed and left its selection to Archie, who picked out a gold pencil, a gold case for the world-famous eyeglasses, and an expandable gold ruler ("small and would not take up much room"). The lot came to $35. Archie composed a two-line inscription to be engraved on the ruler:

> *Theodore Roosevelt From William Howard Taft*
> *Good-bye—Good luck*

Taft added four words:
> *and a safe return.*[25]

Captain Butt made his way through a crush of Roosevelt's admirers on the deck on the SS *Hamburg* to hand the ex-president the letter and the parcel. Not until the ship began to move down the Hudson River did Roosevelt find time to read his old friend's letter assuring him that he did:

*nothing in the Executive Office without considering what you would
do under the same circumstances and without having in a sense a mental talk with you over the pros and cons of the situation. I have not the
facility for educating the public as you had through talks with correspondents, and so I fear that a large part of the public will feel as if I
had fallen away from your ideals;* but you know me better and will
understand that I am still working away on the same old plan
*and hope to realize in some measure the results that we both hold valu-
able and worth striving for. I can never forget that the power that I
now exercise was a voluntary transfer from you to me, and that I am
under obligation to you to see to it that your judgment in selecting me
as your successor and in bringing about the succession shall be vindicated according to the standards which you and I in conversation have
always formulated. (WHT's emphasis)*

Roosevelt scribbled a reply to be taken ashore and mailed by the pilot:
"Am deeply touched by your gift and even more by your letter. Greatly
appreciate it. Everything will turn out all right, old man. Give my love to
Mrs. Taft."[26]

Archie Butt was left with the impression his new employer had not yet
realized that

*for seven years he has been living on the steam of Theodore Roosevelt
and that the latter has been his motive power and the things he has
accomplished have been largely under the high pressure of Mr. Roosevelt.
With Roosevelt out of the country, the president will find, and I think
has already found, that his steam has been cut off. He will have to find
his own fuel and now, like a child, will have to learn to walk alone.*[27]

Dr. Washington had persuaded the president-elect to soften the wording of
his inaugural address but not to remove its ban on Negro appointments in
the South that could be expected to result in race friction. This was the new
president's "Southern Policy," and he lost no time in carrying it out. In his
first six months he followed up Dr. Crum's resignation by ousting the chief
black officeholder in Georgia and a Tuskegee lieutenant in Texas. Blacks
who had held public office in the South since the Harrison administration
were not reappointed, and when they applied for jobs as 1910 census enu-

merators, they found their numbers had been reduced, even in predominantly black districts.[28]

The year 1909 ended without a single major black appointment by the new president. He had, however, appointed two southern Democrats to his Cabinet. When the center seat of the Supreme Court fell vacant, Taft passed over Justice Harlan, the court's distinguished senior member, a Republican whose 1883 dissent in the Civil Rights Cases had pointed out that the prevailing opinion would leave Negroes "at the mercy of corporations and individuals wielding power under the States." Harlan might have been describing Taft's choice to preside over the Court, Associate Justice Edwin D. White, a wealthy, conservative, Louisiana planter appointed to the bench by Grover Cleveland.

On December 10, 1910, Chief Justice White was sworn in by Justice Harlan, who in 1896 had declared in his *Plessy v Ferguson* dissent, "Our Constitution is color-blind, and neither knows nor tolerates classes among citizens. In respect of civil rights all citizens are equal before the law."[29]

A few days after the Confederate veteran (and former Klansman) settled down in the Supreme Court's center seat, Foraker happened to be in Washington, and when he called at the White House "to pay my respects to the President," Taft asked his opinion of the appointment. Foraker said he couldn't help wondering "how my old comrade of the Army of the Cumberland, Mr. Justice Harlan, must have felt when administering the oath to him."

"Oh, Senator, the war is over!" Taft remarked.

"Yes, I know the war is over with a great many people," Foraker said, "but I know also that with most of these the war never commenced."

Taft called in one of his secretaries and "laughingly" directed him to send the senator an invitation to the judicial dinner to be held at the White House a few evenings later. After "a very agreeable conversation" with the new chief justice, Foraker sought out Justice Harlan. In administering the oath, the jurist said, "I placed emphasis on the requirement that he should uphold the Constitution."[30]

Looking back on the first twenty months of the new Administration, Du Bois reminded readers of *The Crisis*:

> Not only is Mr. Taft particeps criminis *with the late Mr. Roosevelt in the crime of Brownsville, but he added to that the Taft Doctrine of recognizing race prejudice, instead of fitness, in Federal appointments.*

On top of this, and in the face of a record of murder, lynching and
burning in this country which has appalled the civilized world and
loosened the tongue of many a man long since dumb on the race prob-
lem, in spite of this, Mr. Taft has blandly informed a deputation of
colored men that any action on his part is quite outside his power, if not
his interest.[31]

"Edith R[oosevelt] writes to W. S. [Bigelow] in Paris that people tell her to keep T[heodore] out of the country for a year and a half longer," Henry Adams reported to his friend Elizabeth Cameron on January 24, 1910, and then added: "Why not for life? The ostrich business won't work forever even among the Hottentots." A month later he noted: "Poor dear Taft can't stand alone. He is feebly wabbling all over the place, and tumbling about the curbs."[32]

The inevitable break between Roosevelt and Taft was foreshadowed January 17 when a Press Agency runner reached the Colonel on the banks of the White Nile with a cable informing him that Chief Forester Gifford Pinchot had been fired. "I most earnestly hope it is not true," Roosevelt wrote Lodge, not at all confident the letter would reach him ("the postman is a wild savage, who runs stark naked with the mail").[33]

The Colonel was in hot pursuit of the giant eland when Pinchot's letter confirming his removal from office found its way to Gondokoro in late February. "Is there any chance of your meeting me in Europe?" Roosevelt wrote his conservationist friend.[34]

The two men, despite Lodge's misgivings, met in Italy, on April 11. "One of the best & most satisfactory talks with T. R. I ever had," Pinchot wrote in his diary. "Lasted nearly all day, and till about 10:30 P.M." In a letter to their mutual friend, James Garfield, son of the slain president, Pinchot reported he had "found everything just exactly as you and I had foreseen. There was nothing changed, nothing unexpected."[35]

Roosevelt immediately wrote a long, confidential letter to Lodge: "I very earnestly hope that Taft will retrieve himself yet, and if, from whatever causes, the present condition of the party is hopeless, I most emphatically desire that I shall not be put in the position of having to run for the Presidency, staggering under a load which I cannot carry, and which has been put on my shoulders through no fault of my own."[36]

On June 10, when Roosevelt boarded the ship at Southampton that would bring him home after a fifteen-month absence, he found two thousand invitations to make speeches, along with an equally impressive number urging him to take an active role in American politics.

There was also a poignant letter from Taft: "It is now a year and three months since I assumed office and I have had a hard time. I do not know that I have had harder luck than other presidents but I do know that thus far I have succeeded far less than have others. I have been conscientiously trying to carry out your policies, but my method of doing so has not worked smoothly."

His luckless presidency had sustained a devastating blow when Nellie suffered a nervous collapse resulting in "an aphasia that for a long time was nearly complete." She "is not an easy patient," he explained, "and an attempt to control her only increased the nervous strain. Gradually she has gained in strength and she has taken part in receptions where she could speak a formula of greeting, but dinners and social reunions where she has had to talk she has avoided."[37]

"Indeed you have had a hard time, as you say, and of course the sickness of the one whom you love most has added immeasurably to your burden," Roosevelt replied from London, and politely ducked the president's invitation to visit the White House.[38]

British imperialists were heartened by Roosevelt's Guildhall speech, in which he praised the work their settlers and their officials, military and civil, had done in Africa, notably Sudan. "Independence and self-government in the hands of the Sudanese proved to be much what independence and self-government would have been in a wolf pack," he said, and Kipling saluted this "one simple single-minded person, saying and doing, quite casually, things which ought to set the world flaming." The Liberal statesman, John Morley, denounced the speech for giving "powder and shot to our war men, and heaven knows they have plenty of ammunition already."[39]

When Roosevelt reached New York, Saturday, June 18, 1910, Archie Butt climbed aboard the *Kaiserin Auguste Victoria* with a letter from Taft repeating his invitation. In going over the president's first draft, Archie had suggested removal of "the jocular portion." Taft agreed to rewrite the letter but with the proviso that there be nothing that "might mislead Roosevelt into thinking that I expect or desire advice." The letter began "My dear Theodore," and, Archie recorded, it was "written in such a vein as to offer no suggestion that there has come the slightest rift of their old friendship."[40]

The following day, when Archie was back at his post, the president showed him the letter Roosevelt had written him from London. It began, "My dear Mr. President," not "My dear Will," Archie noted, and it contained only one important sentence: "I shall make no speeches nor say anything for two months, but I shall keep my mind as open as I keep my mouth shut."

Roosevelt had changed, Archie felt. "He had ceased to be an American, but had become a world citizen. . . . He is bigger, broader, capable of greater good or greater evil I don't know which, than when he left."[41]

Chapter Fifteen

"I do not know whether Taft or the Titanic
is likely to be the furthest-reaching disaster."

—*Henry Adams,*
April 16, 1912

Foraker was rebuilding his law practice and living comfortably on a refurbished estate in Cincinnati in the summer of 1910 while Roosevelt was dodging "the ultra Taft people," explaining to friends that his endorsement of the president in the off-year elections would not only be insincere but would also "cause me to lose all hold on my own supporters." Taft, on August 19, sat quietly at the breakfast table of the Massachusetts governor in Hopedale reading a *Boston Herald* report that Roosevelt had admitted to friends the possibility of having to run for the presidency in 1912 in order to have his policies carried out.[1]

"The process of coaxing Roosevelt into politics," the *Philadelphia Public Ledger* quipped, "was made difficult by the fact that he never had been out."[2]

At a John Brown memorial ceremony in Osawatomie, Kansas, on August 31, Roosevelt touched off a lively debate with a brief, borrowed paragraph: "Labor is prior to and independent of, capital. Capital is only the fruit of labor and could never have existed if labor had not first existed.

Labor is the superior of capital, and deserves much the higher consideration." He was quoting Abraham Lincoln.

The judiciary should be "interested primarily in human welfare, rather than in property," he argued, and insisted that "the man who wrongly holds that every human right is secondary to his profit must now give way to the advocate of human welfare, who rightly maintains that every man holds his property subject to the general right of the community to regulate its use to whatever degree the public welfare may require it."

The ebullient prophet of what he called the "New Nationalism" was now advocating laws regulating not only industrial combinations but also the labor of women and children, along with protection of natural resources, public exposure of campaign expenditures, a graduated income tax, an inheritance tax, and a comprehensive workmen's compensation law.[3]

"Harding in Ohio who is most anxious to have me come in and speak for him, as a method of getting me to do so, sent me word that if I would come he would announce that my Osawatomie speech was the platform on which he stood!" the Colonel wrote to amuse Lodge.[4]

Harding's thirteen-year-old Marion neighbor Nan Britton entered high school that fall and was thrilled to discover that her English teacher's brother was running for governor. When she first saw Mr. Harding, she wrote many years later, she "knew he was for me my 'ideal American.'" She also knew she "was in love with Warren Harding" and began stalking him, calling his home, looking for his car (a Stevens-Duryea), cutting pictures from election posters and hanging them on her bedroom wall.[5]

In New Jersey that summer and fall, Woodrow Wilson, having resigned as Princeton's president, was running for governor on the Democratic ticket. His defense of the university's intellectual vitality against the assaults of its trustees in 1907 had awakened him to the realization that the campus struggle "went to the roots of the national life." While he preached the gospel of a New Freedom, and Roosevelt a New Nationalism, Taft ended up "unfairly, the guardian of the Old Regime." When asked why he did not make a vigorous response to Roosevelt's western fulminations, he said, "That is not my method." To the suggestion that he "try a new method," he responded, "My methods are the best for me."[6]

"The West loves and understands Roosevelt," declared the Denver *Republican*, and a reporter in Cheyenne wired the Democratic *New York World* that the region "takes it for granted that Theodore Roosevelt will be the next Republican candidate for President."[7]

Inevitably, he would find himself confronted by the specter of Brownsville, which had cropped up again in *The Independent*, with Horace Bumstead, former president of Atlanta University, presenting an ironic soliloquy on the "marvelous exhibition of race loyalty which those dismissed colored soldiers have given us in the complete success of their alleged 'conspiracy of silence.'"

In the last three and a half years, he pointed out, not one of them had "peached," although the resources of the United States government had been "exhausted in shooting up, so to speak, the Twenty-fifth Infantry, with a view to bagging some individual guilty game."

Bumstead was moved to speculate: "Suppose, after all, the colored troops did not shoot up the town, and it should be shown that other persons did who, in a more or less drunken condition, could have been more likely to do so and either with forethought or afterthought, wish to put it off on the soldiers. Can we say that this possibility has ever been investigated with the same unrelenting earnestness as the other, or with any earnestness at all?" The Atlanta educator found it easier to believe that the soldiers had told "the simple truth when they all declared, 'We're not guilty.'"[8]

Like most black Americans of his generation, especially those with a bit of sporting blood, ex-Private Dorsie Willis of Company D, 25th Infantry never forgot where he was and what he did on the Fourth of July, 1910.

"I was working in a barber shop at 110 South Main Street, Tulsa, Oklahoma," Dorsie recalled more than sixty years after Jack Johnson, the world's first black heavyweight champion, climbed into a Reno, Nevada, ring with Jim Jeffries, who in 1899, at the age of twenty-four, had taken the title away from Bob Fitzsimmons.[9]

The color line drawn around the boxing ring by the first American heavyweight champion, John L. Sullivan (1882–92), had been adhered to by Corbett, Fitzsimmons, and Jeffries, none of whom would fight Negroes. After Jeffries retired, unbeaten, in 1905 the title passed to a scrappy Canadian, Tommy Burns (five feet seven, one hundred and seventy-five pounds).[10]

Jack Johnson, "haughty, articulate, stubborn, determined to express his nature openly and to assert all his rights in the face of prejudice," hounded Burns in America, England, and Ireland before catching up with him in Australia in 1908 and knocking him out in the fourteenth round.[11]

When the black champion came home, the first white hope to face him was Victor McLaglen. As a Negro, Johnson was said to have a thicker skull than white contenders, but John Lardner who got to know Jeffries in his later years, when he was working as a museum attraction, recalls that his "chief asset in the ring was intelligence coupled with speed and an airtight defense, and practically no one hit him on the skull." He had no trouble decking McLaglen who ended up in Hollywood with roles in, among other films, *The Informer* and *What Price Glory?*[12]

Jeffries was thirty-five, three years older than Johnson, when he was talked into redeeming his race's honor by returning to what Joyce Carol Oates regards as "the most tragic of all sports because more than any human activity it consumes the very excellence it displays." Jeffries was quoted as saying: "I am going into this fight for the sole purpose of proving that a white man is better than a negro."[13]

Dorsie didn't place a bet on the fight, but he ducked across Main Street to the Turf Exchange to get the round-by-round results coming in by ticker-tape. In the first three rounds, Johnson fought cautiously, letting Jeffries tire himself taking the offensive. In the fourth round, Johnson went on the attack, and by the seventh white supremacy was on the ropes. When Jeffries was counted out in the fifteenth round, a stunned silence fell over the Turf Exchange.

Returning to his shoeshine stand, Dorsie found the barbers and their white customers stunned by the news from Reno. "I bust out laughing," Dorsie told a friend years later, "and the boss got sore. He says, 'Why in the hell didn't you do your laughing across the street?'"

On August 13, 1910, the fourth anniversary of the Brownsville raid, a Committee of Colored Ministers responded to the slaughter of twenty or more black Texans in Anderson County by appealing to President Taft to "use the powers of your great office to suppress lynching, murder, and other forms of lawlessness in this country."

"Men were killing negroes as fast as they could find them, and so far as I have been able to ascertain without any real cause," a Texas sheriff reported, and told of the gunning down of three unarmed Negroes at a wake for a victim of the mob the night before. Two more were found lying in a road, apparently killed while "trying to get out of the country for they had their bundles of clothes with them."[14]

In Texas during a single month, approximately one hundred citizens "have been lynched, murdered, burned and persecuted, the State apparently powerless to help them," the ministers wrote in their petition to the president, and the Houston *Chronicle* declared editorially, "It would puzzle Satan to find a satisfactory excuse for such an outbreak."[15]

In his Osawatomie speech, Roosevelt had not only quoted Lincoln but had also spoken feelingly of the Civil War and praised its generals and its foot soldiers. He had, however, made no mention of the men, women, and children whose forebears were delivered from bondage during the first Republican administration.

Now, after nearly fifty years of loyalty to the Emancipator's party, New York Negroes had banded together to form the United Colored Democracy and do what they could to help defeat the Colonel's candidate for governor of New York, forty-three-year-old Henry L. Stimson, an earnest, austere corporate lawyer who, it was said, "had been known to laugh right out loud."[16]

Black activists had nothing against the hardworking, fair-minded lawyer except that he was Roosevelt's creature. "Remember Brownsville," a United Colored Democracy leaflet proclaimed and posed the question: "Do you remember that when white soldiers in Ohio were proven to be murderers they escaped with one fine and one man imprisoned, while of the black soldiers of Brownsville against whom not a single crime was ever proven, 134 [actually, 167] were unceremoniously kicked out of the army in disgrace. Who did this? Theodore Roosevelt."

Black voters, who would help defeat Stimson, were reminded that, while addressing the National Negro Business League, Roosevelt had praised his audience for having learned "not to whine and cry about privileges you do not have." Dissidents now urged blacks to *"Remember Brownsville*, and bury Theodore Roosevelt so deep on Election day that his advice to 'stop whining' will be buried with him."[17]

New Yorkers by the thousands voted their "direct hostility to me," Roosevelt wrote his twenty-three-year-old son, Ted, after the Democratic victory, and recalled that it was "just thirty years this fall since I began my work in politics." He expressed happiness, not convincingly, at the thought that this rejection of his Republican candidate would put an end to "the talk of nominating me in 1912."[18]

Speaking in his personal forum, *The Outlook* (November 19, 1910), he reaffirmed the principles set forth in Osawatomie. Writing more candidly in a letter to William Allen White, he attributed the Democratic victory to Tammany's ability to strike a deal with the "crooks in Wall Street," who had won the support of "the silk-stockings and professional high-brows." A handwritten postscript dismissed the criticism that he had not stood "strongly enough by Taft" and should have made it clear that he would not be a candidate in 1912. "I felt I did just right on both counts."[19]

Roosevelt's Osawatomie speech brought Foraker bounding back to the lectern. Speaking in Marysville, he denounced the heresies of the New Nationalism "set forth in the nature of a platform for a new party. Possibly they are intended for that use only in the event that the distinguished author be not nominated for the Presidency by either of the old parties." The Colonel's followers in Ohio responded in angry telegrams, speeches, and interviews.

When the State Republican Committee wired a request for the senator to omit from his speeches criticisms of other Republicans, Foraker requested cancellation of his scheduled appearances throughout the state. The committee backed down, inviting him to rejoin the campaign and speak without restrictions. In the meantime, however, James R. Garfield, a Cleveland lawyer, son of the slain president, had taken it upon himself to read Foraker out of the party.

"Before Mr. Garfield reads anybody out of the Republican Party it might be well for him to make it a little plainer that he is himself in the Party," Foraker suggested, and pointed out that Garfield had "failed to speak a word in behalf of President Taft or to even mention the name of Governor Harding."[20]

As 1910 drew to a close and Republicans were still shaken by their humiliating defeat in the off-year elections, the president's closest advisers warned him that Roosevelt would be a candidate for the nomination in 1912.

"Theodore wouldn't do that," Taft said.[21]

Boston's black gadfly, William Monroe Trotter, congratulated Woodrow Wilson on his "magnificent majority" as governor of New Jersey that fall. His declaration that he would "treat all citizens alike," had led to an endorsement by "the independent Colored men of the country. . . . We trust that no word or action of yours on the great question of equal rights will ever cause us to regret our stand."[22]

The *Boston Guardian* editor referred to Wilson's campaign assurances that he would be governor of all the people. As Link points out in a footnote to Trotter's letter, "There is no record of any statements by Wilson addressed specifically to blacks." In the fall of 1909 he had explained to an

Alabama oculist: "I wish very much that I could express an opinion that was worth publishing on the future of the American negro in the United States, but though it is a subject to which I have given a great deal of thought, I have never been able to bring my thinking to a satisfactory conclusion. I feel that men resident among the Southern negroes are the only men who can really answer this question with any degree of confidence."[23]

Crossing Lafayette Square early in the new year, Henry Adams ran into a "hippopotamus," who turned out to be his White House neighbor "wandering about with Archie Butt." The president looked "bigger and more tumble-to-pieces than ever," he wrote Elizabeth Cameron, "and his manner has become more slovenly than his figure; but what struck me most was the deterioration of his mind and expression."[24]

A few weeks later, Adams reported seeing no chance that come June the Republican Convention could be prevented "from voting Theodore by a general yell. Whether Theodore can be elected I doubt, but no one doubts that Taft will be defeated. His only hope is in getting Bryan to run for the Democrats."[25]

"I am pretty well convinced that Taft will be nominated," Roosevelt wrote Nick Longworth (February 7, 1912). "I think the sentiment among the people is two or three to one in my favor, but I cannot and will not make an active campaign, and he very properly can and will."[26]

On Saturday, February 24, Roosevelt responded to an appeal by eight Republican governors: "I will accept the nomination for President if it is tendered to me." The following evening the Tafts were going in to dinner with two White House guests when a short note was handed the president. He read it and passed it around. The Associated Press had carried Colonel Roosevelt's announcement. No comment was made until everyone was seated; then, Archie Butt recorded, Nellie Taft broke the silence, addressing her husband.

"I told you so four years ago, and you would not believe me."

"I know you did, my dear," the president replied, "and I think you are perfectly happy now. You would have preferred the Colonel to come out against me than to have been wrong yourself." The president, Archie Butt tactfully recorded, "laughed good-naturedly" as he spoke.[27]

Major Butt (he had been promoted the year before) lay awake that night, trying to decide whether he should put off his Italian holiday. "I hate to leave the Big White Chief just at this time." he wrote his sister-in-law, Clara

Butt, and reminded her that all his papers were "in the storage warehouse." Next morning he told the president he intended to cancel his sailing orders. Taft insisted he proceed with his plans, and the following Saturday Archie boarded the SS *Berlin*. "If the ship goes down," he told Clara, "you will find my affairs in shipshape condition."

He wound up his month-long, trans-Atlantic vacation in London on the morning of Wednesday, April 10, when he walked into Waterloo Station and made his way through the crowded concourse to Platform 12, where a new liner, said to have cost $75 million, was berthed. Inscribed on the bow in gold letters was the name, "Titanic."[28]

Four days later, when his White House neighbors were mourning the loss of their courtly southerner, Henry Adams, preparing to cross the Atlantic, was in doubt as to "whether Taft or the *Titanic* is likely to be the furthest-reaching disaster." He booked passage on the *Titanic*'s sister-ship, *Olympic*, but his nerves were "now so shaken that no ship seems safe." As for politics that spring, "We are drifting at sea, in the ice, and can't get ashore. No one can guess what is ahead, but it can hardly be anything good. Our dear Theodore is not a bird of happy omen. He loves to destroy."[29]

Taft, in the meantime, had decided that Roosevelt's "lies and unblushing misrepresentations" would have to be answered. A few days later he changed his mind, but finally, on April 23, he wrote a friend that "the time has come when it is necessary for me to speak out in my own defense. I shall do so sorrowfully. I dislike to speak with directness about Theodore Roosevelt, but I cannot longer refrain from refuting his false accusations."[30]

"I am a man of peace," he was quoted as saying two weeks later in Hyattsville, Maryland. "But when I do fight I want to hit hard. *Even a rat in a corner will fight.*"

The last words, a biographer points out "do not appear in the stenographic transcript of his speech. Perhaps a discreet stenographer did not take them down. Perhaps Taft never said them. But it did not matter. They were carried by the newspapers. Their effect was just the same."[31]

Years later a *New York World* reporter recalled an evening when he followed the exhausted president back to one of the lounges in his special train and found him slumped over, his head between his hands.

"Roosevelt was my closest friend," he said brokenly, and began to cry.[32]

Chapter Sixteen

"It will take a very big man
to solve this thing."

—*Woodrow Wilson,*
on racial segregation,
October 7, 1913

As Republican delegates descended on Chicago in mid-June, 1912, Taft was determined to stay the course in order to block Roosevelt's nomination. "His constitutional views are of such character, and his mendacity, his unscrupulousness displayed in deceiving the public and arousing one class against the other, all alike make him a man to be avoided if possible as a candidate. Were I now to withdraw I am very sure that of the delegates pledged to me a number would go at once to Mr. Roosevelt, and that I cannot permit."[1]

The colonel had polled more primary votes than the president (1,157,397 761,716), but the Republican National Committee awarded 235 disputed seats to Taft and only 19 to Roosevelt, who "probably deserved about 30 more delegates than he received." The colonel, arriving in Chicago "as strong as a bull moose," assured his followers he would "fight in honest fashion" and concluded with a peroration that would live in the memories of the faithful and in the history books of their great-grandchildren: "We stand at Armageddon and battle for the Lord."[2]

"It was magnificent," Pringle wrote some 20-odd years later. "It was epic, even if nobody knew where Armageddon was, exactly, and why the Lord had suddenly become an opponent of William Howard Taft. Roosevelt probably believed, as he spoke, that he was telling the truth. But the weight of the evidence is against him. He had forgotten that precisely the same methods had been used to achieve his own nomination in 1904 and that he had used them for Taft in 1908. He did not know that in 1916 he would be back in the ranks of the G.O.P. and would be working with the very bosses whom he now condemned. Roosevelt was a child of the moment. When, as he rarely did, he looked back across the years he remembered things as he wished to remember rather than as they were. He seldom looked into the future at all." As a reviewer of his books observed, "He seems to have been born with his mind made up."[3]

Democrats assured their first national victory in eighty years by nominating a literate, conservative southern governor of a northern state who had sponsored "the strictest regulatory legislation ever passed in New Jersey." What people wanted, Governor Woodrow Wilson told the liberal New York editor, Oswald Garrison Villard, was "a modified Rooseveltism."[4]

The editor of the *New York Age*, the voice of Tuskegee, could not see how any Negro could vote for Wilson, who as a child had absorbed "most of the prejudices of the narrowest type of Southern white people against the Negro," and who, at Princeton, had presided over "the one large institution in a Northern State that closed its doors to Negroes." As governor, elected by black voters, he had never "by the turn of the finger recognized a single Negro in New Jersey."

William Monroe Trotter, Harvard A.B. *magna cum laude*, '95, editor of Boston's anti-Tuskegee *Guardian*, sent Wilson a copy of the *Age* editorial, identifying it as coming from "the leading Republican Colored paper" and thus offering the Democratic candidate an opportunity to make "a public statement on your attitude when elected toward Colored Americans."[5]

Wilson "carefully hedged" in assuring black militants and their white allies "they had nothing to fear in the way of inimical legislation," but he refused "to commit himself on patronage or the use of his veto power." Three weeks before the election he told Negroes they could "count upon me for absolute fair dealing and for everything by which I could assist in advancing the interests of their race in the United States."[6]

Disillusioned with Taft ("fat, genial and mediocre") because of his treatment of the Brownsville soldiers and "his general cynical attitude toward the race problem," Du Bois turned to Roosevelt and the Bull Moose movement on the eve of the Progressive Party's convention. "I saw there a splendid chance for a third party movement, on a broad platform of votes for Negroes and the democratization of industry." Seated at his desk in the office of *The Crisis*, the spokesman for the National Association for the Advancement of Colored People, drafted a plank for the Colonel's platform, which would offer "Americans of Negro descent the repeal of unfair discriminatory laws and the right to vote on the same terms on which other citizens vote."[7]

When the Progressives descended on Chicago that summer, representing what Du Bois's biographer refers to as "the aroused middle class of small-town America, they trumpeted "Onward Christian Soldiers" and "The Battle Hymn of the Republic." It was a Jim Crow chorus. "At the end of the day, Roosevelt, who was busily courting southern lily-white delegates, approved the denial of convention seats to most of the African-American delegates, and instructed the platform committee to ignore the Du Bois plank." The man was "dangerous." In the northern city where Republicans had nominated Abraham Lincoln, black Republicans were turned away from the "most religious-like convention in American political history."[8]

Villard wrote an "I told you so" letter to Booker Washington. The Tuskegee Wizard "could have walked out on Theodore Roosevelt and the whole political game after the Brownsville affair," his biographer points out, but he lacked "one essential attribute for the leader of an oppressed minority—the capacity for righteous public anger against injustice. Washington could and did work with dogged persistence against a great variety of racial injustices that white men perpetrated. He could chide or cajole with great skill and subtlety. But somewhere back in his life the power to lose his temper with a white man had been schooled out of him."[9]

Roosevelt decried the "venality" of Negro delegates from the South's "rotten boroughs" who came to Republican conventions "representing nothing but their own greed for money or office." He refused to help "create another impotent little corrupt faction of would-be office-holders," falling back on the cliché that southern Negroes could "ultimately get justice" by putting the Progressive movement in the hands of "the best white men in the South."[10]

Du Bois dismissed Roosevelt because of black men's "memory of Brownsville" and wrote off Taft because of his "abject surrender to Southern prejudice." He would have supported Gene Debs, the Socialist nominee ("if it lay in our power to make him President"), but ended up gambling on Wilson, "a cultivated scholar" who "will treat black men and their interests with farsighted fairness."

The NAACP editor was gratified not so much by a southern Democrat's victory as by the defeat of his two mainstream opponents. Taft "allowed the enemies of the Negro race in the South practically to dictate his policy toward black men. Theodore Roosevelt not only made and gloried in the wretched judicial lynching at Brownsville, but gave Negro disfranchisement its greatest encouragement by disfranchising 1,000,000 colored voters in the councils of his new party of social progress."[11]

In a pre-inaugural "Open Letter to Woodrow Wilson," the NAACP editor noted that for the first time since Emancipation, all three branches of the federal government had passed into "the hands of the party which a half century ago fought desperately to keep black men as real estate in the eyes of the law." This historic transition "shows not simply a splendid national faith in the perpetuity of free government in this land, but even more, a personal faith in you."

"We black men," he reminded the president, "by our votes helped to put you in your high position. It is true that in your overwhelming triumphs at the polls you might have succeeded without our aid, but the fact remains that our votes helped elect you this time, and that the time may easily come in the near future when without our 500,000 ballots neither you nor your party can control our government."

Du Bois expressed the belief that "the Negro problem is in many respects the greatest problem facing the nation" and called for "the education of colored children, the opening of the gates of industrial opportunity to colored workers, absolute equality of all citizens before the law, the civil rights of all decently behaving citizens in places of public accommodation and entertainment, absolute impartiality in the granting of the right of suffrage," along with "the just fight of humanity against crime, ignorance, inefficiency and the right to choose one's own wife and dinner companions."

"You will be urged to surrender your conscience and intelligence in these matters to the keeping of your Southern friends," he warned the president-elect. "They 'know the Negro,' as they will continually tell you. And this is true. They do know 'the Negro,' but the question for you to settle is whether or not the Negro whom they know is the real Negro or the Negro of their vivid imaginations and violent prejudices."[12]

Wilson was sworn in by a chief justice who had ridden with the Ku Klux Klan in Louisiana, but racism knew no geographical or political boundaries. William Allen White, the progressive Kansas editor, warned against dilution of "clean Aryan blood" and found comfort in the thought that "we are separated by two oceans from the inferior races and by an instinctive race revulsion to cross breeding that marks the American wherever he is found."[13]

On May 14, Villard called on the president to ask a favor, something the liberal editor had promised the candidate during the campaign he would never do. The favor was appointment of a National Race Commission to make a "nonpartisan, scientific study of the status of the Negro with particular reference to his economic situation." Wilson seemed to like the proposal and was ready to proceed if "his relations with the Senate and House permitted it." By July, when Villard came home from a European trip, the White House was not returning his calls. Dr. Washington wrote to say he had "never seen the colored people so discouraged and bitter."[14]

"It is beyond question that the Senate *will not confirm* any nomination of a negro for any position in the federal service in which he is to be in command of white people—especially white women," Villard's Washington correspondent wrote him on October 1, 1913, and then, with heavy use of emphasis, explained that "the white men and women in the Government service always have resented being compelled to associate with negroes. *Never before has there been an Administration that dared to cater to this feeling except in surreptitious ways.* There has always been in the Departments in Washington a *wish* to do it, but not the *courage*."[15]

When Wilson, "absolutely blocked by the sentiment of Senators from various parts of the country," turned down his request for a racial study, Villard warned him that "if his policy did not change, precedents would be established which might injure the colored people for "generations to come." Wilson said he understood perfectly, and finally, "with shame," he went on to add, "I have thought about this thing for twenty years and I see no way out. It will take a very big man to solve this thing."[16]

In "Another Open Letter to Woodrow Wilson" (September, 1913), Du Bois declared that "not a single act and not a single word of yours since election has given anyone reason to infer that you have the slightest interest in the colored people or desire to alleviate their intolerable position. A dozen worthy Negro officials have been removed from office, and you have nominated but one black man for office, and he, such a contemptible cur, that his very nomination was an insult to every Negro in the land."

Du Bois was probably referring to Adam E. Patterson, a black Texas Democrat, who withdrew his name when the president's offer of the position of registrar of the Treasury created a firestorm of protest on both sides of the color line.[17]

Thomas Dixon, the white supremacist author of *The Clansman* (1905), was "heartsick over the announcement that you have appointed a Negro to boss white girls." Wilson, whose friendship with Dixon dated back to their days as graduate students at Johns Hopkins, replied testily that he was trying to handle the matter "in the spirit of the whole country, though with entire comprehension of the considerations which certainly do not need to be pointed out to me." He called Dixon's attention to a plan being tried out in the Treasury, which would "not in any one bureau mix the two races."[18]

In the Treasury and the Post Office, Du Bois wrote in *The Crisis*, "colored clerks have been herded to themselves as though they were not human beings. We are told that one colored clerk who could not actually be segregated on account of the nature of his work has consequently had a cage built around him to separate him from his white companions of many years. . . . There are foolish people who think that such policy has no limit and that lynching, 'Jim Crowism,' segregation and insult are to be permanent institutions in America."[19]

Moorfield Storey, president of the NAACP, reminded the scholar in residence at the White House that:

> *the very presence of the Capitol and of the Federal flag has drawn*
> *colored people to the District of Columbia in the belief that living there*
> *under the shadow of the National Government itself they are safe from*
> *persecution and discrimination which follow them elsewhere because of*
> *their dark skins. Today they learn that, though their ancestors have*
> *fought in every war in behalf of the United States, in the fiftieth year*
> *after Gettysburg and Emancipation, this Government, founded on the*
> *theory of complete equality and freedom of all citizens, has established*

two classes among its civilian employees. It has set the colored people apart as if mere contact with them were contamination.[20]

When Howard Allen Bridgman, editor-in-chief of *The Congregationalist and Christian World*, asked the president whether he approved of this racial segregation, Wilson replied "that it is distinctly to the advantage of colored people themselves" and had been approved by "some of the most thoughtful colored men I have conversed with." He would not have approved the separation of the two races, he continued, "if I had not thought it to their advantage and likely to remove many of the difficulties which have surrounded the appointment and advancement of colored men and women."[21]

"Washington is essentially a Southern city," John Palmer Gavit, the *New York Evening Post* Washington correspondent, wrote editor Villard a few weeks later, after an off-the-record conversation with the president about Negroes in public service.

> *The great majority of the white people here hold the Southern view of the negro, and as for the Northerners here, it takes but a little while for them to become infinitely more anti-negro than any Southerner. The white men and women in the Government service always have resented being compelled to associate with the negroes.* Never before has there been an Administration that dared to cater to this feeling, except in surreptitious ways. *There has always been in the Departments in Washington a wish to do it, but not the courage." (emphasis in Gavit text)*[22]

Gavit's interview and *Evening Post* article, "The Negro in Washington" (October 21, 1913), brought about a White House luncheon invitation for his employer at which Villard was given an hour to explain where he and the NAACP stood. Likening the president and his segregationist secretary of the treasury, William G. McAdoo, to "atoms on the current of our national life," Villard explained that this "administration would soon pass but that if his policy did not change, precedents would be established which might injure the colored people for generations to come."

Crusading against the president's segregation policy, Villard pointed out that nowhere in the 1910–12 speeches collected in his book *The New Freedom* "do we find any indication that his democracy is not limited by the sex line and the color line."[23]

Gavit wondered whether "historians would say that 'there was much talk in those days of a "New Freedom," but it was exclusively for white men?'" Arthur S. Link, who spent years presiding over the editing of the Wilson Papers, suggests that "this introduction of the caste system into federal government was perhaps inevitable." He quoted Gavit, who described it as "a meeting of the irresistible and the impenetrable; a tragic situation culminating the crimes and hypocrisies of three centuries."[24]

In early January, 1914, six months after ratification of the Seventeenth Amendment providing for a United States Senate "composed of two Senators from each State, elected by the people thereof," Foraker was asked to become a candidate. He welcomed the prospect of vindication and agreed to run if his campaign could be tailored to fit both his requirements and those of the newly mandated direct primary as well.

"I do not like the idea of having to first engage in an election contest with friends as a preliminary to the general election contest with the common enemy," he explained. "With our party already more or less divided, this first fight among ourselves seems to me particularly unfortunate for it will no doubt leave some sore spots."

The requirement that the platform be drawn up after the nomination struck him as being "in conflict with common sense." It was "not only conceivable, but even probable, that some planks of the platform might be such that I could not, even by silent acquiescence, appear to either believe in them or approve them. In such event the only alternative would be the embarrassing one for both the party and myself of withdrawal from the ticket."[25]

Ohio Republican Regulars in the new legislature, setting out to lure Progressive strays back into the fold, talked the state central committee into arranging a reunion banquet in Columbus on February 26. As a goodwill gesture to Bull Moosers, Senator William E. Borah, the Idaho liberal, was asked to be the main speaker at what was variously called a "forgettogether" and a "love feast." Senator Burton and ex-Senator Foraker listened to the Republican Glee Club's rendition of "Hail, Hail, the Gang's All Here" and to the reading of telegrams from absent notables, including Warren G. Harding, who wanted to replace Senator Burton but had promised Foraker he would not oppose him.[26]

Burton bowed out of the race on April 8, leaving Foraker with no serious opposition in view. He announced his candidacy and sounded a still-familiar Republican theme, blaming Democrats for the "general industrial depression," which had been "made worse by hostile legislation heretofore enacted and now threatened by which business activity and enterprise are restricted and restrained far beyond what wise and necessary supervision and regulation require."

In a passage that would have sounded bully to Roosevelt, he attacked Wilson's proposed treaty with Colombia, extending an apology for the "alleged injury done by us through President Roosevelt in connection with the secession of Panama, and the acquisition of the canal zone." Speaking from "personal knowledge," he characterized the Colonel's conduct as "highly honorable." Colombia's only injury was "brought upon herself by her own unwise and indefensible conduct. To pay her $25,000,000, or any other sum, would be like submitting to blackmail; and to apologize to her would be an abject national humiliation . . ."[27]

Two weeks before the May 31 deadline for entering the primaries, the only opponent Foraker faced was Ralph D. Cole, who had lost his Congressional seat in 1910. Party leaders, sensing disaster if they went before the voters with an anti-Roosevelt, Standard Oil lawyer, appealed to Harding, who agreed to enter the race if Mark Hanna's son Dan, publisher of the *Cleveland Leader*, would stop making personal attacks on Foraker.

Hanna agreed and Harding took off for Cincinnati, where he told his old friend and mentor he intended to run against him. Foraker was surprised but raised no objection. On May 27, "with genuine reluctance," Harding announced his candidacy. Next day, Dan Hanna called on Progressives to help eliminate a "man so out of date, so tainted by reactionary activities, so out of harmony with the spirit of the times as Senator Foraker."[28]

Harding carried more than twice as many counties as Foraker (51 to 21), winning 88,540 votes to Foraker's 76,817. Cole, with 16 counties, had picked up 53,237 votes. "On the Republican side," according to the *Akron Beacon-Journal*, "the most significant feature of the vote was the failure of Joseph B. Foraker to 'come back.' Despite his old popularity and his ability as a speaker, Foraker had no chance. What he didn't realize apparently, and what the party did, was that the day of the Forakers has passed in Ohio."[29]

In a letter to Foraker written nine days after his nomination, Harding spoke of "my admiration for you, ever growing for nearly thirty years." He had entered the race, he said, hoping his old friend would retire. "I could not and would not ask it, but I hoped for it. I knew the drift of Republican sentiment. It would gratify you, it would compensate you for your distinguished public service, to know how highly you are esteemed, how much you are admired and how many loyal friends you have in every county in Ohio." The candidate's only regret was that his victory "had to be won in your defeat." He hoped that Foraker would "continue to inspire and encourage Ohio Republicans, and give them the benefit of your counsel and assistance."[30]

Foraker thanked him for his "kind expressions" and made the customary promise to support the ticket. With the help of anti-Papist votes, which he had done nothing to discourage, Harding defeated his Irish-Catholic opponent by a plurality of 102,373 votes, thus helping Ohio Republicans elect a full slate of state officers, a majority in both houses of the legislature, and thirteen congressmen, including Roosevelt's lecherous son-in-law.

"You will have a great future before you," Taft wired the senator-elect.[31]

"Naturally," Foraker wrote in his memoirs, "I felt some mortification and disappointment—mortification that I should have been wheedled into a candidacy I disliked only to be defeated, and largely by the active work of the very men who had especially solicited me to become a candidate—and disappointment because deprived of what I thought would afford me an opportunity to utilize my experience in the public service in a helpful way at a critical time."

He wasted "no time regretting results" and easily persuaded himself "that it was better for me and the country to have the contest end as it did. I shall be more humble and have more time for meditation and reflection and to set my house in order for the 'inevitable hour;' while the State will be represented by a man in the prime of a vigorous manhood, and able, therefore, to make a record that will be a credit both to the Nation and our Commonwealth."[32]

Nan Britton, on a dare from her high school teacher, the senatorial candidate's sister Abigail, called at the Harding home in Marion to offer her congratulations. Mrs. Harding came to the door in a pink linen dress. "It was late afternoon and he was playing cards with his regular 'bunch.' He came out, and I shall never forget his smile—I do not think now it would be too much to say it was a smile of genuine appreciation, for so he assured me in later years—and I thrilled unspeakably under the touch of his hand."[33]

On election night as he was heading for a victory celebration in an open touring car, a man called out: "The next President of the United States is sitting in the back of that auto."[34]

Foraker, still crushed by the sudden death of his son, Benson, on whom he had expected to lean in his last days, was working on *Notes of a Busy Life* in 1915 when he read the first reports of a new and sinister attempt to "rewrite and falsify the history of the Civil War and the reconstruction of the States that followed." He had not seen "the motion picture show entitled 'The Birth of a Nation,'" but understood that it "undertakes to rescue the Ku Klux Klan from the unenviable place assigned them in history as midnight marauders and murderers by portraying them as patriotic citizens banded together for the protection of women and the doing of other things of praiseworthy character."[35]

Booker T. Washington had also spared himself the discomfort of sitting through the film spectacle, but from time to time in the last ten years he had tangled with Tom Dixon, the North Carolina negrophobe whose novel, *The Clansman*, had given David Wark Griffith the foundation on which to build his skewed masterpiece. Dixon "apparently wants to work the colored people into fever heat," Washington wrote a friend, "and reap the reward of the advertising."[36]

Lashing out at "sinister forces" determined to suppress "the noblest defense of the South ever given," Dixon applied to his friend in the White House. At the start of his half-hour with the president "he told Wilson that he had a favor to ask him—not as President, but as a scholar and student of history—that he view this motion picture because it made clear for the first time that a new universal language has been invented."

Wilson, still in mourning for the death of his wife, Ellen Axson, could not go to a theater, but he offered to invite his Cabinet members and their wives to join him in viewing the film if Dixon could set up his projector in the White House. He insisted that the private showing not be mentioned in any way in the press.

"Of course," Dixon later wrote Joe Tumulty, Wilson's secretary, "I didn't dare allow the President to know the *real big purpose back of my film—which was to revolutionize Northern sentiments by a presentation of history that would transform every man in my audience into a good Democrat. . . .* What I told the President was that I would show him the birth of a new art—the launching of the mightiest engine for moulding public opinion in the history of the world." (emphasis in Dixon's text)[37]

Dixon also called on another North Carolina acquaintance, Navy Secretary Josephus Daniels, who helped clear the way for a meeting with Chief Justice White.

"You tell the true story of the Klan?" the chief justice asked when Dixon invited him to see the photoplay.

"Yes," Dixon replied, "for the first time."

White removed his glasses, leaned back in his swivel chair and began to speak of the nights he had walked his Klansman beat "through the ugliest streets of New Orleans with a rifle on my shoulder." He promised to attend the White House screening.[38]

Dixon and his projector crew showed the film in the East Room two weeks later. Milton MacKaye, writing about "The Birth of a Nation" in *Scribner's* (November, 1937), quoted the president as saying: "It is like writing history with lightning. And my only regret is that it is all so terribly true." The editor of the *Wilson Papers* talked to the last survivor of the private screening in the summer of 1977 and was told that "Wilson seemed lost in thought during the showing and that he walked out of the room without saying a word when the movie was over." The quotation does not appear in Dixon's memoirs, "Southern Horizons."[39]

Booker Washington, writing a former Tuskegee librarian who had moved to Boston, denounced the film as "thoroughly harmful and vicious," but when it opened in New York that spring, with seats fetching an unheard-of price for photoplays (two dollars), it proceeded to gross almost $18 million. In Atlanta that winter a diminutive Peachtree Street teenager, inspired by Dixon's prose, produced her own adaptation of his novel, *The Traitor: A Story of the Fall of the Invisible Empire*. Just as the young author-actor-producer, playing the hero, Steve, was about to be hanged, "two of the clansmen had to go to the bathroom, necessitating a dreadful stage wait which made the audience scream with delight," Margaret Mitchell remembered. Twenty-odd years later, when her Civil War novel was about to go to press, she changed the name of her heroine, Pansy O'Hara, and instead of killing off Frank, her second husband, with pneumonia, she had him done in more dramatically, as a Klansman fighting to protect Scarlett O'Hara and Southern womanhood.[40]

In 1856, the year Thomas Woodrow Wilson was born in Staunton, Virginia, Foraker was a ten-year-old Ohio campaigner for the infant "Free Soil" Republican party. Nearly sixty years later he had nothing new to say about the treatment of the emancipated Negro by southern Democrats. In closing his memoirs he referred his readers to a chapter in volume 1 recalling an 1887 invasion of Ohio by a Georgia governor determined to "answer Governor Foraker's assaults on the South."

Foraker had responded immediately, pointing out that between the spring and fall elections of 1868, the Republican vote had fallen off without any corresponding increase in Democratic votes. Almost 100,000 votes were lost in Georgia, Louisiana, and South Carolina, he said, "because of whipping, of lashing, intimidation, assassination and murder. It was the work of the Ku Klux Klan," carried out "for no other purpose than to destroy the free exercise of the right of suffrage and turn the south and the whole country over to the Democratic party."[41]

Now, as Foraker's life was drawing to a close, a revolutionary new form of entertainment not only portrayed the hooded night riders as "patriotic citizens banded together for the protection of women," but also cast reflections "upon the deeds of every soldier who wore the blue." Francis Hackett, who would later become a distinguished screenwriter, denounced the film as "spiritual assassination. It degrades the censors that passed it and the white race that endures it."[42]

Chapter Seventeen

The Champion of People
"Who Had No Champion"

—*Colonel Roosevelt's farewell to
Senator Foraker, June 26, 1916*

Foraker, at work on his memoirs in 1915, recalled that when he left the Senate, "I was 'down and out,' and my enemies were everywhere triumphant." In his first hour in his law office he was given "employment of a most satisfactory and complimentary character. Except by choice I have not had an idle day since, but I have taken time to read the newspapers, to make a few speeches, and to *join my fellow citizens in welcoming back to private life one after another in rapid succession every man who took part in the work of retiring me.*" (Foraker's emphasis)

He mentioned no names but took an unmistakable dig at Taft: "I, too, am so tender-hearted that 'I can't strike a man when he is down,' but I will say that I have no distress on account of what has happened to any of these individuals. I have been able to bear their defeats and disappointments with Christian resignation and fortitude. *I have even found pleasure in the fact that I have been permitted to live long enough to see my worst enemies saying worse things about each other than either of them ever said about me.*" (Foraker's emphasis)[1]

Professor Taft of Yale Law School, who had once referred to Colonel Roosevelt as "the most dangerous man that we have had in this country since its origin," was serving as president of the League to Enforce Peace, an organization founded at the Century Club in 1915, the second year of the European war. "We are not peace-at-any-price men," Taft made clear, but he had no doubt that his affiliation with the peacekeepers would be "like a red flag to a bull to Theodore," who was "obsessed with his love of war and the glory of it."[2]

The Republican party's "one chance of winning was with me," Roosevelt wrote University of California president Benjamin Ide Wheeler, when Wilson won reelection after campaigning on the slogan, "He Kept Us Out of War." The Colonel could have been paraphrasing "Fire Alarm" Joe Foraker when, in a letter to Lodge, he attributed Wilson's victory "to the fact that the negroes of the south, who are not allowed to vote, are nevertheless used to give to the southern whites (and therefore to the Democratic Party), fifty electoral votes and fifty Congressmen, to which they are no more entitled than the people of Kamchatka."[3]

After managing to maintain a seven-week silence following Germany's renewal of "submarine warfare against neutrals and noncombatants," he spoke out at the Union League Club the following March: "Let us face the accomplished fact, admit that Germany is at war with us, and in our turn wage war on Germany with all our energy and courage, and regain the right to look the whole world in the eyes without flinching." The next day he wrote Secretary of War Newton D. Baker, asking permission "to be allowed to raise a division for immediate service at the front."[4]

On April 10, four days after Wilson had signed the joint resolution formally declaring a "state of war between the United States and the Imperial German Government," Colonel Roosevelt bounded into his old White House office, gave presidential secretary, Joe Tumulty, "a hearty slap on the back" and "shook hands cordially" with the president, who, a friend later reported, seemed to appreciate the Colonel's "intense virility, picturesque personality, and love of fighting."[5]

Roosevelt had come to the White House to dramatize his availability to form a division that could be shipped out quickly and, on its arrival in France, demonstrate to the Allies that the Americans were now fighting at their side. Harding led the successful Senate fight to send the White House a conscription bill that would create a "Roosevelt Division." The bill left it up to the president to decide whether the Colonel would be called on to create it.[6]

"I doubt whether the President lets me go," he later wrote his beloved sister Bye; "and surely he will try his best to cause me to fail if he does let me go."[7]

The country had been at war for a month, and Roosevelt still was waiting to hear whether he was to be permitted to reprise his Cuban adventure in France when a Cincinnati stringer for the *New York Times* reported on May 10, 1917: "Joseph Benson Foraker, formerly United States Senator from Ohio, lawyer, orator, and soldier died at his home here today at the age of 70 years." He was known for many years as the "bulldog of politics," the obituary continued, "because he was always fighting and always fought as a bulldog is supposed to fight never asking quarter and never giving it." In the headline and in the text he was identified as "old foe of Roosevelt." The obituary made no mention of the Brownsville Affray or of the many times Roosevelt had turned to him for advice and support.

Nearly a year earlier, on June 28, 1916, after reading Foraker's memoirs, the Colonel had written him a long, generous letter:

> *My dear Senator: I have just finished your two volumes, which I have read with great interest. Of course there are certain portions as to which you and I will continue to differ; but if I ever get the chance to speak publicly, I shall elaborate what I said in speaking of you in the libel suit.[8]*
>
> *Not only do I admire your entire courage and straightforwardness (in the railway legislation I respected you a thousand times more than I did many of the men who voted for the bill) but I also grew steadily more and more to realize your absolute Americanism, and your capacity for generosity and disinterestedness. Besides, you knew the need that the freeman shall be able to fight, under penalty of ceasing to be a freeman.*
>
> *Too many of our representatives in the senate and the lower house could not be persuaded to take any interest in any matter in which they or their districts were not personally concerned. But, as far as you were concerned, when the question came up of dealing with the Philippines or Porto Rico or Panama, or the navy, or anything involving America's*

*international good name, or the doing of our duty to help people who
had no champion; I knew that if I could convince you that my view was
right I could count upon your ardent championship of the cause. I had
much the same feeling about O. H. Platt of Connecticut and Cockrell
of Missouri; but in neither case did they look upon international affairs
as you and I did.*

*There is no use in raking up the past now, but there were some
things told me against you, or in reference to you, which (when I consider what I know now of my informants) would have carried no weight
with me at the time had I been as well informed as at present.*

*Now for something entirely different. If you are ever in this neigh-
borhood I wish you would let me know, and come down for lunch or
dinner. I have some questions I wish to ask you about the battle of Chickamauga; this being in connection with the work of a cousin of mine, now
dead, a man named Gracie.*[9]

*Faithfully yours,
(signed) Theodore Roosevelt*[10]

The Colonel, who had played at being a soldier in the War between the
States never got to discuss Chickamauga with the teenage officer who
stormed Missionary Ridge, but in his friendly letter to the elderly senator,
he had provided Foraker's epitaph:

*The Champion of People
Who Had No Champion*

"I am exceedingly glad that you fearlessly told the truth about the Administration," Roosevelt wrote Lodge, May 17, 1917, the day after his old friend
had taken the Senate floor to denounce, among other usurpations of power,
the president's appointment of Herbert Hoover as the nation's food "dicta-
tor." Three days later, in a letter congratulating General Pershing on his
"selection to lead the expeditionary force to the front," the Colonel requested that his two oldest sons, twenty-seven-year-old Ted and twenty-
three-year-old Archie, "both of Harvard, be allowed to enlist as privates
under you, to go over with the first troops." His postscript indicated he had
finally given up hope of fighting in France: "If I were physically fit, instead
of old and heavy and stiff, I should myself ask to go under you in any capacity down to and including a sergeant."[11]

General Pershing, during a farewell meeting with Secretary of War Newton D. Baker, May 27, squared an old debt by asking, "If I cable requesting that the two Roosevelt boys be sent to France, will you grant the request?"

"Certainly," Secretary Baker replied.[12]

The two young Roosevelts came ashore in France on the eve of Independence Day, when their father was writing a letter to their brother, Kermit, who was hoping to get his sailing orders at any moment. The last to leave was the youngest, Quentin, who had signed on as an aviator.

"It was hard when Quentin went," his mother admitted. "But you can't bring up boys to be eagles, and expect them to turn out sparrows."[13]

When Quentin brought down a German plane near Chateau-Thierry the following summer, his father saluted his son's San Juan Hill. "He has now had his crowded hour and his day of honor and triumph," he wrote his daughter Ethel (July 12, 1918).[14]

Six days later the *New York Times* ran a "semi-official" report from Paris: "Lieutenant Quentin Roosevelt, youngest son of the former President, has been killed in an air fight." He had last been seen in combat three days earlier, on a "Sunday morning with two enemy airplanes about ten miles inside the German lines in the Chateau-Thierry sector."

"Quentin's mother and I are very glad that he got to the front and had a chance to render some service to his country, and to show the stuff there was in him before fate befell him," the Colonel wrote in his statement to the press.[15]

The story was confirmed July 21, and Roosevelt, responding to the British Royal Family's cable of condolence, recalled that when the four young Roosevelts "sailed from our shores over a year ago, their mother and I knew their temper and quality; and we did not expect to see all of them come back."[16]

"The fine gallantry of Quentin's death has stirred our whole people," the Colonel wrote Ted, and in a letter to Archie he pointed out, "If our country did not contain such men it would not be our country."[17]

Roosevelt, who had made his peace with Taft, demurred when his old friend proposed that he run for governor of New York. "As in your case," he pointed out, "my heart is wrapped up in my boys at the front, and I am not thinking in terms of New York State conditions."[18]

"Only those are fit to live who do not fear to die," he wrote; "and none are fit to live who have shrunk from the joy of life. Both life and death are parts of the same Great Adventure." But it was sadly apparent to his friend

Hermann Hagedorn that the boy in the old Colonel had died with Quentin. "The days of exuberance had gone, life became heavy," Stefan Lorant notes, "his own Great Adventure was closing."[19]

"This is the crisis of the world," Du Bois wrote in the summer of 1918, and warned his NAACP readers that "we of the colored race have no ordinary interest in the outcome. That which the German power represents today spells death to the aspirations of Negroes and all darker races for equality, freedom and democracy. Let us not hesitate. Let us, while this war lasts, forget our special grievances and close our ranks shoulder to shoulder with our own white fellow citizens and the allied nations that are fighting for democracy."[20]

While young, able-bodied Negroes signed up for Selective Service and were bundled off to Jim Crow camps run by white officers, tens of thousands of southern Negroes were heading North to take jobs thrown open by the draft and by an abrupt decline in immigration. Barred from most labor unions, they were forced to work for low wages, forced by fellow-workers who, Du Bois pointed out, "have in reality common cause with him."[21]

The problem dated back to the earliest days of the Negro's freedom, when striking members of Jim Crow labor organizations found their jobs put at risk by employers who could draw replacements from a bountiful pool of liberated slaves. In 1866, when white New Orleans bricklayers struck for higher wages and found themselves replaced by freed men, the *New Orleans Tribune*, a Negro newspaper, spoke up for workers on both sides of the color line: "Labor equalizes all men; the handicraft of the worker has no color and belongs to no race. The best worker—not the whitest—is the honor and pride of his trade."[22]

Forty-five years later the *International Molders' Journal* insisted that "so long as the Negroes remain unorganized they will continue to be exploited and used to break down the standard of living of not only their own race, but of all men who are forced to compete with them in the industrial field." The *Detroit Labor News* had concluded that "never again can the Negro be ignored. Unionism must welcome to Negro to its ranks."[23]

The message was lost on Samuel Gompers, president of the American Federation of Labor and on the white workers in East St. Louis, Illinois, the "Pittsburgh of the West," where by 1917 some 10,000 to 12,000 southern Negroes had shown up looking for jobs.

"The Aluminum Ore Co. brought hundreds and hundreds of them to the city as strike breakers, to defeat organized labor," a Kentucky congressman would report later that year. "White men walked the streets in idleness, their families suffering for food and warmth and clothes, while their places as laborers were taken by strange negroes who were compelled to live in hovels and who were used to keep down wages."[24]

The displaced southern Negroes found themselves caught up in the intolerable conditions they had hoped to escape. They worked in segregated gangs and, despite an 1885 public accommodations law, they ate in Jim Crow cafes, attended Jim Crow theaters, and sent their children to Jim Crow schools. Both races began patronizing a pawnshop with a window displaying the warning: "Buy a Gun for Protection."[25]

On Sunday evening, July 1, 1917, after receiving reports of white marauders shooting into Negro homes from a passing Ford car, four lawmen, a driver, and a newspaper reporter piled into a squad car, also a Ford, and were fired upon by Negroes who may have mistaken them for drive-by assassins. One policeman was killed instantly, a second died the following day. On their way to work that morning, white laborers stopped by the police station to examine the bullet-ridden Ford in which the officers had been riding when attacked. A local attorney offered his services to "any man that would avenge the murders."[26]

Union men held a protest meeting and then, "in good humor," started shooting Negroes along a bloody half-mile of a principal business street. They were encouraged by white neighbors crowding the sidewalks, "cheering and hand-clapping" while dead and wounded black men and women were being loaded into an ambulance. Reporters were struck by the "visible coolness and premeditation" of the violence. It "was not the hectic and raving demonstration of men suddenly gone mad."

When a journalist appealed to a group of militiamen to stop a lynching, he "was not able to interest them in it." Carlos F. Hurd of the St. Louis Post-Dispatch described the scene: "To put the rope around the negro's neck, one of the lynchers stuck his fingers inside the gaping scalp and lifted the negro's head by it, literally bathing his hand in the man's blood. 'Get hold, and pull for East St. Louis,' called the man as he seized the other end of the rope."[27]

On the third day "white people roamed the downtown area, exchanging souvenirs from the rampage, ghoulishly touring the morgues, and cheering whenever an increase in the black body count was announced. Mangled black corpses ('horribly mutilated floaters') bobbed to the surface of the

Mississippi. By July 5, almost $400,000 worth of property had been destroyed and thirty-nine black and eight white people were dead.[28]

Witnesses who had no reason to avoid the truth "agreed in condemnation of the police for failure to even halfway do their duty," a congressional investigating committee reported. "They fled the scene where murder and arson held full sway. They deserted the station house and could not be found when calls for help came from every quarter of the city."[29]

The state militia came in for its fair share of condemnation. The officer in charge, Colonel S. O. Tripp "answered the call to duty in a seersucker suit and a dainty straw hat." He spent the morning in city hall, then repaired to a restaurant, where he had a leisurely lunch before returning to his post in city hall. While he was eating his lunch, three men were killed within three blocks of the restaurant.[30]

The soldiers serving under him "were scattered over the city," congressional investigators reported, "many of them being without officers to direct or control them. In only a few cases did they do their duty. They seemed moved by the same spirit of indifference or cowardice that marked the conduct of the police force. As a rule they fraternized with the mob, joked with them and made no serious effort to restrain them." One militiaman in uniform led a section of the mob. Another boasted of having "fired his gun seventeen times during the riot and every time at a 'black target.' Soldiers shared a common expression: 'Have you got your nigger yet?' "[31]

Casualty estimates, inflated by both races, ranged from 100 to 400 fatalities (Du Bois stuck with 125). The coroner counted nine dead whites. No accurate figures were available for Negroes, because so many of them were disposed of like "dead hogs." Only two were examined by the coroner.[32]

"What chance on earth, has a poor innocent Negro in a place like this?" a California congressman exclaimed when Colonel Tripp completed his testimony.

It was Colonel C. B. Clayton of the 4th Infantry, next in command, who finally brought the riot under control at 7:30, the Monday evening of July 2. "Several hundred persons were arrested," The Crisis reported. "Most of these were turned loose by the police as soon as they were indicted. They were dismissed as rapidly as they could walk out."[33]

"The city's Fourth of July celebration was called off," the New York Times reported July 5, and followed up on the story two days later, after Colonel Roosevelt had been drawn into the controversy while sharing Carnegie Hall's stage with AFL president Samuel Gompers and the city's mayor in welcoming envoys from Russia's revolutionary new Bolshevik government. The two men were brought to the brink of a fistfight when Gompers tossed the Illinois race riot into play by attacking the employers who lured Negroes from the South "to be used in undermining the conditions of the laborer in East St. Louis. . . . The poor devil working under debasing conditions in old Russia was no worse off than the man on whom there are imposed the same conditions in free America. [Applause.]"

Roosevelt sprang up angrily, "unwilling that a meeting called to commemorate the birth of democracy in Russia shall seem to have given any approval of or apology for the infamous brutalities that have been committed on negroes at East St. Louis. Justice with me is not a mere phrase or form of words. It is to be translated into living action."

He strode over to Gompers, shaking his fist in the labor leader's face. "We must have investigations," he began.

Gompers interrupted, "Investigations afterward—."

"I'd put down the murderers first and investigate afterward," Roosevelt snapped, "amid a chorus of groans from the gallery."[34]

"A few years ago," the Colonel later reminded an Illinois labor official, "certain negro troops shot up a Texas town, and the other members of their companies shielded them from punishment. The government proceeded to the limit of its power against them all, and dismissed them from the army; not because they were black men who had committed a crime against white men, but because they had acted criminally; and justice should be invoked against wrong-doers without regard to the color of their skins."[35]

Roosevelt's "justice" was given to two of the Brownsville battalion's five white officers, who were tried by their peers and acquitted; the 167 black enlisted men, all of whom swore to their innocence, were summarily dismissed and sent home in disgrace. East St. Louis white militiamen appeared before a military board of inquiry which based its findings on testimony of officers rather than on civilian witnesses who had seen some soldiers turn their backs on the violence and others take part in it. They too were cleared.[36]

Survivors of the East St. Louis riot received, among other relief-fund contributions, a check for $146.60 from 654 black soldiers of the 3rd Battalion, 24th Infantry, who had been ordered to Texas with eight white officers to take over guard duties at a $2 million Camp Logan construction site about three and one-half miles from the center of Houston. The 24th, like members of their sister regiment stationed in Brownsville in 1906, had fought in Cuba and the Philippines. The regiment had also served in Mexico with General Pershing's Punitive Expedition.[37]

The black battalion arrived on Saturday, July 28, and bivouacked on a ten-acre tract a mile east of Camp Logan. Houston's chamber of commerce, eager to swell the profits of cotton farmers and oil producers with additional government contracts, had assured federal authorities "that in a spirit of patriotism, the colored soldiers would be treated all right." But, along with the city's 30,000 black residents, the men found themselves compelled to travel on Jim Crow streetcars between the city's two separate and unequal worlds.[38]

"In most cases the soldiers obeyed the law or the white conductors disregarded minor violations," Robert V. Haynes wrote in his initial study of the Houston mutiny, but on their first Saturday night, when the men set out to explore the town, "a few black troopers openly defied the system of discrimination by removing Jim Crow screens which they either kept as 'souvenirs' or tossed out the windows."[39]

After a more serious confrontation the following evening, an agreement was worked out which left punishment of such violations to the army. The battalion's commanding officer appeased the white townspeople and insulted his men by stripping military police of the pistols they carried while on duty. The soldiers, forbidden to congregate outside the camp in groups larger than three, avoided white neighborhoods, preferring to entertain black visitors at the camp. "On weekends the numerous visitors from the city's most respected black families gave the camp, according to one curious white officer, the appearance of a 'very orderly . . . big picnic.' "[40]

Black soldiers and black townspeople alike resented "the strong-armed tactics of the city police." They might have got on peacefully had the local constabulary been less "intent on catching 'a penny-ante' Negro thief than in uncovering a syndicate of white criminals."[41]

On Thursday morning, August 23, Mrs. Sara Travers, a Negro housewife, the mother of five children, was working at her ironing board, dressed to accommodate the summer heat and humidity. When a notorious racist bully, Officer Lee Sparks, chasing a young black crapshooter, ran into her house, she objected to the intrusion. "You all God damn nigger bitches," she quoted him as replying, "since these God damn sons of bitches of nigger soldiers came here, you are trying to take the town."

As the policeman, with Mrs. Travers in custody, was calling for a patrol wagon, Private Alonzo Edwards, in town on a twenty-four-hour pass, offered to pay the woman's fine. Sparks "raised his six-shooter" and beat the soldier over the head "about four or five times."

"I wasn't going to wrestle with a big nigger like that," he later explained, so "I hit him until he got his heart right."

Edwards was shoved into the patrol wagon with Mrs. Travers and taken to the city jail. When Corporal Charles W. Baltimore, a model senior member of the provost guard, came to the jail that afternoon to inquire about the prisoner, Sparks hit him "over the head with the barrel of his gun." Baltimore, unarmed, ran off and hid in an unoccupied house. Sparks tracked him down and packed him off to jail in a patrol wagon. Asked about the soldier's head wounds, the policeman calmly explained: "He ran against the home there and liked to have killed himself."[42]

That night, inflamed by a false report that Baltimore had died in prison, some hundred or more mutineers, rallying to the cry: "To hell with going to France. . . . Get to work right here," passed out ammunition, loaded their rifles, and headed for the town, where a white civilian had once remarked to the battalion's medical officer: "In Texas it costs twenty-five dollars to kill a buzzard and five dollars to kill a nigger."[43]

During the next two hours, four soldiers and fifteen whites, including four police officers, were killed. None of the four dead infantrymen were killed by whites. Vida Henry, who led the march on Houston, committed suicide. A wounded soldier died of medical negligence and two others were shot by fellow-soldiers who mistook them for police officers.[44]

The Houston riot was unique on two counts. "It was the first race riot where more whites were killed than blacks, and it was one of the few where no civilian Negroes were involved. Instead the Houston riot was a conflict between black soldiers and white citizens in which the former made a conscious effort to keep black Houstonians from participating." After the soldiers went to the gallows and to penitentiary cells for taking their lawless stand against rogue lawmen, Houston ended up with the most active branch of the NAACP in Texas.[45]

In an effort to avoid a repetition of what the editor of a racist weekly, State Topics, characterized as "the Brownsville joke," Wilson's secretary of war praised the townspeople for their "tolerance and restraint" and promised to "leave no stone unturned" in apprehending and punishing the guilty men. Despite recommendations by the army's top investigators, however, no officers were put on trial, although one could well have been charged with negligence, another with cowardice.[46]

A court-martial convened at Fort Sam Houston in San Antonio to try sixty-three enlisted men charged with premeditated murder and mutiny in time of war found fifty-four men guilty of both crimes. Thirteen men were sentenced to death by hanging; forty-one got life at hard labor. Of the remaining nine men on trial, five went free and four got two-year sentences.[47]

"Nothing since the Brownsville incident," John Hope Franklin would write for a later generation of students, "had done so much to wound the pride of Negro Americans, or to shake their faith in their government."[48]

In the darkness before dawn, December 22, without public notice, the thirteen condemned men were taken to a common gallows. The editors of the *Messenger* (The Only Radical Negro Magazine in America) objected to this "dark lantern" administration of the law, denying the thirteen black soldiers "the right of appeal granted to the vilest criminal."[49] Readers were reminded that "Theodore Roosevelt started this thing and the South's desire to 'go him one better' is the logical conclusion of the Brownsville starter."[50]

In the spring of 1919, black soldiers, including Napoleon B. Marshall, the Harvard lawyer who ten years earlier had defended the Brownsville infantrymen at their court of inquiry, returned from the battlefields of Europe's colonial powers. They were coming home to a "shameful land," Du Bois wrote in *The Crisis*, a land that for fifty years has lynched "two Negroes a week," a land that "disfranchises its own citizens," a land that "encourages ignorance," a land that:

> *keeps us consistently and universally poor and then feeds us on charity and derides our poverty. . . . This is the country to which we Soldiers of Democracy return. This is the fatherland for which we fought! But it is our fatherland. It was right for us to fight. The faults of our country are our faults. Under similar circumstances, we would fight again. But by the God of Heaven, we are cowards and jackasses if now that the war is over, we do not marshal every ounce of our brain and brawn to fight a sterner, longer, more unending battle against the forces of hell in our own land.[51]*

Woodrow Wilson was in Paris preparing for the Peace Conference when Theodore Roosevelt died, on January 6, 1919. "I saw him in the hospital six weeks ago," Taft told reporters, "and he seemed to be very vigorous. He was suffering from rheumatism, but his voice was strong, his personality was as vigorous as ever, and his interest in the questions of the day as tense and acute as always."[52]

The Colonel was buried "near the summit of a steep hill which looks out on Oyster Bay cove and across the cove to the Roosevelt home on Sagamore Hill," the *New York Times* reported. "Ex-President William Howard Taft, the picture of grief, stood near the grave, with his head bent forward and tears in his eyes. Senator Henry Cabot Lodge, who appeared hardly able to command himself, stood a short distance away."[53]

The morning Roosevelt's death blanketed the nation's front pages, Ohio's Senator Harding awakened to find his name in accompanying headlines that, by nightfall, had made him the Republican front-runner for 1920. He "has steered a strictly party career during his first term in the Senate," the *Times* pointed out, "but he has advanced with the trend of political events which have put progressive theories more to the fore than ever before."

"He is straight on all leading public issues," the *New York World* declared, and mention was made of his support of Prohibition and Woman Suffrage. His home state, it was also pointed out, had come to be "known as the maker of Presidents." Ohio's two leading Progressive newspaper editors, Dan Hanna of the *Cleveland Leader* and Robert F. Wolfe of the *Ohio State Journal*, took a fresh look at the handsome, reassuring face of the state's presidential prospect. It seemed sculpted for postage stamps.[54]

On one of these early January evenings, Nan Britton checked into a downtown Washington hotel and "Mr. Harding" whisked her off to the Senate Office Building. "We stayed quite a while there that evening, longer, he said, than was wise for us to do, because the rules governing guests in the Senate Offices were rather strict. It was here, we both decided afterward, that our baby girl was conceived."

"We must go at this thing in a sane way, dearie," the startled sire said the following month when she gave him the news in their room at the Willard Hotel. Nan noticed the sweat forming on his forehead. "You know, Nan," he remarked ("wistfully"), "I have never been a father."

He left the room and returned "with some Dr. Humphrey's No. 11 tablets, which, he said, 'Mrs. Harding used to take and found in some instances effective.'" Nan didn't think the pills would work and hoped "Mr. Harding would tell me definitely to go on and have the baby," but "our problem was left in the air, or rather for me to solve."[55]

In the enlightened fall of 1920, thanks to the Nineteenth Amendment, women could join men in going to the polls to choose between Warren G. Harding and Calvin Coolidge (Republican) and James M. Cox and Franklin D. Roosevelt (Democrat). In the South's polling places, however, black women were no more welcome than black men. Some well-educated black women in South Carolina, *The Nation* reported, failed to qualify when they were unable to "explain *mandamus*" or "define civil code" to a local white official who would have had trouble defining "civility."

When even more black women showed up the second day, registrars made them step aside while white voters were registering, at which point "the high sheriff came in and shouted: 'Yo' niggahs git out o' de way, git out an' let de whahte people register—an' stay out! An' if yo' don' stay out, dey'll be some buckshot to keep yo' out.'—And still the colored people came. The women especially defied all opposition."[56]

Throughout his campaign, Harding had been hounded by William Eastabrook Chancellor, a white supremacist college professor who distributed flyers tracing the senator's ancestry to a West Indian Negro, Amos Harding, and a colored wife, Hulda. Their marriage, he insisted, could be "verified by a hundred people in Marion, Ohio." On the closing night of the campaign, Harding's manager referred to the persistent rumor in a coded aside: "No lip of libel nor tongue of slander can harm your cause or you."[57]

In an open letter to the newly elected president, Du Bois noted that his enemies had sought to count him among the country's 10 million Negroes "whose destiny rests so largely with you in the next four years." Negroes would be deeply satisfied "to welcome you to the old and mystic chrism of Negroland," the NAACP spokesman continued, "but blood and physical descent are little and idle things as compared with spiritual heritage. And here we would see you son of the highest: a child of Abraham Lincoln and Lloyd Garrison and Frederick Douglass." He called for "an administration which will say and mean: *the first and fundamental and inescapable problem of American democracy is Justice to the American Negro. If races cannot live together in peace and happiness in America, they cannot live together in the world.*" (emphasis in original text)[58]

Six weeks after Chief Justice White died on May 19, 1921, Professor Taft was rescued from the classroom and seated in the center chair of what he called the "sacred shrine." Four years later, when Warren Harding's death installed Calvin Coolidge in the White House, Chief Justice Taft told a friend that "in my present life I don't remember that I ever was President."[59]

Roosevelt's old friend had been two years dead and Coolidge's secretary of commerce, Herbert Hoover, was about to lose his lease on the White House to the Colonel's cousin Franklin in 1932, when Julia Bundy Foraker, now in her eighty-fifth year, brought out her lively memoir, *I Would Live It Again*.

She had not forgotten "the wrecking of the Republican Party" in 1912, when "Theodore Roosevelt let down President Taft as completely as President Taft ever let down anybody." Political enemies, now long-dead, "flocked back to my husband, begged him to come over into Progressive Macedonia and help them." He stood by his party. "He had voted for Mr. Taft in 1908; he voted for him again in 1912. He was a Taft man to the end; lonely, of course, but incorrigibly loyal."[60]

Toward the close of her book, Julia reproduced the text of the letter Roosevelt wrote her husband in the summer of 1916 after reading *Notes of a Busy Life*. She singled out the sentence in which the Colonel praised the senator's "courage and straightforwardness" and then cited the significance of his statement, "You knew the need that the freeman shall be able to fight, under penalty of ceasing to be a freeman." That, she wrote, was her husband's "whole code; it was at the root of every one of his differences with Roosevelt. The two men never saw each other again."[61]

She forgave the Colonel because of his generosity and, most of all, his "human-beingness," but she never forgave Taft, who turned away when his benefactor was battling for his public life. She died believing Theodore Roosevelt was "disaster" for her husband, "but, different in every other way, Mr. Roosevelt and Foraker were oddly alike in natural fearlessness, independence of thought and utter inability to yield. If this similarity made their battles inevitable, it made them, also, the odds being as they were, perfectly helpless.

"Were it all to be lived over again, I am afraid that everything would happen just as it did."[62]

Afterword

Olive Allen was working as a waitress at Jim's Barbecue in Minneapolis in the fall of 1944 when her best friend, Ruth Brown, met her ex-husband's roommate, a widower named Dorsie Willis, who asked her to find him a girlfriend.

"I don't want to hear about him," Ollie said when Ruth suggested she meet Dorsie. She had been married twice and was now "through with men."

"He's nice and he's got a car that he doesn't drive, and you haven't any car, and he's got his own home."

"I'm not interested," Ollie said, but a moment later she asked, "How old is he?"

"Age has nothing to do with it," Ruth snapped, shielding Ollie from the discovery that she was younger than Dorsie's son.

Ollie likes to pick up the story at this point: "Ruth took me over there for Thanksgiving dinner and Dorsie was ready to marry right after he seen me. 'No, no,' I told him, 'no marrying for me.' Every morning, while I'm laying in my bed trying to get my rest, Dorsie would call me before he went to work. He asked me would I come live with him, and I said, 'No, I didn't believe in that. If I'm not good enough to marry, I'm not good enough to live with.'"

Three weeks later, when Ruth returned from a vacation in Louisiana, Ollie was wearing an engagement ring. She and Dorsie were married at

Zion Baptist Church February 11, 1945, the groom's fifty-ninth birthday. The bride was forty-eight hours short of being twenty-eight.[1]

On February 11, 1973, Harriett and I sent a telegram congratulating them on their wedding anniversary and on Dorsie's "historic birthday present," the honorable discharge he was to receive from the army at Zion Baptist Church. Ollie called that evening to share with us a sad secret she had withheld from him until after the ceremonies. His seventy-one-year-old sister, Julia, had died in Los Angeles the day before.

Dorsie, when told of her death, insisted on flying out to California for the funeral. Even though he had not fully recovered from a bout with flu, his family doctor knew there was no point in forbidding him to make the trip. He was accompanied by Ollie and Reginald, the son born of his first marriage.

We met them that afternoon in the white bungalow Dorsie's younger brother, Orville, had rented in the south-central section of the city. Reginald, who in his youth had toured the country as an entertainer, was no stranger to Los Angeles, but neither Dorsie nor Ollie had ever visited California before.

"When we left Minneapolis it was seven below and snow was about a foot deep," Ollie marveled. "When I got out of the car here at Orville's house, I said, 'Oh, I'm stepping on grass!' I couldn't believe it."

The house overflowed with family and friends. Many elderly couples had brought their grandchildren. "It's something we want them to remember," they explained, and took pictures of the freshly scrubbed young black faces staring up at the old man whose name would now be in history books.[2]

Shortly before Dorsie's arrival I had received a letter from Harriet Lyon, the older daughter of his company's commanding officer, Captain Samuel P. Lyon. Harriet, who still lived at Pasture House, the family home in Shirley Center, Massachusetts, had slept through the Brownsville raid at the age of three and, with her younger sister, Mary, had grown up with its cruel consequences not only for the soldiers but for her parents as well, especially her father.

"That miserable display of rank injustice and flagrant abuse of power left scars on his spirit, and also on my mother's, that never faded," Harriet Lyon wrote me. "In my own background it has been an enduring bitterness."[3]

"Of the five white officers at Brownsville on the night of the shooting, only your father had the courage and decency to stand up to the military bureaucracy from the outset," I replied.[4]

Mary Lyon, who worked in the administrative office of the University of California at Santa Barbara drove down to Los Angeles that Sunday to meet Dorsie. Both were in tears when I made the introductions. Mary brought out a snapshot of her father taken in the late 1930s. A generation after the Brownsville raid, he still stood tall and straight as an exclamation mark. Dorsie started chuckling at memories the photograph evoked.

"Every inch a soldier. We'd be out on a practice march after a rain and there'd be mudholes in the road full of water. Captain Lyon would never walk to one side or the other, he'd just plow straight ahead. He used to say he could take D Company and lead it through a burning hell. All he'd have to say is, 'Come on,' and they'd follow him, every man."[5]

Dorsie remembered Mary's mother sitting on her front porch in the evening, with little Harriet in her lap. He also remembered how men sent to the guardhouse would get permission from their first sergeant to speak to their company commander and then try to pick a time when Mrs. Lyon would be on hand to hear their appeal.

"They knew what Captain Lyon was gonna say," Dorsie said. "'Take him back to the guardhouse,' he'd tell the sergeant, but your mother, she'd fight the battle for 'em. The men used to take advantage of him. D Company had great admiration for that family."

"We felt the same way about D Company," Mary said.

She had brought her copy of *The Brownsville Raid* for Dorsie to sign. He rested the book on his lap and struggled to place his twisted, arthritic right hand in control of the ballpoint pen she handed him.

"They were two wonderful people," he said, and tears came to his eyes as his crippled hand slowly and painfully forced his name, letter by letter, onto the title page.[6]

A few weeks before Dorsie flew out to Los Angeles, Congressman Gus Hawkins's search for other survivors had led to the discovery of Edward Warfield, a former member of Company B. The eighty-nine-year-old veteran was living alone in a small furnished apartment on Avalon Boulevard in Gus's district. Warfield was one of the fourteen members of the black battalion the court of inquiry, in 1910, had permitted to reenlist (as eleven chose to do). In 1919, after serving in France during the first World War, he had left the army with an honorable discharge, taken a civil service examination, and gone to work for the government as a security guard. He had been drawing a pension from the Veterans Administration for twenty years.

Warfield was ill, feverish and weakened by a wrenching cough, when I visited him one rainy afternoon in late January, 1973. I had brought along a photocopy of his court of inquiry testimony. He adjusted his spectacles, squinting at the words my father had recorded and my mother had typed and sent to the Government Printing Office.[7]

"It's like hearing yourself talk after you're dead," he muttered to himself.

"Who do you think did the shooting?" I asked.

"The people in town," he replied, and then spotted the answer he had given to the same question sixty-three years earlier. He read it to me: "The citizens did it."[8]

We were joined by Chuck Knox, Hawkins's special assistant, and a young black woman, a journalism major who was preparing an article for a community paper. Warfield put the testimony aside and brought out his army papers, along with a photograph of himself taken in his dress uniform shortly before his outfit was ordered to Texas, where he had enlisted in the summer of 1905, the same year Dorsie had signed up.

"There was just a mean bunch of people in Brownsville," Warfield said. "They didn't want Negro soldiers there. They had a sign in the park, 'No Niggers and No Dogs Allowed.'"

When Gus Hawkins's field office arranged a press conference for the two Brownsville survivors, I drove Dorsie, Ollie, and Reginald to the assigned meeting room in Exposition Park, where Knox was waiting with members of the press. Warfield had not yet arrived.

None of the reporters had bothered to check the spate of newspaper articles about the exoneration of the Brownsville soldiers, and Gus's staff had not had time to prepare the sort of press release so many of them, especially the young ones in radio and television, had come to depend on. As a result, all they seemed to know was that the old man in the checked sports jacket, hobbling toward them, leaning on my arm, had just received his honorable discharge after having left the army in 1906.

"What took so long?" one reporter asked Dorsie. "Didn't they have discharge papers in 1906?"

We were not, I could see, in the presence of potential Pulitzer Prize winners, but gradually, as the morning wore on, the shadowy outlines of the Brownsville affair began to emerge, like a Polaroid snapshot. At this early stage of the conference, before Warfield arrived, it was Dorsie's show, and he enjoyed it as much as the reporters enjoyed the warmth of his company.

"Is it too late for you to get any benefits?" a young woman asked.

"I don't know, but I'm trying," Dorsie said.

Chuck Knox interrupted to explain that Congressman Hawkins was drafting legislation to provide a cash payment and all the benefits to which veterans of that period were entitled.

When Edward Warfield showed up, a sudden chill came over the room. The two old soldiers took an instant dislike to each other, and the relationship worsened as their joint interview proceeded.

"Do you remember Mr. Willis?" Warfield was asked as he entered the room.

He nodded. "Court of inquiry. Washington, D.C. February 2, 1910. We met together then."

"No," Dorsie said when asked if he recalled that meeting in Washington.

"We testified the same day," Warfield insisted, and when I tactfully pointed out that Dorsie was right, he had not gone to Washington to appear before the court of inquiry, Warfield snapped, "I was there. You weren't."

Shortly before Warfield's arrival I had explained to the reporters that his case differed from Dorsie's. He was one of the fourteen soldiers who, for reasons never set forth, the court of inquiry had cleared for reenlistment.

"Do you want to explain how you were allowed to reenlist?" he was asked.

"I was one of the men who went to Washington, D.C., for that Senator from Ohio," he began, and Dorsie was delighted when the old man's memory failed to come up with the senator's name.

"Senator Foraker," Dorsie said, beaming.

"Senator Foraker, right," Warfield grunted. "He's the one that had caused the court of inquiry. I was one of the three men out of B Company that was found not guilty. There was Corporal Coltrane, Corporal Daniels and myself. When the shooting began, Corporal Daniels was the first man to come out of the barracks onto the parade ground. I was the second man out, and I formed No. 1 of the first section, first rank. After Corporal Coltrane finally came out, he taken the position of right guide."

I too had tried to find out why Warfield had ended up among the fourteen men selected for reenlistment. Each time I put the question to him, he recited the same story of the formation of B Company on the parade ground on the night of the raid. It was a set piece, like an address a high school valedictorian had committed to memory. If anybody interrupted him, he went back to the first sentence and started anew: "Corporal Daniels was the first man to come out."

The official rationale for the old soldier's reenlistment was still a mystery on the morning of September 25, 1973, the eve of his ninetieth birthday, when I drove to a military chapel in West Los Angeles for his interment. The *Washington Post* obituary had quoted a comment he made to Dial Torgerson of the *Los Angeles Times* the day we called on him: "To get ganged up in something like that thing in Brownsville—it's just got to make you sorrowful."

The service ended with the hymn, *He Knows How Much We Can Bear.*[9]

Among the letters waiting for Dorsie and Ollie when they got home from Los Angeles was one from Senator Hubert Humphrey, who had called on the Congress to act "immediately with appropriate legislation which would authorize a just recognition, financially and in terms of eligibility for benefits, of the treatment you have received." The proposed bill, worked out in conjunction with Gus Hawkins, would grant Dorsie a payment of $40,000 along with a veterans' pension computed with interest from the date due, bringing the total to $100,000.

"Time is running out," I noted in a letter to Gus, who had introduced a bill in the House similar to Humphrey's. "If justice is to be done, it must be done now."[10]

Some weeks later, on a spring morning in 1973, when I was watching the Watergate hearings on television, Gus called to ask if I could come back to Washington to help his staff and Humphrey's prepare arguments for their Brownsville compensation bills to be presented to the House and Senate veterans' committees.

"The Administration is opposed to our bills because they might set a precedent," Gus said, and neither of us could imagine a more desirable precedent for the beleaguered Nixon Administration to set.

Bill Higgs, Gus's legal adviser on Brownsville, cleared a desk for me near his and brought out a sheaf of reports, letters, and memoranda.

"But first you might want to see this," he said, and gave me a copy of the statement Gus had prepared for next day's meeting of the Compensation and Pension Subcommittee of the House Veterans' Affairs Committee.

"First, even if the bill did establish a precedent," Gus had written, "I never thought there was anything wrong in establishing a precedent to do justice. Second, by the admission of the Department of the Army itself, the Brownsville incident is unique as a case of mass punishment, so no 'precedent' could possibly be established."

From Gus's prepared statement I learned that veterans' pension benefits had been granted to nearly half of the soldiers or to their widows (seventy-nine of the one hundred and sixty-seven men), because they had served in the Spanish-American War or, like Edward Warfield, in the first World War. Dorsie Willis was to represent the families of the men for whom nothing had been done.

"My mother, who passed away April 5, 1971, tried a number of times to get a veterans' pension but to no avail," Mrs. M. G. Greenfield, a Los Angeles schoolteacher, had written Gus. Her father, James E. Armstrong, was Company C's trumpeter. On the night of the raid he had sounded the call to arms.

Calvin W. Parker of Baltimore was a nephew of Charles H. Hawkins, a D Company corporal. He and his wife were dead and had left no children or grandchildren, Parker wrote. His Uncle Charles, he had been told by his aunt, had "refused to come home after his discharge. He went to Chicago and started a new life for himself."

"I consider the Army is part of my home," Corporal Hawkins had told the court of inquiry. "I have been in the Army since 1898, April 3. I soldiered with Colonel Daggett at El Caney and San Juan Hill." He had found work in Chicago as a Pullman porter, he told the generals. He was not among the six men of his company they cleared for reenlistment.

"Our family Bible shows that James Wadsworth Newton was born on November 20, 1880," Mrs. Lya W. Hamilton of Greenville, South Carolina, wrote of her uncle, the C Company soldier who had been pistol-whipped by a white customs officer on the main street of Brownsville. After his appearance before the court of inquiry had failed to get him back into uniform, he had gone home to work as a house painter, taken an active part in the work of his A.M.E. Church and died in 1932, when his niece was eighteen years old.

"Mrs. Hamilton said Newton had told her about 'the rough way they had to fight in the Philippines,' about the 'jungle' in the Spanish-American

War and about the time 'they got lost and had to eat dog meat,'" Nellie Dixon reported in the *Charlotte (North Carolina) Observer.* "She said she doesn't remember his mentioning what happened in Brownsville, although she believes it must have been uppermost in his memory."

Robert Hollomon, former president and board chairman of Mammoth Life and Accident Insurance Company of Louisville, Kentucky, wrote to say that his father, the "finance man" of Company B, had died in that city in 1947. John Hollomon, he said, had opened his saloon in Brownsville as a "protest" against the town's racial discrimination.

"It was his feeling that the opening of the saloon and the subsequent economic loss to the white community was the real cause behind the false charges and the expulsion of the soldiers," he continued, and added that he was spending his declining years on a small island off the coast of British Columbia, conducting research on the former slaves who had settled in this part of Canada a few years before emancipation.

Someone in the Hawkins office had drawn brackets around the following paragraph: "I have been a permanent resident of Canada for the past twenty years, and a Canadian citizen since 1960. My father's experience at Brownsville and my personal experience in World War II convinced me that the U.S. was unable or unwilling to defend the rights of the black people who go forth to defend it."[11]

I had heard Dorsie make much the same comment at the Los Angeles press conference, when a reporter asked whether black troops in the Army had always been treated poorly.

"In all the wars we've had," Dorsie had told the young man, "we've had many a Negro soldier to die—in the Philippines, the First World War, the Second World War—and when they come back to the United States, the country they were fighting for, and they'd go to a public place, they'd get the Hitler salute: 'Go round to the back door.'"[12]

The House subcommittee hearing on the Brownsville compensation bill was set for ten o'clock, June 14, 1973. I got to Gus's office shortly after nine, had a cup of coffee with Bill Higgs, and picked up the wheelchair I'd arranged to borrow for Dorsie. A family friend drove him up to the street-level entrance of the Rayburn Building, where Ollie and I could transfer him to the wheelchair with the least possible discomfort.

"Back home he was watching Watergate on the TV and he hated to leave it, but he's having the time of his life," Ollie said, "He's seen the White House, the Monument, everything."

Dorsie was wearing a sport coat, striped shirt, and tan gabardine slacks, and as I wheeled him through a marble labyrinth, he held his Zion Church cane between his knees. Ollie followed us, carrying on a lively conversation with Val Fleischhacker, an aide to Representative Donald M. Fraser, a Minneapolis attorney who, like Senator Humphrey, had taken a personal interest in Dorsie's case.

Gus Hawkins was on the phone when we got to his office. Higgs introduced Dorsie and Ollie to the members of the staff, and someone produced coffee. Gus joined us, shook hands with Dorsie and Ollie, and then, beaming, removed a two-page letter from the breast pocket of his coat and handed it to Higgs and me.

The letter, written on Department of the Army stationery and dated June 13, 1973, was addressed to W. Bryan Dorn, chairman of the House Veterans' Affairs Committee. The first page was a summary of the compensation issue, written in the Pentagon's murky prose. On the second page, signed by Howard H. Callaway, who had succeeded Bob Froehlke as Secretary of the Army, a clearly worded sentence leaped out at us.

"The Department of the Army believes that some compensation to surviving members of the Brownsville Incident or their widows is a fair objective through legislation," Secretary Callaway had written, and the letter ended with word that the president's advisers at the Office of Management and Budget had "no objection to the presentation of this report for the consideration of the committee."[13]

Higgs was delighted. "Now we won't be fighting the Pentagon and the White House," he explained to Dorsie and Ollie, "but we still have to get it through the Congress."

Before leaving Washington I met with members of the staff of both the House and Senate Veterans' Affairs Committees. A compensation bill of some sort could now be passed, they agreed, but not one as broad as the Hawkins-Humphrey proposal.

"There's no question about Dorsie Willis," they said. "He's entitled to something, but grandchildren are out. We've never given pension benefits to grandchildren. That would set a precedent, and a costly one. There's also a problem with children. These aren't little tots toddling off to school. They're middle-aged men and women, and any sort of payment to them

Left to right: Dorsie Willis, Burk Conyers, son of a young Company B private, and John D. Weaver.

could be regarded as an undeserved windfall. Our best bet is a lump-sum payment to Mr. Willis and to widows who haven't remarried."[14]

When I dropped by Gus's office to say good-bye, he agreed that the inclusion of children and grandchildren might jeopardize the chance of getting something done quickly for Dorsie and the dozen or so widows he had located.

"I want to get a bill through this session of Congress," he said, "so they will hold a check in their hands, not have it go to their estates."[15]

When I got home, one of Ollie's familiar "Hi There Harriett and John" cards was on my desk. It had been written on a Sunday evening, while Dorsie was watching television.

"I hope your back is O.K. from pushing Willis around in the wheel-chair," she wrote. "We certainly did enjoy ourselves. Everyone was so nice to us."

"My back held up beautifully," I replied, and told her I'd talked to the House and Senate lawyers who would be working on a bill to compensate Dorsie. "They assured me they were eager to see the bill go through as quickly as possible, but summer is a bad time in Washington, and they seemed to think it would take until October or November."[16]

Three weeks later, on another Sunday night, when Dorsie was getting out his fishing tackle ("he is going fishing at 5 A.M. & I will be at work at that time"), Ollie wrote another "Hi There Harriett and John" note: "I have begun to feel bad. Couple of girls here said Willis is not going to get anything."

"I know how discouraged you both must feel at times (and goodness knows, I feel the same way)," I replied, "but I'm convinced that some sort of payment will be made and that it will probably be made this year."

A month later, on August 21, Ollie wrote to say that Dorsie's doctor had ruled out the trip they were planning to make to Los Angeles the following month.

"Dorsie's leg and feet keep swelling on him so and he had gained so much weight, the Doc said he is too heavy on his legs," she explained, and then went on to add, "Senator Humphrey called Dorsie three weeks ago and said they had passed his bill. Now it's up to the House. Today while I was at work Congressman Hawkins' secretary called here and said they would be starting his case around the first of Sept."[17]

Under Section 8 of the veterans' benefits bill passed by the Senate, $25,000 would be paid to any survivor of the Brownsville battalion who had not been cleared for reenlistment by the court of inquiry. This provision applied only to Dorsie Willis. The bill also called for payment of $10,000 to unremarried widows.

"The Brownsville veterans and their families have endured years of economic deprivation, denial of opportunity and personal anguish because of this tragic episode in American history," Humphrey reminded Representative Olin ("Tiger") Teague of Texas, urging him to use his influence on the House Veterans Affairs Committee to expedite passage of the bill. "It was a tragic mistake of the government which injured these men, and I hope we may right that wrong while Mr. and Mrs. Willis, and the others, still live to see it."

Gus Hawkins sent me a copy of the Senate bill on September 5, along with the comment, "It is not perfect, but it is a lot better than nothing." I agreed. "My overriding desire," I wrote him, "is to get a bill passed as promptly as possible, so Dorsie will get to enjoy its benefits. He wants to come out here and sit in the sun, and goodness knows he's entitled to its warmth."[18]

The presentation of a $25,000 government check to the last survivor of the Brownsville battalion in Minneapolis, January 10, 1974. *Left to right:* Augustus F. Hawkins, who launched the exoneration crusade in Congress, Dorsie Willis, Maj. Gen. De Witt Smith, and Mrs. Olive Willis. *Courtesy U.S. Army Signal Corps*

"The legislation shows clearly that justice can be done—at least in substantial measure—in spite of the passage of time and changing of events," Gus said on November 16, when the House passed the bill calling for payment of $25,000 to Dorsie and $10,000 to unremarried widows. "My original bill would have awarded compensation to each surviving veteran or his surviving relatives of about $85,000. I believe that this original bill would have done more adequate justice; however, I do feel that it is of the utmost importance to grant some meaningful relief without further delay."[19]

Ollie sent us a clipping from the *Minneapolis Tribune*, quoting Dorsie: "If that's the best we can do, it's the best we can do. It doesn't make up for what happened to me, but it's better than nothing."

"Well," Ollie wrote, "I hope the President signs it. (Smiles)."

He signed it on December 6, and when Dorsie turned up on Walter

Cronkite's news summary that night, he was asked what he intended to do with the $25,000.

"I'm not going to throw it away," he said.[20]

The Pentagon brushed aside suggestions that Dorsie's $25,000 check be presented to him at the Capitol. Privately, the army grumbled at the prospect of being upstaged by Congress. Publicly, it expressed concern that the trip east might be too much for the government's elderly guest of honor. It was decided to send General De Witt Smith back to Minneapolis to preside over "a luncheon-type ceremony."

Gus Hawkins, who flew out from Washington in a snowstorm, was seated next to Dorsie on January 10, 1974, when a dozen of his friends and relatives joined the general at the Marquette Inn for a luncheon of veal cordon bleu, peas, potatoes, salad, and chocolate sundaes. The Pentagon had agreed to blow $200 on Dorsie's first army meal in sixty-seven years.

"Mr. Willis rose early on this special day," the *New York Times* reported. "'I had to,' he said, 'just to get to the bathroom before all the womenfolk.'"

When Jack Cornelius was called on to speak, he told how his friend Willis had come upstairs to his office twice a year with twenty-five dollars in loose change to help send youngsters to the Minneapolis Boys Club camp.

"The way I figure it, that's two hundred shoe shines every twelve months," he said, and presented Dorsie a gold statuette, the club's Man and Boys Award.

Dorsie's eyes filled with tears. "It's wonderful," he said, his voice cracking. "It's wonderful."

General Smith, deeply moved by his involvement in this historic moment, recalled his visit to Minneapolis a year earlier, when he had been "privileged to make amends in a very small way for a very large wrong done to Mr. Willis." He traced the roots of Brownsville back to the country's beginnings, when "we created the ultimate contradiction—a slave-holding democracy," and referred to Dorsie's honorable discharge as a symbol of progress.

"We are here," he said in closing, "to pay tribute to a man whose full life has been marked by hard work, human decency, and honor."

"Oh, Harriett," Ollie said when she called us that evening, "you and John should've seen Willis. When Mr. Cornelius was telling how he gave money to send poor boys to camp every year, Willis got to crying. Then the general got up, and he was crying, everybody was crying, but when the general said the check was tax-free, Willis stopped crying."[21]

We urged Dorsie and Ollie to come out to Los Angeles to spend February 11 with us. It would mark the eighty-eighth anniversary of Dorsie's birth and the twenty-ninth anniversary of their marriage. By coincidence the date fell on a Monday, the start of what was then Black History Week, and Mayor Tom Bradley had told us he would like to have Dorsie take part in City Hall ceremonies that morning.

"Doc Brown says we can come," Ollie announced in a phone call in late January, and we arranged with a friend at Western Airlines to provide a wheelchair for Dorsie when he boarded the plane in Minneapolis and when he got off in Los Angeles.

"Willis won't ever be the same," Ollie said when they reached her brother-in-law's house a couple of days before the birthday-wedding anniversaries. "Reginald drove us out to the airport in Minneapolis and there was a man waiting with a wheelchair. He took us to this room where they had a bar and color TV, and suddenly all these pretty girls started coming over to Dorsie with little sandwiches and champagne, and I said to myself, 'Oh my, what's this gonna cost?' and Reginald said, 'You know, Dad, they're giving you the V.I.P. treatment,' and Dorsie said, 'Whatever it is, I like it.'"[22]

We drove down to the beach and turned Ollie and Harriett loose on the Santa Monica pier. Dorsie stared after them, smiling. "This wife's a good one," he said, "a worker. My other two didn't care for work, and they didn't save nothing. They spent it all. This one saves. She don't waste nothing. She never met the first two, but every Decoration Day she goes out to the Crystal Lake Cemetery and puts flowers on their graves."[23]

On the Sunday afternoon before their reception in City Hall, we took them for a drive and ended up at our house for dinner. While Harriett was showing Ollie the garden, I sat in the living room with Dorsie, whose thoughts drifted back to his boyhood in Oklahoma Territory.

"Grandmother Willis used to worry us kids every day to study and accomplish something," he said. "I'd argue with her. 'What's the use of going to school and learning a trade?' I'd say. 'If we learn it, we can't get nothing like that to do.' And she'd say, 'It's not always gonna be like that. Things gonna change, and you can't wait till they do to try to learn something. Learn it now, so when the change comes, you'll be qualified to step right in.'"

Next morning, when I was wheeling him into the mayor's office, I asked him which would have been more astonishing to his grandmother, the sight of television cameras waiting to focus on him as he received the key to the country's third largest city or the discovery that it would be presented by a mayor whose parents were black Texas sharecroppers.

Dorsie looked up at Tom Bradley, grinned and shook his head. "She never would of believed that."[24]

"We congratulate you for your courage and determination," Mayor Bradley said. "The trials and tribulations of Dorsie Willis and all of the other members who were involved in that gross miscarriage of justice are a part of the history of this country, and the fact that justice finally was done in terms of absolving them of the charges made against them is at least some help. The money obviously is not enough to ever repay him for the suffering that he went through, or that the others went through."

A respectful hush fell over the room, even the television crews standing silent for a moment as they watched Dorsie sitting in his wheelchair, secure in his personal conviction that Providence had some mysterious reason for reaching down into the rear ranks of Company D, 25th Infantry, and picking Private Dorsie W. Willis to be the black battalion's last survivor.[25]

Dorsie died on August 24, 1977, at the age of ninety-one. Toward the end of his life, when he required more attention than any one person could be expected to provide, especially someone holding down an eight-hour job, friends and family urged Ollie to put him in a nursing home.

"I told 'em no, not as long as I've got the strength to take care of him," she said, and as death drew near, she took two weeks off from her job to be with him. "I went back to work on a Monday and he died that Wednesday. A man came out of the office and said, 'Telephone, Ollie.' When I seen him go in to tell the manager something, I figured Dorsie had died. I'd sat with him a long time the night before and he was unconscious. I kinda slapped his face, and he said, 'Baby, Baby.' That's the last words he said to me."[26]

The last survivor of the Brownsville Affray was buried with military honors at Fort Snelling, Minnesota, on August 29, 1977.

"No," he had replied some years earlier when a young black reporter asked if he were bitter, but he pointed out, "They can't pay me for the sacrifice I've made, the sacrifice that my family had to undergo. You can't pay for a lifetime. Some people feel the world owes them a living. I never thought that, but I did figure the world owed me an opportunity to earn a living. They took that away from me. That dishonorable discharge kept me from improving my station. Only God knows what it done to the others."[27]

Appendix

BIBLIOGRAPHIC ESSAY

Theodore Roosevelt ignored the Brownsville brouhaha in his 1913 *Autobiography* and seven years later Joseph Bucklin Bishop, his authorized biographer, dismissed it as the cause of "a bitter partisan debate in the Senate, led by Senator Foraker of Ohio, which continued for many weeks, but in the end the President's course was sustained." In 1930, when Black History week was created to "emphasize not Negro history, but the Negro in history," the Brownsville soldiers and Senator Foraker's role as their champion were given five paragraphs by journalist Mark Sullivan in *Our Times*. The following year, Henry F. Pringle, also a journalist, devoted six well-documented pages to the subject in his biography of Theodore Roosevelt. As the decade drew to a close, Pringle completed his biography of William Howard Taft, who paid the penalty for "Roosevelt's error."[1]

By this time the Brownsville Affray had faded so far from the memories of old crusaders for racial justice that it went unmentioned in *Fighting Years* (1939), the memoirs of Oswald Garrison Villard, editor of *The Nation* and, in 1910, a founding father of the National Association for the Advancement of Colored People. Walter White, who became the NAACP's general secretary in 1931, was an Atlanta, Georgia teenager the summer of Brownsville's midnight raid, but in *A Man Called White* (1948) he had it confused with the Houston mutiny, which occurred eleven years later. Roosevelt's treatment of the black infantrymen in 1906 had become "an event in our World War One jimcrow army."[2]

In 1948, James A. Tinsley, a graduate student at the University of North Carolina at Chapel Hill, concluded his examination of the episode with "some doubt whether the punishment would have been inflicted and whether, if inflicted, public opinion would have tolerated it, had the troops been white." The thesis was approved by Tinsley's faculty adviser, Howard K. Beale, "one of the most outspoken advocates of racial equality and Negro rights in the historical profession."[3]

It was at Chapel Hill that Beale, in 1935, first met C. Vann Woodward, who had introduced his white students to Du Bois' classic study, *Black Reconstruction*. In *Origins of the New South, 1877–1913* (1951), Woodward took the position that "war and Reconstruction, while removing some of the South's peculiarities, merely aggravated others and gave rise to new ones." In reviewing recent scholarship on race relations, Woodward cited Gunnar Myrdal's *An American Dilemma* (1944) and his friend John Hope Franklin's "superior synthesis of Negro history," *From Slavery to Freedom* (1947).[4]

In the fall of 1953, when called on to help Thurgood Marshall persuade the Warren Court to outlaw the Jim Crow caste system sanctioned by *Plessy v. Ferguson* (1896), Woodward and Franklin supported a broad approach, "arguing that the original equalitarian intentions of the post-Civil War amendments had been eroded in ensuing decades by unbearable political and economic pressures and extra-legal tactics. . . ."[5]

During his tenure as chairman of the history department at Brooklyn College (1956–64), Franklin sparked Ann J. Lane's interest in the Brownsville shooting spree. Her graduate work at Columbia produced *The Brownsville Affair: National Crisis and Black Reaction* (1971). Along with just about everyone else of her generation who has looked into the ramifications of this murder mystery, Lane acknowledged her indebtedness to James A. Tinsley's article, "Roosevelt, Foraker and the Brownsville Affray," *The Journal of Negro History* 41 (January, 1956): 43–65, and to Emma Lou Thornbrough for "The Brownsville Episode and the Negro Vote," *Mississippi Valley Historical Review* 44 (December, 1957): 469–93.[6]

Present-day students enjoy access not only to the papers and writings of Frederick Douglass, Booker T. Washington, and W. E. B. Du Bois, but also to important biographies by William McFeely (Douglass), Louis R. Harlan (Washington), and David Levering Lewis (Du Bois). They can also benefit from "the rainbow of voices" speaking out in Edward L. Ayers's *The Promise of the New South*, and in addition to the latest edition of Franklin's *From Slavery to Freedom*, they have *Long Memory: The Black Experience in America*, by Mary Frances Berry and John W. Blassingame, as well as August Meier's *Negro Thought in America, 1880–1915*.[7]

I have spent much of the last thirty years in the company of the black infantrymen who fell victim to Roosevelt's executive order. For much of the latter's side of the story I am indebted to Elting E. Morison, who selected and edited Harvard's eight-volume *Letters of Theodore Roosevelt* (1951–54). I have also drawn from the work of William Henry Harbaugh (*Power and Responsibility: The Life and Times of Theodore Roosevelt*, 1961), Edmund Morris (*The Rise of Theodore Roosevelt*, 1979), David McCullough (*Mornings on Horseback*, 1981), and Willard B. Gatewood, Jr. (*Theodore Roosevelt and the Art of Controversy*, 1970). To Lewis L. Gould, I am lastingly grateful not only for *The Presidency of Theodore Roosevelt* (1991) and *The Presidency of William McKinley* (1980) but also for a friendship that goes back nearly thirty years to my initial research in Austin under the guidance of Llerena Friend of the Eugene C. Barker Texas History Center.

Most of the soldiers I know only from official records, but I got to meet two of them and still correspond regularly with Dorsie Willis's widow and with Mary Lyon, the daughter of his commanding officer, who told me her father never fully recovered from the part he was forced to play in carrying out Special Order 266. Its victims also included Joseph Benson Foraker and his wife, Julia. Throughout the presidencies of Johnson, Ford, Carter, Reagan, Bush, and Clinton, the Ohio Senator's *Notes of a Busy Life* (1916) and his wife's lively recollections, *I Would Live It Again* (1932, 1975), along with Everett Walters's biography, *Joseph Benson Foraker: An Uncompromising Republican* (1948), have been within reach of my desk.

When I returned to Ohio in 1992 to reexamine the Foraker Papers at the Cincinnati Historical Society, I was distressed to find that in the fifteen years since I first made my way through the Senator's scrapbooks, the yellowing newspaper clippings had begun to crumble. I made arrangements for them to be microfilmed.

"A fascinating man," Scott Lewis Gampfer wrote the following fall, after supervising the microfilming of ninety-one volumes of personal and political scrapbooks (1855–1913) and nineteen volumes on special subjects (1883–1913). "There was scarcely a significant historical event in this country during his adult life in which he was not a participant."[8]

In *The Souls of Black Folks* (1903), Du Bois singled out the color line as "the problem of the twentieth century." Ninety years later, John Hope Franklin, Duke University's James B. Duke Professor Emeritus of History, found the color line was "alive, well, and flourishing in the final decade of the twentieth century." He found "nothing inherently wrong with being aware of color as long as it is seen as making distinctions in a pleasant, superficial, and unimportant manner," but when "a whole galaxy of factors that spell the difference between success and failure in our society are tied to color," we become "two nations, black and white, separate, hostile, unequal."[9]

Since "we cannot escape history," as Abraham Lincoln warned his contemporaries, we would do well to follow the admonition African-American poet Sarah Webster Fabio has given her generation, "We must heal our history." Our history was ill-served in the fall of 1996, when a four-hour documentary film designed for classrooms attended by contemporaries of Colonel Roosevelt's great-grandchildren spent no footage on black faces except for brief coverage of the white hunter's 1910 African safari. Booker T. Washington and W. E. B. Du Bois, along with the black regiments who fought alongside the Rough Riders in the taking of the San Juan Heights, were unmentioned and unseen.[10]

Notes

PREFACE

Unless otherwise noted, material on the writing of *The Brownsville Raid*, on exoneration of the soldiers, and on the last survivors has been taken from letters and interviews conducted at various times and places. Notes, correspondence, documents, and related items are in the John D. Weaver Collection No. 1206, Special Collections, University Research Library, University of California at Los Angeles. Cited as JDW, 1206. The basic document drawn from this material is a 219-page typescript, "The Last Survivor," in Box 273.

For additional material on the exoneration process, see "The Papers of Augustus F. Hawkins, Legislative Files, 93rd Congress" in Special Collections, UCLA Research Library. Archivist Jane H. Odom notes that the files contain "bills; background material; a Senate bill and report; drafts of legislation; correspondence with the Army Department, the media, and John Weaver, the author of the book on the subject; press releases; floor statements; newsclippings; and other materials."

1. JDW, 1206, Box 262. Typewritten letter, dated Thursday, 26 [September, 1968]. See Box 273, "The Last Survivor," 5–7.
2. Joseph Benson Foraker, *Notes of a Busy Life*, 2:327.
3. "The Last Survivor," 137–38.
4. Ibid., 142–43.
5. *California Eagle*, November 2, 9, 1934.
6. Maurine Christopher, *Black Americans in Congress*, 222; John H. Averill, "Silent Fighter For Decent Justice," *Los Angeles Times*, June 13, 1976.
7. *Congressional Record*, 92nd Congress, 1st sess., March 19, 1972.
8. John D. Weaver, *The Brownsville Raid*, 164.

9. "The Last Survivor," 149.

10. Ibid., 149–51.

11. Ibid., 152.

12. Ibid., 157.

13. Ibid., 158–59.

14. Ibid., 161.

15. Ibid., 163.

16. Ibid., 163–65.

17. Ibid., 166.

18. Ibid., 170.

19. Ibid., 171–74.

20. Everett Walters, *Joseph Benson Foraker: An Uncompromising Republican*, ix; Elting E. Morison, ed., *The Letters of Theodore Roosevelt*, 8:1081.

21. Lewis L. Gould, *Southwest Historical Quarterly* 74 (April, 1971): 577–78.

22. Morison, *Letters of Theodore Roosevelt*, 6:1476.

23. Undated clipping. Foraker Papers. Scrapbook, vol. 82.

24. Joseph B. Foraker, *Busy Life*, 2:298; Morison, *Letters of Theodore Roosevelt*, 8:1081.

CHAPTER I

1. J. P. Mayer, ed., *Alexis de Tocqueville, Democracy in America*, 345–46.

2. Joseph Benson Foraker, *Notes of a Busy Life*, 1:1; David A. Gerber, *Black Ohio and the Color Line, 1860–1915*, 3–7; Frank Quillin, "The Color Line in Ohio," (Ph.D. dissertation, Knox College, n.d.), 38–39.

3. Philip S. Foner, *The Voice of Black America*, 101; Joan Hedrick, *Harriet Beecher Stowe: A Life*, 208.

4. Hedrick, *Harriet Beecher Stowe*, 223, 234; Julia Bundy Foraker, *I Would Live It Again*, 54–55.

5. Joseph B. Foraker, *Busy Life*, 1:9.

6. Ibid., 10–11.

7. Julia B. Foraker, *I Would Live*, 12, 16.

8. Joseph B. Foraker, *Busy Life*, 1:17, 20, 27.

9. Julia B. Foraker, *I Would Live*, 12, 14–15, 20–21.

10. Ibid., 23.

11. David Herbert Donald, *Lincoln*, 385; Joseph B. Foraker, *Busy Life*, 1:26, 179.

12. Eric Foner, *Reconstruction: America's Unfinished Revolution, 1863–1877*, 8–9.

13. Theodore Roosevelt, *An Autobiography*, 4; see also David McCullough, *Mornings on Horseback*, 53–54; Edmund Morris, *The Rise of Theodore Roosevelt*, 38–40.

14. Roosevelt, *Autobiography*, 5.

15. Ibid., 5.

16. Morris, *Rise of Theodore Roosevelt*, 38–39.

17. Everett Walters, *Joseph Benson Foraker: An Uncompromising Republican*, 10.

18. Joseph B. Foraker, *Busy Life*, 1:35–36.

19. Ibid., 1:44–45.

20. William Tecumseh Sherman, *Memoirs*, 1:666.

21. Joseph B. Foraker, *Busy Life*, 1:35.

22. John Sherman, *Recollections of Forty Years in the House, Senate and Cabinet: An Autobiography*, 2:859.

23. Joseph B. Foraker, *Busy Life*, 1:64.

24. Ibid., 1:34–35, 179.

25. Julia B. Foraker, *I Would Live*, 53.

26. Joseph B. Foraker, *Busy Life*, 1:87. Foner, *Reconstruction*, 333.

27. Julia B. Foraker, *I Would Live*, 11.

28. Ibid., 58, 56.

29. Theodore Roosevelt, *Diaries of Boyhood and Youth*, 109; Lillian Rixey, *Bamie: Theodore Roosevelt's Remarkable Sister*, 3, 21.

30. Roosevelt, *Diaries*, 103.

31. Sylvia Jukes Morris, *Edith Kermit Roosevelt: Portrait of a First Lady*, 60.

32. Herman Hagedorn, *The Roosevelt Family of Sagamore Hill*, 9.

33. Joseph B. Foraker, *Busy Life*, 1:82–83; Julia B. Foraker, *I Would Live*, 67.

34. Ibid., 68, 65.

35. Ibid., 11, 65.

36. Walters, *Joseph B. Foraker*, 19; Herbert G. Gutman, "The Worker's Search for Power," in H. Wayne Morgan, ed., *The Gilded Age*, 35.

37. Julia B. Foraker, *I Would Live*, 69; Joseph B. Foraker, *Busy Life*, 1:93.

38. Dee Brown, *The Year of the Century: 1876*, 279–80; John D. Bergamini, *The Hundredth Year: The United States in 1876*, 44–48; Louis W. Koenig, *Bryan: A Political Biography of William Jennings Bryan*, 26–27.

39. Thomas J. Schlereth, *Victorian America: Transformations in Everyday Life, 1876–1915*, 5, 67–69; William Safire, *Safire's New Political Dictionary, The Definitive Guide to the New Language of Politics*, 511.

40. Kenneth E. Davidson, *The Presidency of Rutherford B. Hayes*, 42; Wayne Morgan, *From Hayes to McKinley: National Party Politics, 1877–1896*, 25.

41. David Saville Muzzey, *James G. Blaine: A Political Idol of Other Days*, 100.

42. Joseph B. Foraker, *Busy Life*, 1:93; Muzzey, *Blaine*, 101; John W. Blassingame and John R. McKivigan, eds., *The Frederick Douglass Papers, 1864–1880*, 4:441, 442; *New York Times*, June 15, 1876.

43. *New York Times*, June 16, 1876; Hedrick, *Harriet Beecher Stowe*, 359.

44. Muzzey, *Blaine*, 110.

45. Muzzey, *Blaine*, 108; H. Wayne Morgan, *From Hayes to McKinley*, 70–71.

46. McCullough, *Mornings*, 155–59; Theodore Roosevelt, *Letters from Theodore Roosevelt to Anna Roosevelt Cowles, 1870–1918*, 9.

47. Morgan, *From Hayes to McKinley*, 74–75.

48. Edmund Morris, *Rise of Theodore Roosevelt*, 81–82; David Levering Lewis, *W. E. B. Du Bois: Biography of a Race, 1868–1919*, 85.

49. Henry F. Pringle, *The Life and Times of William Howard Taft*, 1:35, 41, 44.

50. T. Harry Williams, ed., *Hayes: The Diary of a President, 1875–1881, Covering the Disputed Election, the End of Reconstruction, and the Beginning of Civil Service*, 44–47; Hoogenboom, *The Hayes Presidency*, 31, 32.
51. Hoogenboom, *Hayes Presidency*, 32–33.
52. Ibid., 34–35.
53. Williams, *Hayes Diary*, 74–75.
54. Foner, *Reconstruction*, 582.
55. Williams, *Hayes Diary*, 96; Hoogenboom, *Hayes Presidency*, 72, 73.
56. Williams, *Hayes Diary*, 86; Morgan, *From Hayes to McKinley*, 35–38; Sherman, *Recollections*, 2:678.
57. Sherman, *Recollections*, 2:680–82.
58. Morgan, *From Hayes to McKinley*, 37; Sherman, *Recollections*, 2:683–84.
59. Williams, *Hayes Diary*, 107.
60. McCullough, *Mornings*, 179–80.
61. Elting E. Morison, ed., *The Letters of Theodore Roosevelt*, 1:35.
62. McCullough, *Mornings*, 226.
63. Rixey, *Bamie*, 31.

CHAPTER 2

1. Joseph Benson Foraker, *Notes of a Busy Life*, 1:87; David McCullough, *Mornings on Horseback*, 232, 235; William Henry Harbaugh, *Power and Responsibility: The Life and Times of Theodore Roosevelt*, 17.
2. McCullough, *Mornings*, 231; Julia Bundy Foraker, *I Would Live It Again*, 228; H. Wayne Morgan, *From Hayes to McKinley: National Party Politics, 1877–1896*, 41.
3. Morgan, *From Hayes to McKinley*, 93–95.
4. Ibid., 100.
5. Justus D. Doenecke, *The Presidencies of Garfield and Arthur*, 29–30.
6. Morgan, *From Hayes to McKinley*, 99; Doenecke, *Garfield and Arthur*, 29–30.
7. *Inaugural Addresses of the Presidents of the United States*, 143–44.
8. H. H. Alexander, *The Life of Guiteau and the Official History of the Most Exciting Case on Record, Being the Trial of Guiteau for Assassinating Pres. Garfield*, 47; T. Burton Smith, "Assassination Medicine," *American Heritage* (September, 1992).
9. Edmund Morris, *The Rise of Theodore Roosevelt*, 146; Harbaugh, *Power and Responsibility*, 18–19; Henry F. Pringle, *Theodore Roosevelt: A Biography* (New York: Harcourt, Brace, 1931), 61.
10. Roosevelt, *Autobiography*, 55; McCullough, *Mornings*, 254–55.
11. McCullough, *Mornings*, 255–57.
12. Richard E. Welch, Jr., *The Presidencies of Grover Cleveland*, 24.
13. McCullough, *Mornings*, 266.
14. Hermann Hagedorn, *Roosevelt in the Badlands*, 45.
15. McCullough, *Mornings*, 283.
16. Stefan Lorant, *The Life and Times of Theodore Roosevelt*, 196.

17. Elting E. Morison, *The Letters of Theodore Roosevelt*, 1:6.

18. Everett Walters, *Joseph Benson Foraker, An Uncompromising Republican*, 22.

19. Julia B. Foraker, *I Would Live*, 79; Walters, *Joseph B. Foraker*, 25.

20. Walters, *Joseph B. Foraker*, 26.

21. Joseph B. Foraker, *Busy Life*, 1:167, 168.

22. John A. Garraty, *Henry Cabot Lodge: A Biography*, 75; Morgan, *From Hayes to McKinley*, 178, 180–81.

23. Joseph B. Foraker *Notes*, 1:158; Garraty, *Lodge*, 77–78.

24. Morris, *Rise of Theodore Roosevelt*, 264; Joseph B. Foraker, *Busy Life*, 1:162, 163; Walters, *Joseph B. Foraker*, 28.

25. Joseph B. Foraker, *Busy Life*, 1:161, 167.

26. Morgan, *From Hayes to McKinley*, 205–206.

27. Morison, *Letters of Theodore Roosevelt*, 1:73n., 77; W. A. Swanberg, *Pulitzer*, 82.

28. W. A. Swanberg, *Citizen Hearst: A Biography of William Randolph Hearst*, 29.

29. Welch, *Presidencies of Grover Cleveland*, 37; Allan Nevins, *Grover Cleveland: A Study in Courage*, 162–68.

30. Morgan, *From Hayes to McKinley*, 214–15.

31. Welch, *Presidencies of Grover Cleveland*, 37–38.

32. Morgan, *From Hayes to McKinley*, 231.

33. Swanberg, *Pulitzer*, 99–100; David Saville Muzzey, *James G. Blaine: A Political Idol of Other Days*, 307–308; Morgan, *From Hayes to McKinley*, 235.

34. Edward L. Ayers, *The Promise of the New South: Life After Reconstruction*, 47–48.

35. R. Hal Williams, "Dry Bones and Dead Language: The Democratic Party," in H. Wayne Morgan, ed., *The Gilded Age*, 133.

36. Ayers, *New South*, 50.

37. *Inaugural Addresses*, 152.

38. Joseph B. Foraker, *Busy Life*, 1:181.

39. Henry Cabot Lodge, ed., *Selections from the Correspondence of Theodore Roosevelt and Henry Cabot Lodge 1884–1918*, 1:15.

40. Joseph B. Foraker, *Busy Life*, 1:197.

41. Ibid., 1:176–80.

42. Walters, *Joseph B. Foraker*, 33, 38.

CHAPTER 3

1. Henry Cabot Lodge, ed., *Selections from the Correspondence of Theodore Roosevelt and Henry Cabot Lodge 1848–1918*, 1:30; Sylvia Jukes Morris, *Edith Kermit Roosevelt: Portrait of a First Lady*, 79.

2. Lodge, *Correspondence* 1:36; S. J. Morris, *Edith Kermit Roosevelt*, 81.

3. Ray Ginger, *The Bending Cross: A Biography of Eugene Victor Debs*, 50–52.

4. Lothrop Stoddard, *Master of Manhattan: The Life of Richard Croker*, 84–86; John Morton Blum, *The Republican Roosevelt*, 13; H. Wayne Morgan, *From Hayes to McKinley: National Party Politics, 1877–1896*, 218; Allan Nevins, ed., *Selected Writings of Abram S. Hewitt*, 386.

5. Lodge, *Correspondence*, 1:47.

6. S. J. Morris, *Edith Kermit Roosevelt*, 89ff.

7. Lillian Rixey, *Bamie: Theodore Roosevelt's Remarkable Sister*, 66.

8. Julia Bundy Foraker, *I Would Live It Again*, 146–48.

9. William Safire, *Safire's New Political Dictionary, The Definitive Guide to the New Language of Politics*, 436; William Safire applies the term to "anyone who bolted his political party" and traces it back to 1663, when it appeared as the Algonquin word *mugquomp*, "used to define a chief or another individual in high rank."

10. Julia B. Foraker, *I Would Live*, 83; Everett Walters, *Joseph Benson Foraker: An Uncompromising Republican*, 36.

11. Walters, *Joseph Benson Foraker*, 41–43.

12. Frank U. Quillin, *The Color Line in Ohio: A History of Race Prejudice in a Typical Northern State*, 96.

13. Unless otherwise indicated, all Dorsie Willis material has been taken from UCLA Research Library's Collection 1206, John D. Weaver Papers. See Box 273, typescript, "The Last Survivor."

14. Edwin C. McReynolds, *Oklahoma: History of the Sooner State*, 289–93, 307.

15. Joseph B. Foraker, *Busy Life*, 1:236; Richard E. Welch, Jr., *The Presidencies of Grover Cleveland*, 64.

16. Allan Nevins, *Grover Cleveland: A Study in Courage*, 333–34.

17. Joseph B. Foraker, *Busy Life*, 1:240–42.

18. Walters, *Joseph B. Foraker*, 56–57.

19. Ibid., 81–82.

20. Zane L. Miller, *Boss Cox's Cincinnati: Urban Politics in the Progressive Era*, 77.

21. David Saville Muzzey, *James G. Blaine: A Political Idol of Other Days*, 361–62.

22. R. Hal Williams, "Dry Bones and Dead Language: The Democratic Party," in *The Gilded Age*, edited by H. Wayne Morgan, 136–37.

23. Morgan, *From Hayes to McKinley*, 281; Walters, *Joseph B. Foraker*, 63.

24. Walters, *Joseph B. Foraker*, 68.

25. Joseph B. Foraker, *Busy Life*, 1:356; Walters, *Joseph B. Foraker*, 69.

26. They were quietly returned by Congress in 1905, when Foraker was a United States senator. Gaines M. Foster, *Ghosts of the Confederacy: Defeat, the Lost Cause, and the Emergence of the New South, 1865 to 1913*, 154.

27. Walters, *Joseph B. Foraker*, 69.

28. Joseph B. Foraker, *Busy Life*, 1:356.

29. Walters, *Joseph B. Foraker*, 63; John Sherman, *Recollections of Forty Years in the House, Senate and Cabinet: An Autobiography*, 2:1027.

30. Joseph B. Foraker, *Busy Life*, 1:362; Morgan, *From Hayes to McKinley*, 288.

31. Walters, *Joseph B. Foraker*, 72–79.

32. Julia B. Foraker, *I Would Live*, 107–108; Joseph B. Foraker, *Busy Life*, 366–72; Walters, *Joseph B. Foraker*, 76–77.

33. Morgan, *From Hayes to McKinley*, 298.

34. Sherman, *Recollections*, 2:1028–29.

35. Joseph B. Foraker, *Busy Life*, 1:368–72.
36. Walters, *Joseph B. Foraker*, 76–77.

CHAPTER 4

1. Homer E. Socolofsky and Allan B. Spetter, *The Presidency of Benjamin Harrison*, 14.
2. Julia B Foraker, *I Would Live It Again*, 134.
3. Foraker, *I Would Live It Again*, 135; H. Wayne Morgan, *From Hayes to McKinley: National Party Politics, 1877–1915*, 2n.; Socolofsky, *Presidency of Benjamin Harrison*, 2; Morgan, *From Hayes to McKinley*, 326,2n.; *Inaugural Addresses of the Presidents of the United States*, 154.
4. *Inaugural Addresses of the Presidents of the United States*, 156.
5. Morgan, *From Hayes to McKinley*, 318; John A. Garraty, *Henry Cabot Lodge: A Biography*, 103.
6. Morgan, *From Hayes to McKinley*, 322–23; Everett Walters, *Joseph Benson Foraker: An Uncompromising Republican*, 84.
7. Garraty, *Lodge*, 147, 100–102.
8. Ibid., 103–104.
9. Edmund Morris, *Rise of Theodore Roosevelt*, 392.
10. Garraty, *Lodge*, 147.
11. William Henry Harbaugh, *Power and Responsibility: The Life and Times of Theodore Roosevelt*, 76.
12. R. Hal Williams, *Years of Decision: American Politics in the 1890s*, 12–13.
13. Dorothy Ganfield Fowler, *John Coit Spooner: Defender of Presidents*, 135; Morgan, *From Hayes to McKinley*, 340–41.
14. Williams, *Years of Decision*, 31.
15. Ibid., 37.
16. Morgan, *From Hayes to McKinley*, 342; William E. Leuchtenburg, "The Old Cowhand From Dixie," *The Atlantic Monthly* (December, 1992), 96; see also Richard E. Welch, Jr., "The Federal Elections Bill of 1890," *The Journal of American History* 52 (December, 1965), 511, 525.
17. Walters, *Joseph B. Foraker*, 88–89; Joseph Benson Foraker, *Notes of a Busy Life*, 1:400.
18. Ibid., 1:414, 419.
19. Julia B. Foraker, *I Would Live*, 144.
20. Henry F. Pringle, *The Life and Times of William Howard Taft*, 1:94; Joseph B. Foraker, *Busy Life*, 1:421, 238.
21. Joseph B. Foraker, *Busy Life*, 1:239.
22. Pringle, *Taft*, 1:106–107, 109.
23. Julia B. Foraker, *I Would Live*, 306.
24. Walters, *Joseph B. Foraker*, 98.
25. John Sherman, *Recollections of Forty Years in the House, Senate and Cabinet: An Autobiography*, 2:1118–19.

26. Walters, *Joseph B. Foraker*, 101–103.

27. Pringle, *Taft*, 1:106–107, 122.

28. Lewis L. Gould, *The Presidency of William McKinley*, 3; Henry L. Stoddard, *As I Knew Them: Presidents and Politics from Grant to Coolidge*, 208; H. Wayne Morgan, "Election of 1892," *A History of American Presidential Elections*, edited by Arthur M. Schlesinger, Jr., 2:1723.

29. Edward L. Ayers, *The Promise of the New South*, 261.

30. Morgan, *From Hayes to McKinley*, 430.

31. Ayers, *New South*, 42.

32. Morgan, *From Hayes to McKinley*, 431–32.

33. Gould, *Presidency of William McKinley*, 28.

34. *Plessy v. Ferguson*, 163 U.S. 537 (1896); John D. Weaver, *Warren: The Man, The Court, The Era*, 20–21.

35. Worthington Chauncey Ford, ed., *Letters of Henry Adams, 1892–1918*, 350; Page Smith, *John Adams*, 2:1050.

36. Morris, *Rise of Theodore Roosevelt*, 455.

37. Elting E. Morison, *The Letters of Theodore Roosevelt*, 1:314; Morris, *Rise of Theodore Roosevelt*, 457.

38. Lillian Rixey, *Bamie: Theodore Roosevelt's Remarkable Sister*, 82.

39. Morris, *Rise of Theodore Roosevelt*, 476.

40. Ibid., 478.

41. W. A. Swanberg, *Pulitzer*, 194.

42. Lincoln Steffens, *Autobiography of Lincoln Steffens*, 258.

43. Walters, *Joseph B. Foraker*, 109; Morgan, *From Hayes to McKinley*, 490.

44. Walters, *Joseph B. Foraker*, 110.

45. Joseph B. Foraker, *Busy Life*, 1:456–57; Walters, *Joseph B. Foraker*, 127.

46. Joseph B. Foraker, *Busy Life*, 1:458; Morgan, *From Hayes to McKinley*, 493.

47. Margaret Leech, *In the Days of McKinley*, 81–82.

48. Bascom N. Timmons, ed., *Charles G. Dawes: A Journal of the McKinley Years, 1893–1913*, 86.

49. Leech, *McKinley*, 82.

50. Murat Halstead, *Illustrious Life of William McKinley, Our Martyred President*, 160.

51. Howard K. Beale, *Theodore Roosevelt and the Rise of American Power*, 57; see also Allan Nevins, *Grover Cleveland: A Study in Courage*, 549, 743.

52. Beale, *American Power*, 57–63; Morison, *Letters of Theodore Roosevelt*, 1:504.

53. Rixey, *Bamie*, 93.

54. Morris, *Rise of Theodore Roosevelt*, 513, 540; Steffens, *Autobiography*, 258–60.

CHAPTER 5

1. Everett Walters, *Joseph Benson Foraker, An Uncompromising Republican*, 132; William Jennings Bryan and Mary Baird Bryan, *The Memoirs of William Jennings Bryan*, 107; Louis W. Koenig, *Bryan: A Political Biography of William Jennings*

Bryan, 178, 197–98; William Jennings Bryan, *The First Battle: A Story of the Campaign of 1896*, 199–206.

2. R. Hal Williams, *Years of Decision: American Politics in the 1890s*, 104.

3. Koenig, *Bryan*, 223, 224.

4. Joseph Benson Foraker, *Notes of a Busy Life*, 1:494.

5. H. Wayne Morgan, *From Hayes to McKinley, National Party Politics, 1877–1896*, 516–17; Lewis L. Gould, *The Presidency of William McKinley*, 10.

6. Morgan, *From Hayes to McKinley*, 518; Edmund Morris, *Rise of Theodore Roosevelt*, 550.

7. *Inaugural Addresses of the Presidents of the United States*, 173, 176, 175; Gould, *Presidency of William McKinley*, 28.

8. March 5, 1897.

9. Walters, *Joseph B. Foraker*, 141–42.

10. Gould, *Presidency of William McKinley*, 8.

11. Walters, *Joseph B. Foraker*, 137.

12. Morris, *Rise of Theodore Roosevelt*, 555.

13. M. R. Werner, *Tammany Hall*, 330; Henry Cabot Lodge, ed., *Selections from the Correspondence of Theodore Roosevelt and Henry Cabot Lodge*, 1:244.

14. Lodge, *Correspondence*, 1:247.

15. Morris, *Rise of Theodore Roosevelt*, 556–57.

16. Lodge, *Correspondence*, 249.

17. Elting E. Morison, ed., *The Letters of Theodore Roosevelt*, 1:588; William Henry Harbaugh, *Power and Responsibility: The Life and Times of Theodore Roosevelt*, 92.

18. Harbaugh, *Power and Responsibility*, 91; Margaret Leech, *In the Days of McKinley*, 157–58.

19. Lodge, *Correspondence*, 1:278.

20. Pringle, *Theodore Roosevelt*, 172.

21. *Congressional Record*, 55th Congress, 1st sess., 1159.

22. *Washington Post*, May 20, 1897.

23. Morison, *Letters of Theodore Roosevelt*, 1:709.

24. Walters, *Joseph B. Foraker*, 147.

25. W. A. Swanberg, *Citizen Hearst: A Biography of William Randolph Hearst*, 132–34.

26. Leech, *McKinley*, 167. Gould, *Presidency of William McKinley*, 74.

27. Harbaugh, *Power and Responsibility*, 96.

28. Ibid., 96, 98.

29. Morison, *Letters of Theodore Roosevelt*, 1:798; Sylvia Jukes Morris, *Edith Kermit Roosevelt: Portrait of a First Lady*, 170–73.

30. Gould, *Presidency of William McKinley*, 80; Bascom N. Timmons, ed., *Charles G. Dawes: A Journal of the McKinley Years, 1893–1913*, 150.

31. Morison, *Letters of Theodore Roosevelt*, 2:803.

32. Timmons, *Charles G. Dawes*, 156.

33. Mary Church Terrell, "A Sketch of Mingo Saunders [sic]," *The Voice* (March, 1907), 128.

34. John H. Nankivell, *History of the Twenty-fifth Regiment United States Infantry 1869–1926*, 38.
35. Ibid., 48–49.
36. Ibid., 54.
37. Ibid., 66.
38. Morris, *Rise of Theodore Roosevelt*, 615.
39. Julia Bundy Foraker, *I Would Live It Again*, 221–22.
40. Morison, *Letters of Theodore Roosevelt*, 2:822; Pringle, *Theodore Roosevelt*, 184.
41. Pringle, *Theodore Roosevelt*, 183.
42. Morison, *Letters of Theodore Roosevelt*, 2:817.
43. Lodge, *Correspondence*, 1:315.

CHAPTER 6

1. Henry F. Pringle, *Theodore Roosevelt: A Biography*, 473.
2. Edmund Morris, *The Rise of Theodore Roosevelt*, 654.
3. Richard Slotkin, *Gunfighter Nation: The Myth of the Frontier in Twentieth-Century America*, 79–80; Morris, *Rise of Theodore Roosevelt*, 629.
4. Frank E. Vandiver, *Black Jack: The Life and Times of John J. Pershing*, 1:171; Marvin Fletcher, *The Black Soldier and Officer in the United States Army*, 34.
5. Samuel P. Lyon Papers, Archives, U.S. Military History Institute, Carlisle Barracks, PA, Box 1, 9 (June, 1898); Edward A. Johnson, *History of Negro Soldiers in the Spanish-American War, and Other Items of Interest*, 37.
6. Johnson, *History of Negro Soldiers*, 39.
7. Theodore Roosevelt, *The Strenuous Life*, of vol. 15 *The Works of Theodore Roosevelt*, 291–92.
8. W. A. Swanberg, *Citizen Hearst: A Biography of William Randolph Hearst*, 154.
9. Johnson, *Negro Soldiers*, 40.
10. Ibid., 40. Lyon, "Cuban Service," 18, 24, 26.
11. Richard Harding Davis, "The Rough Riders' Fight at Guasimas," *Scribner's* (September, 1898), 24:262.
12. Morris, *Rise of Theodore Roosevelt*, 642.
13. *New York Times*, July 27, 1898; Theodore Roosevelt, *The Rough Riders*, vol. 13 of *The Works of Theodore Roosevelt*, 72.
14. Johnson, *Negro Soldier*, 44.
15. Morris, *Rise of Theodore Roosevelt*, 643–44.
16. John H. Nankivell, *History of the Twenty-fifth Regiment United States Infantry, 1869–1926*, 70; Mary Church Terrell, "A Sketch of Mingo Saunders [*sic*]," *The Voice* (March, 1907), 128–31.
17. Roosevelt, *The Rough Riders*, 13:82.
18. Richard Harding Davis, "The Battle of San Juan," *Scribner's* (October, 1898), 24:394.
19. Swanberg, *Hearst*, 154.
20. Henry Cabot Lodge, *The War With Spain*, 119.

21. Ibid., 121. See also Captain Arthur H. Lee, R.A., "The Regulars at El Caney," *Scribner's* (October, 1898), 24:410.

22. Johnson, *Negro Soldiers*, 47–48.

23. Roosevelt, *Rough Riders*, 101, 107; Lodge, *War with Spain*, 126.

24. Roosevelt, *Rough Riders*, 13:95.

25. Finley Peter Dunne, *Mr. Dooley at His Best*, Elmer Ellis, ed., 101–102.

26. Fredson Bowers, ed., *The Works of Stephen Crane: Reports of War*, 9:155.

27. Roosevelt, *Rough Riders*, 13:108–109.

28. Charles H. Wesley, *The Quest for Equality: From Civil War to Civil Rights*, 92–94.

29. Roosevelt, *Rough Riders*, 13:110.

30. Vandiver, *Black Jack*, 1:204–205.

31. *World's Work* (April, 1919), 693.

32. Nankivell, *History of the Twenty-fifth Regiment*, 84.

33. Charles Morris, *The War With Spain*, 258.

34. Nankivell, *History of the Twenty-fifth Regiment*, 84.

35. William Roscoe Thayer, *The Life and Letters of John Hay*, 2:337.

CHAPTER 7

1. Chauncey M. Depew, *My Memories of Eighty Years*, 160–62.

2. Theodore Roosevelt, *An Autobiography*, 271.

3. Elting E. Morison, ed., *The Letters of Theodore Roosevelt*, 2:888.

4. William Henry Harbaugh, *Power and Responsibility: The Life and Times of Theodore Roosevelt*, 129.

5. *New York Times*, June 23, 1899.

6. Morison, *Letters of Theodore Roosevelt*, 2:1023.

7. Richard W. Leopold, *Elihu Root and the Conservative Tradition*, 22; Philip C. Jessup, *Elihu Root*, 1:215.

8. *New York Times*, June 23, 1899.

9. Lewis L. Gould, *The Presidency of William McKinley*, 155.

10. David Levering Lewis, *W. E. B. Du Bois: Biography of a Race, 1868–1919*, 334.

11. Gould, *Presidency of William McKinley*, 157, 159–60.

12. Henry Cabot Lodge, ed., *Selections from the Correspondence of Theodore Roosevelt and Henry Cabot Lodge*, 1:437.

13. Henry F. Pringle, *The Life and Times of William Howard Taft*, 1:159–60.

14. Ibid., 1:161.

15. Joseph Benson Foraker, *Notes of a Busy Life*, 2:87.

16. Pringle, *Taft*, 1:169.

17. Joseph B. Foraker, *Busy Life*, 2:66.

18. Jessup, *Root*, 1:378.

19. *New York Times*, May 28, 1901.

20. John Tipple, "Big Businessmen and a New Economy," in *The Gilded Age*, edited by H. Wayne Morgan, 15.

21. James Bryce, *The American Commonwealth*, 2:720–21.
22. Bernard Schwartz, *A History of the Supreme Court*, 168–70; William F. Swindler, *Court and Constitution in the Twentieth Century: The Old Legality 1899–1932*, 36, 359, 371.
23. Glenn Porter, *The Rise of Big Business, 1860–1910*, 54–57, 71–74.
24. Joseph B. Foraker, *Busy Life*, 2:88.
25. Ibid., 90.
26. Ibid., 91–92.
27. Henry F. Pringle, *Theodore Roosevelt: A Biography*, 220.
28. Kehl, *Boss Rule*, 227.

CHAPTER 8

1. Mark Sullivan, *Our Times: The United States, 1900–1925*, 1:6n.
2. Claude G. Bowers, *Beveridge and the Progressive Era*, 119.
3. Ibid., 124.
4. Richard Slotkin, *Gunfighter Nation, The Myth of the Frontier in Twentieth-Century America*, 106; Theodore Roosevelt, *The Strenuous Life*, vol. 15 of *The Works of Theodore Roosevelt*, 279.
5. Slotkin, *Gunfighter Nation*, 114; *Raleigh (North Carolina) News & Observer*, May 15, 1993.
6. Samuel and Stuart Lyon Papers, 1889–1901, Box 1, U.S. Army Military History Institute, Carlisle Barracks, PA 17013-5003.
7. Lyon court-martial transcript, National Archives, Record Group 153 (No. 68857), 157; see Garna L. Christian, *Black Soldiers in Jim Crow Texas 1899–1917*, 47–68.
8. Typescript, "The Last Survivor." JDW Papers, UCLA Research Library, Collection 1206. Box 273, 18.
9. Ibid., 160.
10. Ibid., 19.
11. Ibid., 20.
12. Margaret Leech, *In the Days of McKinley*, 587.
13. Ibid., 595–96.
14. Roosevelt, *Autobiography*, 349.
15. Leech, *McKinley*, 602.
16. Elting E. Morison, ed., *The Letters of Theodore Roosevelt*, 3:149.
17. Lincoln Steffens, *The Autobiography of Lincoln Steffens*, 503.
18. Corinne Roosevelt Robinson, *My Brother Theodore Roosevelt*, 206–207.
19. Ibid., 9.
20. William Roscoe Thayer, *The Life and Letters of John Hay*, 2:266.
21. Ibid., 2:268.
22. Henry Adams, *The Education of Henry Adams*, 417.

CHAPTER 9

1. Takahiro Sasaki, "Race or Individual Freedom: Public Reactions to the Roosevelt-Washington Dinner at the White House in October, 1901" (M.A. thesis, University of North Carolina at Chapel Hill, 1984), 9, 13; Mark Sullivan, *Our Times: The United States, 1900–1925. Pre-war America*, 3:128–45.

2. Stephen R. Fox, *The Guardian of Boston: William Monroe Trotter*, 15–19; Louis R. Harlan, *Booker T. Washington: The Wizard of Tuskegee, 1901–1915*, 2:3, 1:218.

3. Joseph Benson Foraker, *Notes of a Busy Life*, 2:105–106.

4. Henry Cabot Lodge, ed., *Selections from the Correspondence of Theodore Roosevelt and Henry Cabot Lodge*, 508, 510; Elting E. Morison, ed., *The Letters of Theodore Roosevelt*, 3:181.

5. Julia Bundy Foraker, *I Would Live It Again*, 192, 193.

6. Ibid., 193.

7. Ibid., 192.

8. Morison, *Letters of Theodore Roosevelt*, 3:644.

9. Lewis L. Gould, *The Presidency of Theodore Roosevelt*, 91.

10. Ibid., 98.

11. *New York Times*, December 18, 1903.

12. Joseph B. Foraker, *Busy Life*, 2:189.

13. Ibid., 2:192, 194, 195.

14. Henry F. Pringle, *The Life and Times of William Howard Taft*, 1:217.

15. Ibid., 1:217.

16. Ibid., 1:214.

17. Ibid., 1:219.

18. Ibid., 1:240.

19. Ibid., 1:241.

20. Ibid., 1:244.

21. Ibid., 1:245.

22. Ibid., 1:246.

23. Ibid., 1:247.

24. Morison, *Letters of Theodore Roosevelt*, 2:425–26.

25. Joseph B. Foraker, *Busy Life*, 2:109–10.

26. Gould, *Presidency of Theodore Roosevelt*, 131.

27. Morison, *Letters of Theodore Roosevelt*, 3:479.

28. Herbert Croly, *Marcus Alonzo Hanna: His Life and Work*, 424–25.

29. Everett Walters, *Joseph Benson Foraker: An Uncompromising Republican*, 201.

30. Ibid., 203.

31. Thomas Beer, *Hanna*, 289.

32. Morison, *Letters of Theodore Roosevelt*, 4:713.

33. Henry F. Pringle, *Theodore Roosevelt: A Biography*, 349.

34. Croly, *Hanna*, 453.

35. Morison, *Letters of Theodore Roosevelt*, 4:730.

36. Joseph B. Foraker, *Busy Life*, 2:121.

37. Julia B. Foraker, *I Would Live*, 93.
38. Morison, *Letters of Theodore Roosevelt*, 4:336.
39. *New York Times*, November 9, 1904.
40. Joseph B. Foraker, *Busy Life*, 2:203.
41. Albert Bigelow Paine, ed., *Mark Twain's Letters*, 766–77.
42. William Roscoe Thayer, *The Life and Letters of John Hay*, 363.
43. *New York Times*, February 14, 1905.
44. Gould, *Presidency of Theodore Roosevelt*, 121–22.
45. *Inaugural Addresses from George Washington to John F. Kennedy*, 184; "The Souls of Black Folk" in W. E. B. Du Bois, *Writings*, Nathan Huggins, ed., 372.
46. Philip S. Foner, ed., *W. E. B. Du Bois Speaks: Speeches and Addresses 1890–1910*, 142; David Levering Lewis, *W. E. B. Du Bois: Biography of a Race, 1869–1919*, 312–13.
47. C. Vann Woodward, *Origins of the New South, 1877-1913*, 466.
48. *Louisville Courier-Journal*, October 21, 1905.
49. Woodward, *Origins*, 466.
50. Lewis, *Du Bois Biography*, 316, 321.
51. Foner, *Du Bois Speaks*, 144, 148.

CHAPTER 10

1. William Henry Harbaugh, *Power and Responsibility: The Life and Times of Theodore Roosevelt*, 124; Lewis L. Gould, *The Presidency of Theodore Roosevelt*, 28–29.
2. Ray Stannard Baker, *An American Chronicle*, 31.
3. Theodore Roosevelt, *Presidential Addresses and State Papers* (Homeward Bound edition), 1:714, 716; see John E. Semonche, *Ray Stannard Baker: A Quest for Democracy in Modern America, 1870–1918*, 147–52.
4. Lincoln Steffens, *Autobiography of Lincoln Steffens*, 462.
5. Ibid., 508. Elting E. Morison, ed., *The Letters of Theodore Roosevelt*, 5:341.
6. Ibid., 5:469, 465.
7. W. A. Swanberg, *Citizen Hearst: A Biography of William Randolph Hearst*, 249.
8. David Graham Phillips, *The Treason of the Senate*, ed. George E. Mowry and Judson A. Grenier, 20.[1]
9. Ibid., 59.
10. Chauncey M. Depew, *My Memories of Eighty Years*, 175, 227. Phillips, *Treason*, 67, 73.
11. William Mosley Miller, as told to Frances S. Leighton, *Fishbait: The Memoirs of the Congressional Doorkeeper*, 146.
12. Julia Bundy Foraker, *I Would Live It Again*, 203.
13. Henry F. Pringle, *The Life and Times of William Howard Taft*, 1:313, 314.
14. Morison, *Letters of Theodore Roosevelt*, 5:354.
15. Pringle, *Taft*, 1:317.
16. Joseph Benson Foraker, *Notes of a Busy Life*, 2:374.

17. John Morton Blum, *The Republican Roosevelt*, 74.
18. Everett Walters, *Joseph Benson Foraker: An Uncompromising Republican*, 218–24; see John Blum, "Theodore Roosevelt and the Hepburn Act: Toward an Orderly System of Control," in Morison, *Letters of Theodore Roosevelt*, 6:1565.
19. Walters, *Joseph B. Foraker*, 1, 3, 218; see Joseph B. Foraker, *Busy Life*, 2:226–27, 282.
20. John H. Nankivell, *History of the Twenty-fifth Regiment United States Infantry, 1869–1926*, 119.
21. Weaver, *Brownsville*, 22.
22. Ibid., 23.
23. Ibid., 28.
24. Ibid., 31, 40.
25. JDW, UCLA Collection 1206, Box 273. Typescript. "The Last Survivor," 36.
26. Weaver, *Brownsville*, 62–63.
27. Ibid., 72.
28. August 15, 1906.
29. Morison, *Letters of Theodore Roosevelt*, 5:226.
30. Ibid., 5:227–28, 309–10; see Willard B. Gatewood, Jr., *Theodore Roosevelt and the Art of Controversy*, 62–89.
31. Weaver, *Brownsville*, 76.
32. Ibid., 77
33. Ibid., 262.
34. August 16, 1906.
35. Weaver, *Brownsville*, 101; Morison, *Letters of Theodore Roosevelt*, 5:227.

CHAPTER 11

1. Everett Walters, *Joseph Benson Foraker: An Uncompromising Republican*, 230; Lewis L. Gould, *The Presidency of Theodore Roosevelt*, 251–52; Henry F. Pringle, *The Life and Times of William Howard Taft*, 1:305.
2. Elting E. Morison, *The Letters of Theodore Roosevelt*, 5:430.
3. Ibid., 5:428–29.
4. Pringle, *Taft*, 1:308, 305.
5. Ibid., 1:310; see Gould, *Presidency of Theodore Roosevelt*, 250–53.
6. *Chattanooga Daily Times*, October 16, 18, 1906.
7. Louis R. Harlan, *Booker T. Washington: The Wizard of Tuskegee, 1901–1915*, 2:32, 309.
8. Stephen R. Fox, *The Guardian of Boston: William Monroe Trotter*, 32–33.
9. W. E. B. Du Bois, *Writings*, Nathan Huggins, ed., 1248–49.
10. Ibid., 850–51.
11. Ibid., 842, 855.
12. Ibid., 855.
13. Ibid., 861.

14. Ibid., 1288.

15. Harlan, *Booker T. Washington*, 2:299; David Levering Lewis, *W. E. B. Du Bois: Biography of a Race, 1868–1919*, 333.

16. Darden Asbury Pyron, *Southern Daughter: The Life of Margaret Mitchell*, 31–32.

17. Harlan, *Booker T. Washington*, 2:299–300; Elliott M. Rudwick, *W. E. B. Du Bois: Propagandist of the Negro Protest*, 107.

18. Du Bois, *Du Bois Writings*, 1125.

19. John D. Weaver, *The Brownsville Raid*, 9; Harlan, *Booker T. Washington*, 2:309–10.

20. Harlan, *Booker T. Washington*, 2:295.

21. Weaver, *Brownsville*, 97–98.

22. Emma Lou Thornbrough, "The Brownsville Episode and the Negro Vote," *Mississippi Valley Historical Review* 44 (December, 1957), 471.

23. Weaver, *Brownsville*, 101.

24. *New York Times*, November 7, 8, 1906.

25. Morison, *Letters of Theodore Roosevelt*, 5:491, 495.

26. Joseph Benson Foraker Scrapbook Collection, the Cincinnati Historical Society, vol. 62.

27. *New York Times*, November 9, 1906. "Summary Discharge," 60th Congress, 1st sess., 1907, 155, 185.

28. *New York Times*, November 21, 1906.

29. "Secretary Taft and the Negro Soldiers," *The Independent*, July 23, 1908. See unpublished typescript, "A Colored Woman in a White World," 274–81, Terrell Papers, Library of Congress, Box 26.

30. Taft Papers, Library of Congress, Series 1, Box 113.

31. Morison, *Letters of Theodore Roosevelt*, 5:498.

32. Weaver, *Brownsville*, 107.

33. Pringle, *Taft*, 1:325.

34. *New York Times*, November 22, 1906.

35. *New York Age*, November 29, 1906.

36. JDW Papers, UCLA, Collection 1206, box 273. Unpublished transcript, "The Last Survivor," 72.

37. Julia Bundy Foraker, *I Would Live It Again*, 277.

38. Weaver, *Brownsville*, 110.

CHAPTER 12

1. Everett Walters, *Joseph Benson Foraker, An Uncompromising Republican*, 235; *Congressional Record*, The Proceedings and Debates, 59th Congress, 2nd sess., December 3, 1906, 41:2, 37, 101.

2. Ibid., *Congressional Record*, December 6, 1906, 41:102.

3. Ibid., 41:550.

4. *New York Times*, October 4, 5, 1906.

5. *Congressional Record*, 59th Congress, 2nd sess., December 6, 1906, 41:101–102.

6. Ibid.; *Congressional Record*, December 20, 1906, 41:570, 571.

7. *Congressional Record*, December 19, 1906, 41:551.

8. Francis Butler Simkins, *Pitchfork Ben Tillman, South Carolinian*, 2–6; *Congressional Record*, January 12, 1907, 41:1030, 1033.

9. *Congressional Record*, January 12, 1907, 41:1034.

10. Ibid., 1035.

11. Darwin Payne, *The Man of Only Yesterday: Frederick Lewis Allen*, 17–18.

12. Elting E. Morison, *The Letters of Theodore Roosevelt*, 5:557–58.

13. Payne, *The Man of Only Yesterday*, 15.

14. Morison, *Letters of Theodore Roosevelt*, 5:559–60.

15. Joseph Benson Foraker, *Notes of a Busy Life*, 2:248–49.

16. Henry F. Pringle, *Theodore Roosevelt: A Biography*, 446.

17. Morison, *Letters of Theodore Roosevelt*, 5:520; Joseph Bucklin Bishop, *Theodore Roosevelt and His Time: Shown in His Own Letters*, 1:422–23.

18. Arthur Wallace Dunn, *Gridiron Nights: Humorous and Satirical Views of Politics and Statesmen as Presented by the Famous Dining Club*, 171–72, 174.

19. Ibid., 7; Julia Bundy Foraker, *I Would Live It Again*, 3.

20. Foraker, *Busy Life*, 2:254–55; *Washington Post*, January 29, 1907.

21. Many members of the audience had reached the age at which hearing becomes faulty. Some, including Foraker, quoted the line as, "Now is the time for bloody sarcasm." Dunn, *Gridiron Nights*, 185.

22. Champ Clark, *My Quarter Century of American Politics*, 446; Joseph B. Foraker, *Busy Life*, 2:250.

23. Joseph B. Foraker, *Busy Life*, 2:252.

24. Clark, *Quarter Century*, 447–48.

25. Julia B. Foraker, *I Would Live*, 4.

26. Sheldon M. Novick, *Honorable Justice: The Life of Oliver Wendell Holmes*, 28.

27. John D. Weaver, *The Brownsville Raid*, 145.

28. *Washington Post*, February 5, 1907.

29. C. P. Connolly, "Senator Warren of Wyoming," *Collier's* (August 31, 1912); Frank E. Vandiver, *Black Jack: The Life and Times of John J. Pershing*, 1:389–90.

30. Morison, *Letters of Theodore Roosevelt*, 5:570–71; see Robert Franklin Jones, M.A. thesis, "The Political Career of Francis E. Warren, 1902–1912," (January, 1949), Historical Research and Publications, Department of Commerce, Parks and Cultural Resources Division, Cheyenne, Wyo.; see also Warren Papers, University of Wyoming, Laramie.

31. Courts-Martial, 60th Congress, 1st sess., S. Doc. 402, pt. 2, (1908) (Penrose), 145–65, pt. 3, (1908) (Macklin), 166–68.

32. Weaver, *Brownsville*, 94–96.

33. *Congressional Record* 60th Congress, 2nd sess., December 19, 1906, 41:550.

34. Ibid., *Congressional Record*, March 11, 1908, 43:3132; Weaver, *Brownsville*, 176–79, 181; Joseph B. Foraker, *Busy Life*, 2:290.

35. Weaver, *Brownsville*, 182–83.

36. March 12, 1908.

37. *Congressional Record*, 60th Congress, 2nd sess., 1909, 43:3122, 3147, 4709.

38. Morison, *Letters of Theodore Roosevelt*, 6:96.

39. Weaver, *Brownsville*, 186–89; *Congressional Record*, 60th Congress, 2nd sess., 1909, 43:4709–23.

40. Julia B. Foraker, *I Would Live*, 281, 286, 287.

41. Ibid., 288.

42. Ibid., 292.

43. Ibid., 293.

44. Ibid., 295–96.

CHAPTER 13

1. Elting E. Morison, *The Letters of Theodore Roosevelt*, 5:695, 696, 705.

2. Everett Walters, *Joseph Benson Foraker: An Uncompromising Republican*, 264; Pringle, *Taft*, 1:323.

3. Morison, *Letters of Theodore Roosevelt*, 5:726–27.

4. Ibid., 5:777; Justin Kaplan, *Lincoln Steffens: A Biography*, 136.

5. Joseph Benson Foraker, *Notes of a Busy Life*, 2:389; Francis Russell, *The Shadow of Blooming Grove: Warren G. Harding in His Times*, 188.

6. Joseph B. Foraker, *Busy Life*, 2:393.

7. Morison, *Letters of Theodore Roosevelt*, 6:916; Pringle, *Taft*, 1:358.

8. Pringle, *Taft*, 1:218.

9. Ibid., 1:319–20.

10. Ibid., 1:319. W. A. Swanberg, *Citizen Hearst: A Biography of William Randolph Hearst*, 230, 266.

11. Swanberg, *Citizen Hearst*, 259, 319. See John K. Winkler, *William Randolph Hearst: A New Appraisal*, 157–65.

12. Joseph B. Foraker, *Busy Life*, 2:556, 558.

13. Morison, *Letters of Theodore Roosevelt*, 6:999.

14. *Indianapolis World*, August 15, 1908. Emma Lou Thornbrough, "The Brownsville Episode and the Negro Vote," *Mississippi Valley Historical Review* 44 (December, 1957), 487.

15. Herbert Aptheker, ed., *Writings in Periodicals Edited by W. E. B. Du Bois, Selections from* The Horizon (June, 1908), 59.

16. Ibid. (August, 1908), 66.

17. John A. Garraty, *Henry Cabot Lodge: A Biography*, 259–61. Pringle, *Taft*, 1:353.

18. Joseph B. Foraker, *Busy Life*, 2:394; Pringle, *Taft*, 1:371.

19. Walters, *Joseph B. Foraker*, 269, 271.

20. Ibid., 272; Pringle, *Taft*, 1:371.

21. Louis R. Harlan, *Booker T. Washington: The Wizard of Tuskegee, 1901–1915*, 2:323.

22. Ibid., 2:324.

23. Aptheker, *Du Bois Periodicals*, The Horizon (September, 1908), 69–70.

24. Joseph B. Foraker, *Busy Life*, 2:328–54.
25. Julia Bundy Foraker, *I Would Live It Again*, 299; Allan Nevins, *John D. Rockefeller: The Heroic Age of American Enterprise*, 2:508–11.
26. Walters, *Joseph B. Foraker*, 274; Joseph B. Foraker, *Busy Life*, 2:329–32.
27. Julia B. Foraker, *I Would Live*, 300.
28. Ibid., 301–302; Joseph B. Foraker, *Busy Life*, 2:330.
29. Julia B. Foraker, *I Would Live*, 302.
30. Joseph B. Foraker, *Busy Life*, 2:330–33.
31. Joseph B. Foraker, *Busy Life*, 2:338–39.
32. Walters, *Joseph B. Foraker*, 251–52.
33. David J. Rothman, *Politics and Power: The United States Senate 1869–1901*, 6.
34. Joseph B. Foraker, *Busy Life*, 2:124–25.
35. David Graham Phillips, *The Treason of the Senate*, ed. George E. Mowry and Judson A. Grenier, 24, 160.[2]
36. Julia B. Foraker, *I Would Live*, 310; Joseph B. Foraker, *Busy Life*, 2:395–96.
37. Julia B. Foraker, *I Would Live*, 311.
38. Joseph B. Foraker, *Busy Life*, 2:396.
39. Morison, *Letters of Theodore Roosevelt*, 6:1244–45.
40. Joseph B. Foraker, *Busy Life*, 2:397.
41. Julia B. Foraker, *I Would Live*, 311.
42. Thornbrough, *Brownsville Episode*, 492–93.
43. Pringle, *Taft*, 1:377–78.
44. Aptheker, *Du Bois Periodicals*, The Horizon (November–December, 1908), 78.
45. November 19, 1908.
46. Pringle, *Taft*, 1:378.
47. Ibid., 1:381
48. Harlan, *Booker T. Washington*, 2:339.
49. Morison, *Letters of Theodore Roosevelt*, 6:1375–76.
50. *Congressional Record*, 60th Congress, 2nd sess., Senate, December 14, 1908, 43:184.
51. Lewis L. Gould, *The Presidency of Theodore Roosevelt*, 283; see *Congressional Record*, (January 12, 1909), 795.
52. *Congressional Record*, (December 14, 1908), 185–86.
53. Ibid., (December 16, 1908), 307–308.
54. Walters, *Joseph B. Foraker*, 283–84.
55. Russell, *Blooming Grove*, 192.
56. Walters, *Joseph B. Foraker*, 283.
57. Ibid., 284; *Washington Post*, March 12, 1908.
58. Joseph B. Foraker, *Busy Life*, 2:309.
59. *Congressional Record*, (January 12, 1909), 802.
60. Weaver, *Brownsville*, 220; Joseph B. Foraker, *Busy Life*, 319–20.
61. *Congressional Record*, 60th Congress, 2nd sess., Senate, (February 2, 23, 1909), 1718, 2948.

62. Ibid., House, (February 27, 1909), 3391.

63. Ibid., Senate, 2nd sess., (February 23, 1909), 2947–48; Joseph B. Foraker, *Busy Life*, 2:313–14.

64. Joseph B. Foraker, *Busy Life*, 2:315–16.

65. Ibid., 2:320.

CHAPTER 14

1. Lawrence F. Abbott, ed., *The Letters of Archie Butt: Personal Aide to President Roosevelt*, 42; Mark Sullivan, *Our Times: The United States, 1900–1925. The War Begins*, 4:419–21.

2. Elting E. Morison, *The Letters of Theodore Roosevelt*, 6:1454.

3. Henry F. Pringle, *The Life and Times of William Howard Taft*, 1:390.

4. Louis R. Harlan, *Booker T. Washington: The Wizard of Tuskegee, 1901–1915*, 2:339; see Willard B. Gatewood, Jr., *Theodore Roosevelt and the Art of Controversy*, 90–134.

5. Morison, *Letters of Theodore Roosevelt*, 6:1538; *Washington Post*, March 2, 1909.

6. Harlan, *Booker T. Washington*, 2:337.

7. Mrs. William Howard Taft, *Recollections of Full Years*, 325.

8. Pringle, *Taft*, 1:392.

9. Ibid., 1:387–88.

10. Sullivan, *Our Times*, 4:331–32.

11. Mrs. Taft, *Recollections*, 325–26.

12. Abbott, *Letters of Archie Butt*, 378.

13. *Washington Post*, March 4, 1909.

14. Gifford Pinchot, *Breaking New Ground*, 380–81.

15. Abbott, *Letters of Archie Butt*, 378, 380; Mrs. Taft, *Recollections*, 326–27.

16. Mrs. Taft, *Recollections*, 327–28.

17. *Washington Post*, March 4, 1909.

18. *New York Times*, March 5, 1909.

19. *Washington Post*, March 5, 1909.

20. Mrs. Taft, *Recollections*, 331.

21. Harlan, *Booker T. Washington*, 2:338.

22. *Washington Post*, March 5, 1909.

23. "Brownsville Texas Affair: Presentation of Loving Cup to Hon. Joseph Benson Foraker." Washington: Murray Brothers Press, 1909. A twenty-five-page pamphlet, Cincinnati Historical Society, Foraker Papers, F692.

24. Lawrence F. Abbott, *Taft and Roosevelt: The Intimate Letters of Archie Butt, Military Aide*, 1:9, 14.

25. Ibid., 1:27.

26. Pringle, *Taft*, 1:400–401.

27. Abbott, *Taft and Roosevelt: Butt Letters*, 1:27.

28. Harlan, *Booker T. Washington*, 2:341–42.

29. Pringle, *Taft*, 1:530. John A. Garraty, ed., *Quarrels That Have Shaped the Constitution*, 156; C. Vann Woodward, "The Case of the Louisiana Traveler."

30. Joseph Benson Foraker, *Notes of a Busy Life*, 2:404–405.

31. Herbert Aptheker, ed., *Writings in Periodicals Edited by W. E. B. Du Bois: Selections from* The Crisis (October, 1911), 30.

32. Worthington Chauncey Ford, ed., *Letters of Henry Adams, 1892–1918*, 531, 536.

33. Morison, *Letters of Theodore Roosevelt*, 7:46.

34. Ibid., 7:50–51.

35. M. Nelson McGeary, *Gifford Pinchot: Forester-Politician*, 176–77.

36. Morison, *Letters of Theodore Roosevelt*, 7:73.

37. Pringle, *Taft*, 1:543.

38. Morison, *Letters of Theodore Roosevelt*, 7:89.

39. Howard K. Beale, *Theodore Roosevelt and the Rise of America to World Power*, 167, 169.

40. Abbott, *Letters of Archie Butt*, 1:389–90.

41. Ibid., 1:395–96.

CHAPTER 15

1. Everett Walters, *Joseph Benson Foraker: An Uncompromising Republican*, 288–89; Elting E. Morison, *The Letters of Theodore Roosevelt*, 7:103; Lawrence F. Abbott, *Taft and Roosevelt: The Intimate Letters of Archie Butt, Military Aide*, 2:483.

2. *The Literary Digest* (July 16, 1910), 88.

3. Theodore Roosevelt, *The Case Against the Reactionaries*, of vol. 19 *The Works of Theodore Roosevelt*, 292, 317.

4. Morison, *Letters of Theodore Roosevelt*, 7:122–23.

5. Nan Britton, *The President's Daughter*, 3–7.

6. Ray Stannard Baker, *Woodrow Wilson: Life and Letters, Princeton 1890–1910*, 263; William Henry Harbaugh, *Power and Responsibility: The Life and Times of Theodore Roosevelt*, 391; Henry F. Pringle, *The Life and Times of William Howard Taft*, 2:569; Abbott, *Taft and Roosevelt: Butt Letters*, 2:506.

7. Harbaugh, *Power and Responsibility*, 392.

8. May 10, 1910, 1036.

9. Typescript, "The Last Survivor." JDW, UCLA Collection 1206, Box 273, 61–63.

10. John Lardner, *White Hopes and Other Tigers*, 22.

11. Ibid., 29–30.

12. Ibid., 23–24.

13. Joyce Carol Oates, *On Boxing*, 16; *The Literary Digest* (July 16, 1910), 84–85.

14. Herbert Aptheker, ed., *A Documentary History of the Negro People in the United States, A History of the Negro people from colonial times to 1910, told in their own words*, 3:16–18; *The Literary Digest* (August 13, 1910), 226.

15. William Henry Harbaugh, ed., *The Writings of Theodore Roosevelt*, 315–33.

16. Elting E. Morison, *Turmoil and Tradition: A Study of the Life and Times of Henry L. Stimson*, 113.

17. Aptheker, *Documentary History*, 3:19–21.

18. Morison, *Letters of Theodore Roosevelt*, 7:160.

19. Ibid., 7:167.

20. Joseph Benson Foraker, *Notes of a Busy Life*, 2:434.

21. Pringle, *Taft*, 2:762.

22. Arthur S. Link et al., eds., *The Papers of Woodrow Wilson*, 22:50.

23. Ibid., 19:386.

24. Worthington Chauncey Ford, ed., *Letters of Henry Adams, 1892–1918*, 2:577.

25. Ibid., 2:578.

26. Morison, *Letters of Theodore Roosevelt*, 7:497–98.

27. Ibid., 7:511; Abbott, *Taft and Roosevelt: Butt Letters*, 2:849–51.

28. Lawrence F. Abbott, *The Letters of Archie Butt: Personal Aide to President Roosevelt*, xxvi–xxvii; Geoffrey Marcus, *The Maiden Voyage*, 19–20.

29. Ford, *Letters of Henry Adams*, 594, 595.

30. Pringle, *Taft*, 2:774.

31. Ibid., 2:783.

32. Ibid., 2:781–82.

CHAPTER 16

1. Henry F. Pringle, *The Life and Times of William Howard Taft* (New York: Farrar, Rinehart, 1939), 2:794–95.

2. Lewis L. Gould, *Reform and Regulation: American Politics from Roosevelt to Wilson*, 156, 157; see *The Outlook* (July 27, 1912); Theodore Roosevelt, *The Works of Theodore Roosevelt*, 19:411.

3. Pringle, *Taft*, 2:803; Edmund Morris, *American Heritage*, (June/July, 1981), 8.

4. Oswald Garrison Villard, *Fighting Years: Memoirs of a Liberal Editor*, 219.

5. Arthur S. Link et al., eds., *Woodrow Wilson Papers*, 24:558–59.

6. Louis R. Harlan, *Booker T. Washington: The Wizard of Tuskegee, 1901–1915*, 2:355–56.

7. W. E. B. Du Bois, *Writings*, Nathan Huggins, ed., 724–25.

8. David Levering Lewis, *W. E. B. Du Bois: Biography of a Race, 1868–1919*, 422–23; William Henry Harbaugh, *Power and Responsibility: The Life and Times of Theodore Roosevelt*, 442–43.

9. Harlan, *Booker T. Washington*, 2:355, 323.

10. Elting E. Morison, *The Letters of Theodore Roosevelt*, 7:589–90.

11. Herbert Aptheker, ed., *Writings in Periodicals Edited by W. E. B. Du Bois: Selections from* The Crisis, 1:40, 46.

12. Ibid., 51–52.

13. George E. Mowry, *The Era of Theodore Roosevelt*, 93.

14. Villard, *Fighting Years*, 236–37.

15. Arthur S. Link et al., eds., *The Papers of Woodrow Wilson*, 28:349.

16. Arthur S. Link, *Wilson: The New Freedom*, 245; Villard, *Fighting Years*, 240.

17. Aptheker, *Du Bois*, The Crisis, 1:64–66.

18. Link et al., eds., *Papers of Woodrow Wilson*, 28:256, 265.

19. Aptheker, *Du Bois*, The Crisis, 64–65.

20. Link et al., eds., *Papers of Woodrow Wilson*, 28:163–64.

21. Ibid., 28:256, 265–66.

22. Ibid., 348–50.

23. Villard, *Fighting Years*, 238–40.

24. Link, *New Freedom*, 254. For a sympathetic look at Wilson and negroes, see Link, "Woodrow Wilson: The American as Southerner," *Journal of Southern History* (February, 1970), 17–18.

25. Joseph Benson Foraker, *Notes of a Busy Life*, 2:447–48; Everett Walters, *Joseph Benson Foraker: An Uncompromising Republican*, 291–94.

26. Randolph C. Downes, *The Rise of Warren Gamaliel Harding, 1855–1920*, 196.

27. Francis Russell, *The Shadow of Blooming Grove: Warren G. Harding and His Times*, 244–45; Joseph B. Foraker, *Busy Life*, 2:449, 450; see Downes, *Harding*, 199–200.

28. Walters, *Joseph B. Foraker*, 291–94.

29. Downes, *Harding*, 206.

30. Russell, *Blooming Grove*, 247.

31. Ibid., 248, 251, 252.

32. Joseph B. Foraker, *Busy Life*, 2:451–53.

33. Nan Britton, *The President's Daughter*, 18.

34. Downes, *Harding*, 215.

35. Walters, *Joseph B. Foraker*, 294–95; Joseph B. Foraker, *Busy Life*, 2:555.

36. Harlan, *Booker T. Washington*, 2:432.

37. Link et al., eds., *Papers of Woodrow Wilson*, 32:142 n1.

38. David M. Chalmers, *Hooded Americanism: The History of the Ku Klux Klan*, 27.

39. Link et al., eds., *Papers of Woodrow Wilson*, 32:267n1.

40. Louis R. Harlan and Raymond W. Smock, eds., *The Booker T. Washington Papers*, June 30, 1915, 13:335; Darden Asbury Pyron, *Southern Daughter: The Life of Margaret Mitchell*, 56, 382.

41. Joseph B. Foraker, *Busy Life*, 1:283–89.

42. Ibid., 2:555. *The New Republic* (March 20, 1915), 185.

CHAPTER 17

1. Joseph Benson Foraker, *Notes of a Busy Life*, 2:473.

2. Henry F. Pringle, *The Life and Times of William Howard Taft*, 2:841, 928, 930–31.

3. Elting E. Morison, *The Letters of Theodore Roosevelt*, 8:1127–28, 1131–32.

4. Ibid., 8:1163–64, 1169–70.

5. Ray Stannard Baker, *Woodrow Wilson: Life and Letters*, 6:11, 11n.

6. Randolph C. Downes, *The Rise of Warren Gamaliel Harding, 1865–1920*, 261–65.

7. Morison, *Letters of Theodore Roosevelt*, 8:1192.

8. In the spring of 1915, defending himself in a libel suit brought by New York boss William Barnes, Jr., Roosevelt was asked whether Foraker was a "boss" like George Cox. "Senator Foraker," the Colonel replied, "was a very powerful man; a very powerful man in politics, a man with whom I disagreed most radically. He was one of my most bitter opponents, but he was not the ordinary type of boss at all." *New York Times*, April 24, 1915.

9. Archibald Gracie, a retired U.S. Army colonel, survived the sinking of the *Titanic* but never fully recovered from the shock of bobbing about in a half-submerged raft committed like a funeral wreath to the cold, dark waves of the North Atlantic. He died the following December. A copy of his book, *The Truth about Chickamauga*, on loan to a wealthy fellow-passenger, went down with its borrower. See *New York Times*, December 5, 1912; Geoffrey Marcus, *The Maiden Voyage*, 110, 151; John Updike, "It Was Sad: Our endless impulse to raise the Titanic," *The New Yorker* (Oct. 14, 1996), 94–98.

10. Morison, *Letters of Theodore Roosevelt*, 8:1081.

11. Ibid., 8:1191, 1193.

12. Frank E. Vandiver, *Black Jack: The Life and Times of John J. Pershing*, 2:694.

13. Hermann Hagedorn, *The Roosevelt Family of Sagamore Hill*, 369.

14. Morison, *Letters of Theodore Roosevelt*, 8:1351.

15. *New York Times*, July 18, 1918.

16. Morison, *Letters of Theodore Roosevelt*, 8:1353.

17. Hagedorn, *Roosevelt Family*, 415.

18. Morison, *Letters of Theodore Roosevelt*, 8:1355.

19. Stefan Lorant, *The Life and Times of Theodore Roosevelt*, 614.

20. Herbert Aptheker, *Writings in Periodicals Edited by W. E. B. Du Bois, Selections from* The Crisis, 159.

21. Philip S. Foner, ed., *Du Bois Speaks: Speeches and Addresses, 1890–1919*, 271.

22. Philip S. Foner, *Organized Labor and the Black Worker, 1919–1973*, 17–18, 174.

23. Ibid., 136.

24. Philip S. Foner and Ronald L. Lewis, eds., *The Black Worker: A Documentary History from Colonial Times to the Present*, 5:285–86.

25. Elliott M. Rudwick, *Race Riot at East St. Louis, July 2, 1917*, 26.

26. Ibid., 38–39, 40.

27. Ibid., 44–47.

28. David Levering Lewis, *W. E. B Du Bois: Biography of a Race*, 536–37.

29. Foner and Lewis, *Black Worker*, 5:290.

30. Ibid., 299, 306.

31. Ibid., 300.

32. Rudwick, *Race Riot*, 50; Lewis, *Du Bois*, 537.

33. Foner and Lewis, *Black Worker*, 5:307.

34. *New York Times*, July 7, 1917; Foner and Lewis, *Black Worker*, 5:307–308.

35. Morison, *Letters of Theodore Roosevelt*, 8:1210.

36. Rudnick, *Race Riot*, 231–32.

37. Robert V. Haynes, *A Night of Violence: The Houston Riot of 1917*, 59, 62; Robert V. Haynes, "The Houston Mutiny and Riot of 1917," *Southwestern Historical Quarterly* 76, no. 4 (April, 1973), 418–21.

38. Haynes, "The Houston Mutiny and Riot of 1917," 419; Haynes, *Night*, 52.

39. Haynes, "The Houston Mutiny and Riot of 1917," 421–22; *Night*, 63–64.

40. Haynes, "The Houston Mutiny and Riot of 1917," 424–25.

41. Haynes, *Night*, 84.

42. Ibid., 94–97.

43. Haynes, "The Houston Mutiny and Riot of 1917," 430, 426.

44. Ibid., 435, 69n.; Haynes, *Night*, 167–70.

45. Haynes, *Night*, 208, 305–307.

46. Haynes, *Night*, 196–97.

47. Ibid., 271; Haynes, "The Houston Mutiny and Riot of 1917," 438.

48. John Hope Franklin, *From Slavery to Freedom: A History of Negro Americans*, 340.

49. Herbert Aptheker, ed. *A Documentary History of the Negro People in the United States from the N.A.A.C.P. to the New Deal*, 3:196–97.

50. Article 48 of the 1916 Articles of War makes no provision for appellate court review of a wartime "conviction of murder, rape, mutiny, desertion, or espionage." That would come in 1920. "Mass Punishment of 24th Infantry." Memorandum from Judge Advocate General's office, 27 April 1973, relating to the Houston riot and the Brownsville raid, JDW, UCLA Collection 1206, Box 494.

51. W. E. B. Du Bois, *Writings*, Nathan Huggins, ed., 1180–81.

52. *New York Times*, January 7, 1919.

53. Ibid., January 9, 1919.

54. Downes, *Rise of Harding*, 294, 299.

55. Nan Britton, *The President's Daughter*, 69, 73–74.

56. William Pickens, "The Woman Voter Hits the Color Line" (October 6, 1920), reprinted in Aptheker, *Documentary History*, 3:305–306, 308.

57. Francis Russell, *The Shadow of Blooming Grove: Warren G. Harding in His Times*, 412–13.

58. Du Bois, *Writings*, 1183–84.

59. Pringle, *Taft* (1964), 2:956, 957, 960.

60. Julia Bundy Foraker, *I Would Live It Again*, 329, 332.

61. Ibid., 316–17, 318.

62. Ibid., 318, 334–35.

AFTERWORD

I have drawn on notes, letters, clippings, government documents, and transcripts of taped conversations, all of which are to be deposited with Special Collections, University Research Library, University of California at Los Angeles as "John D. Weaver Papers, Collection 1206."

1. "The Last Survivor," a 220-page typescript, JDW, UCLA 1206, Box 273, 80–81.
2. Ibid., 174–75.
3. January 27, 1971, JDW, UCLA 1206, Box 275.
4. Ibid., February 4, 1971.
5. JDW, "Last Survivor," 177.
6. Ibid., 178.
7. Court of Inquiry, S. Doc. 701, 61st Congress, 3rd sess., 1911, 1012–25.
8. Ibid., 183. One of the first letters I received when *The Brownsville Raid* appeared in the fall of 1970 came from Dudley T. Cornish, who presided over the history department at Kansas State College of Pittsburg. A white student whose grandparents lived in Brownsville had "once overheard her grandfather and some of his cronies chuckling on the porch over 'the night we blacked our faces, put on uniforms and raised hell.'"
9. UCLA 1206, Box 266.
10. Ibid., Box 271,
11. Ibid., Box 266.
12. Ibid., Box 273.
13. 16 October 1973, Box 270.
14. *Hearing Before the Subcommittee on Compensation and Pensions of the Committee on Veterans Affairs, United States Senate*, 93rd Congress, 1st sess., June 18, 1973, 1012–25.
15. JDW, "Last Survivor," 204.
16. Ibid., 205.
17. Ibid., 205–206.
18. Ibid., 207.
19. UCLA 1206, Box 270.
20. JDW, "Last Survivor," 210–11.
21. Ibid., 211–12.
22. Ibid., 215.
23. Ibid., 216–17.
24. Ibid., 217.
25. Ibid., 218.
26. Ibid., 220.
27. JDW, "Last Survivor," 218.

APPENDIX

1. Joseph Bucklin Bishop, *Theodore Roosevelt and His Time: Shown in His Own Letters*, 2:27–28; Carter G. Woodson, *Journal of Negro History* 12 (April, 1927), 10; Mark Sullivan, *Our Times: The United States, 1900–1925. Pre-War America*,

3:453–54; Henry F. Pringle, *Theodore Roosevelt: A Biography*, 458–64; *Life and Times of William Howard Taft* (1939, 1964), 2:326. In his Roosevelt biography Pringle failed to cite his reference to the black battalion's "six Medal of Honor" soldiers (p. 460), who still keep popping up in print despite the corrective efforts of Edward F. Murphy, president of the Medal of Honor Historical Society. Letter from Murphy, June 25, 1994. JDW, 1206, Box 264.

2. Walter White, *A Man Called White*, 102–103.
3. James Aubrey Tinsley, "The Brownsville Affray," (402747), 137, Davis Library, University of North Carolina, Chapel Hill, 1948; August Meier and Elliott Rudwick, *Black History and the Historical Profession, 1915–1980*, 112.
4. C. Vann Woodward, *Origins of the New South, 1877-1913*, 9:509.
5. Richard Kluger, *Simple Justice: The History of Brown v. Board of Education and Black America's Struggle for Equality*, 2:806.
6. Ann J. Lane, *The Brownsville Affair: National Crisis and Black Reaction*, 1.
7. William McFeely, *Frederick Douglass* (1991); Louis R. Harlan, *Booker T. Washington: The Wizard of Tuskegee, 1901–1905* (1983); David Levering Lewis, *W. E. B. DuBois: Biography of a Race, 1868–1919* (1993); Edward L. Ayers, *The Promise of the New South: Life After Reconstruction* (1992); Mary Frances Berry and John W. Blassingame, *Long Memory: The Black Experience in America* (1982); August Meier, *Negro Thought in America, 1880–1915* (1963).
8. September 14, 1993. JDW, 1206, Box 391.
9. W. E. B. Du Bois, *The Souls of Black Folks* in *Writings* (Library of America, 1986), 372.
10. Benjamin Quarles, *The Negro in the Making of America*, 9–10; Robert Brent Toplin, "Plugged to the Past: TV has become a kind of classroom for the study of history," and William Grimes, "Following the Flow of America's Narration," *New York Times* (August 4, 1996), "Arts & Leisure."

Bibliography

Abbott, Lawrence F. *Impressions of Theodore Roosevelt*. Garden City, N.Y.: Doubleday, Page, 1920.

———. *Taft and Roosevelt: The Intimate Letters of Archie Butt, Military Aide*. Garden City, N.Y.: Doubleday, Doran, 1930.

———, ed. *The Letters of Archie Butt: Personal Aide to President Roosevelt*. Garden City, N.Y.: Doubleday, Page, 1924.

Adams, Henry. *The Education of Henry Adams*. New York: Modern Library, 1931.

———, ed. *Letters of Henry Adams, Contemplating the story of his life as told by himself, 1892–1918*. Edited by Worthington Chauncey Ford. 2 vols. Boston: Houghton Mifflin, 1930, 1938.

Alexander, H. H. *The Life of Guiteau and the Official History of the Most Exciting Case on Record, Being the Trial of Guiteau for Assassinating Pres. Garfield*. Cincinnati, Ohio: Forshee & McMakin, 1882.

Aptheker, Herbert, ed. *A Documentary History of the Negro People in the United States, A History of the Negro people, from colonial times to 1910, told in their own words*. Preface by W. E. B. Du Bois. New York: Citadel Press, 1951.

———, ed. *A Documentary History of the Negro People in the United States From the N.A.A.C.P. to the New Deal*. Preface by Charles H. Wesley. Vol. 3. New York: Citadel Press, Carol Publishing Group, 1973, 1900.

Ayers, Edward L. *The Promise of the New South: Life After Reconstruction*. New York: Oxford University Press, 1992.

Baker, Ray Stannard. [David Grayson]. *American Chronicle*. New York: Charles Scribner's Sons, 1945.

———. *Woodrow Wilson: Life and Letters, Princeton 1890–1910.* Garden City, N.Y.: Doubleday, Page & Co., 1927.

———, with William E. Dodd. *The Public Papers of Woodrow Wilson.* 5 vols. New York: Harper & Brothers, 1925–27.

Beale, Howard K. *Theodore Roosevelt and the Rise of American Power.* Baltimore, Md.: Johns Hopkins University Press, 1956.

Beer, Thomas. *Hanna.* New York: Alfred A. Knopf, 1929.

———. *Stephen Crane.* New York: Alfred A. Knopf, 1923.

Bergamini, John D. *The Hundredth Year, The United States in 1876.* New York: G. P. Putnam's Sons, 1976.

Berry, Mary Frances and John W. Blassingame. *Long Memory, The Black Experience in America.* New York: Oxford University Press, 1982.

Bishop, John Bucklin. *Theodore Roosevelt and His Time Shown in His Own Letters.* 2 vols. New York: Charles Scribner's Sons, 1920.

———. *Theodore Roosevelt's Letters to His Children.* New York: Charles Scribner's Sons, 1923.

Blassingame, John W. and John R. McKivigan, eds. *The Frederick Douglass Papers, 1864–1880.* 5 vols. New Haven, Conn.: Yale University Press, 1991–93.

Blum, John Morton. *The Republican Roosevelt.* College edition, with a new preface by the author. New York: Atheneum, 1972.

———. "Theodore Roosevelt and the Hepburn Act: Toward an Orderly System of Control." Appendix II in Morrison, *The Letters of Theodore Roosevelt.* 6:1558–71.

Boorstin, Daniel J., ed. *An American Primer.* Chicago: University of Chicago Press, 1966.

Bowers, Claude G. *Beveridge and the Progressive Era.* Cambridge, Mass.: The Riverside Press, 1932.

———. *The Tragic Era, The Revolution After Lincoln.* Cambridge, Mass.: The Riverside Press, 1929.

Bowers, Fredson, ed. *The Works of Stephen Crane.* 10 vols. Charlottesville: University of Virginia Press, 1969–75.

Britton, Nan. *The President's Daughter.* New York: Elizabeth Ann Guild, 1927.

Brown, Dee. *The Year of the Century: 1876.* New York: Charles Scribner's Sons, 1966.

Bryan, William Jennings. *The First Battle: A Story of the Campaign of 1896, Together with a collection of his speeches and a biographical sketch by his wife.* Chicago: W. B. Conkey, 1896.

———, and Mary Baird Bryan. *The Memoirs of William Jennings Bryan.* Privately printed, 1925.

Bryce, James. *The American Commonwealth.* Chicago: Charles H. Sergel, 1891.

Burton, Theodore E. *John Sherman.* Boston: Houghton Mifflin, 1906.

Chalmers, David Mark. *Hooded Americanism: The First Century of the Ku Klux Klan, 1865–1965.* Garden City, N.Y.: Doubleday, 1965.

———. *The Social and Political Ideas of the Muckrakers.* New York: The Citadel Press, 1964.

Chessman, G. Wallace. *Theodore Roosevelt and the Politics of Power.* Edited by Oscar Handlin. Boston: Little, Brown, 1969.

Christian, Garna L. *Black Soldiers in Jim Crow Texas 1899–1917.* College Station: Texas A&M University Press, 1995.

Christopher, Maurine. *Black Americans in Congress.* Cincinnati, Ohio: WPA Guide. Reprinted by Cincinnati Historical Society, 1987.

Cincinnati 1788–1943. The WPA Guide to Cincinnati. New introduction by Zane L. Miller. New Preface by Harry Graff. 1943. Reprint. Cincinnati, Ohio: Cincinnati Historical Society, 1987.

Clark, Champ. *My Quarter of a Century of American Politics.* New York: Harper & Bros., 1920.

Cook, Raymond A. *Thomas Dixon.* Boston: Twayne, 1974.

Croly, Herbert. *Marcus Alonzo Hanna: His Life and Work.* New York: Macmillan, 1912.

Crouch, Tom. *The Bishop's Boys: A Life of Wilbur and Orville Wright.* New York: W. W. Norton, 1989.

Curtis, Francis. *The Republican Party, 1854–1904.* New York: G. P. Putnam's Sons, 1904.

Daniels, Josephus. *The Cabinet Diaries of Josephus Daniels.* Lincoln: University of Nebraska Press, 1963.

Davidson, Kenneth E. *The Presidency of Rutherford B. Hayes.* Westport, Conn.: Greenwood Press, 1972.

Davis, Richard Harding. "The Battle of San Juan." *Scribner's Magazine* (October, 1898), 24:387–403.

———. "The Rough Riders' Fight at Guasimas." *Scribner's Magazine* (September, 1898), 24:262–82.

Dawes, Charles G. *A Journal of the McKinley Years, 1893–1913.* Edited by Bascom N. Timmons. Chicago: Lakeside Press, R. R. Donnelley & Sons, 1950.

Depew, Chauncey M. *My Memories of Eighty Years.* New York: Charles Scribner's Sons, 1922.

Doenecke, Justus D. *The Presidencies of Garfield and Arthur.* Lawrence: Regents Press of Kansas, 1981.

Donald, David Herbert. *Lincoln.* London: Jonathan Cape (N.Y.: Simon & Schuster), 1995.

Downes, Randolph C. *The Rise of Warren Gamaliel Harding 1855–1920.* Columbus: Ohio State University Press, 1970.

Du Bois, W. E. B. *Black Reconstruction in America 1860–1880.* Introduction by David Levering Lewis. New York: Atheneum, 1992.

———. *Correspondence. (1877–1934).* 2 vols. Edited by Herbert Aptheker. Boston: University of Massachusetts Press, 1973.

———. *The Souls of Black Folk.* Millwood, N.Y.: Kraus-Thomson Organization Ltd., 1973.

———. *Writings.* Edited by Nathan Huggins. New York: Library of America, 1986.

———. *Writings in Periodicals edited by Du Bois. Selections from* The Crisis. Edited by Herbert Aptheker. 2 vols. Millwood, N.Y.: Kraus-Thomson Organization, 1983.

———. *Writings in Periodicals edited by Du Bois. Selections from* The Horizon. Edited by Herbert Aptheker. Millwood, N.Y.: Kraus-Thomson Organization, 1985.

Duffy, Howard S. *William Howard Taft.* New York: Minton, Balch, 1930.

Dunbar, Paul Laurence. *The Collected Poetry of Paul Laurence Dunbar.* Edited by Joanne Braxton. Charlottesville and London: University Press of Virginia, 1993.

———. *The Paul Laurence Dunbar Reader.* Edited by Jay Martin and Gossie H. Hudson. New York: Dodd, Mead, 1975.

Dunn, Arthur Wallace. *Gridiron Nights, Humorous and Satirical Views of Politics and Statesmen As Presented By The Famous Dining Club.* New York: Frederick A. Stokes, 1915.

Dunne, Finley Peter. *Mr. Dooley in the Hearts of His Countrymen.* Boston: Small, Maynard, 1899.

———. *Mr. Dooley at His Best.* Edited by Elmer Ellis. Foreword by Franklin P. Adams. New York: Charles Scribner's Sons, 1938.

———. *Mr. Dooley in Peace and War.* Boston: Small, Maynard, 1898.

Felsenthal, Carol. *Alice Roosevelt Longworth.* New York: G. P. Putnam's Sons, 1988.

Fletcher, Marvin. *The Black Soldier and Officer in the United States Army.* Columbia: University of Missouri Press, 1974.

Foner, Eric. *Reconstruction: America's Unfinished Revolution, 1863–1877.* New York: Harper & Row, 1988.

Foner, Philip S. *Organized Labor and the Black Worker 1619–1973.* New York: Praeger, 1974.

———. *The Voice of Black America.* New York: Simon & Schuster, 1972.

———, ed. *W. E. B. Du Bois Speaks.* Tribute by Martin Luther King, Jr. New York: Pathfinder, 1970.

———, Ronald L. Lewis, eds. *The Black Worker: A Documentary History from Colonial Times to the Present.* Vol. 5. *The Black Worker from 1900 to 1919.* Philadelphia: Temple University Press, 1980.

Foraker, Joseph Benson. *Notes of a Busy Life.* 2 vols. Cincinnati, Ohio: Stewart and Kidd, 1916.

Foraker, Julia Bundy. *I Would Live It Again.* 1932. Reprint. New York: Arno Press, 1975.

Foster, Gaines M. *Ghosts of the Confederacy: Defeat, the Lost Cause, and the Emergence of the New South, 1865 to 1913.* New York: Oxford University Press, 1987.

Fowler, Dorothy Ganfield. *John Coit Spooner: Defender of Presidents.* New York: University Publishers, 1961.

Fox, Stephen R. *The Guardian of Boston: William Monroe Trotter.* New York: Atheneum, 1970.

Franklin, John Hope. *The Color Line: Legacy for the Twenty-first Century.* Columbia: University of Missouri Press, 1993.

————. *From Slavery to Freedom: A History of Negro Americans.* New York: Alfred A. Knopf, 1974.

Freund, Paul A. et al, eds., *Constitutional Law, Cases and Other Problems.* Boston: Little, Brown, 1961.

Garraty, John A. *Henry Cabot Lodge: A Biography.* New York: Alfred A.Knopf, 1953.

————, ed. *Quarrels That Have Shaped the Constitution.* New York: Harper & Row, 1964.

Gatewood, Willard B., Jr. *"Smoked Yankees" and the Struggle for Empire.* Urbana: University of Illinois Press, 1971.

————. *Theodore Roosevelt and the Art of Controversy.* Baton Rouge: Louisiana State University Press, 1970.

Gerber, David A. *Black Ohio and the Color Line 1860–1915.* Urbana: University of Illinois Press, 1971.

Ginger, Ray. *The Bending Cross: A Biography of Eugene Victor Debs.* Kirksville, Mo.: Thomas Jefferson University Press, 1992.

Gould, Lewis L. *The Presidency of Theodore Roosevelt.* Lawrence: University Press of Kansas, 1991.

————. *The Presidency of William McKinley.* Lawrence: University Press of Kansas, 1980.

————. *Reform and Regulation, American Politics from Roosevelt to Wilson.* 3rd ed. Prospect Heights, Ill.: Waveland Press, 1996.

————. *Wyoming: A Political History, 1869–1896.* New Haven, Conn.: Yale University Press, 1968.

————, ed., with Craig H. Roell. *William McKinley: A Bibliography.* Westport, Conn.: Meckler, 1988.

Gutman, Herbert G. "The Worker's Search for Power," in *The Gilded Age.* Edited by H. Wayne Morgan, 35. Syracuse: Syracuse University Press, 1971.

Hagedorn, Hermann. *Roosevelt in the Badlands.* Boston, Mass.: Houghton Mifflin, 1921.

————. *The Roosevelt Family of Sagamore Hill.* New York: Macmillan, 1954.

Halstead, Murat, ed. *The Illustrious Life of William McKinley Our Martyred President.* Privately printed, 1901.

Harbaugh, William Henry. *Power and Responsibility: The Life and Times of Theodore Roosevelt.* New York: Farrar, Straus and Cudahy, 1961.

————, ed. *The Writings of Theodore Roosevelt.* Indianapolis: Bobbs-Merrill, 1967.

Harlan, Louis R. *Booker T. Washington: The Wizard of Tuskegee, 1901–1915.* Vol. 2. New York: Oxford University Press, 1983.

———— et al., eds., *The Booker T. Washington Papers.* 14 vols. Urbana: University of Illinois Press. 1972–89.

Haynes, Robert V. *A Night of Violence: The Houston Riot of 1917.* Baton Rouge: Louisiana State University Press, 1976.

————. "The Houston Riot of 1917." *Southwestern Historical Quarterly* 75 (April, 1973): 418–39.

Hedrick, Joan D. *Harriet Beecher Stowe: A Life*. New York: Oxford University Press, 1994.

Hine, Darlene Clark, ed. *The State of Afro-American History, Past Present, and Future*. Introduction by Thomas C. Holt. Baton Rouge: Louisiana State University Press, 1986.

Hoogenboom, Ari. *The Hayes Presidency*, Lawrence: University Press of Kansas, 1988.

Hoover, Irwin Hood (Ike). *Forty-two Years in the White House*. Boston: Houghton Mifflin, 1934.

Inaugural Addresses of the Presidents of the United States from *George Washington to John F. Kennedy*. Washington, D.C.: U.S. Government Printing Office, 1961.

Jessup, Philip C. *Elihu Root*. 2 vols. New York: Dodd, Mead & Co., 1938.

Johnson. Edward A. *History of Negro Soldiers in the Spanish-American War, and Other Items of Interest*. Raleigh, N.C.: Capital Printing Co., 1899.

Jones, Robert Franklin. "The Political Career of Francis E. Warren, 1902–1912." M.A. thesis, Historical Research and Publications, Department of Commerce, Cheyenne, Wyo., January, 1949.

Jordan, David M. *Roscoe Conkling of New York*. Ithaca, N.Y.: Cornell University Press, 1971.

Kaplan, Justin. *Lincoln Steffens: A Biography*. New York: Simon and Schuster, 1974.

Kehl, James A. *Boss Rule in the Gilded Age: Matt Quay of Pennsylvania*. Pittsburgh: University of Pittsburgh Press, 1981.

Kennan, George. *Campaigning in Cuba*. New York: Century, 1899.

Kerr, Joan Paterson. *A Bully Pulpit: Theodore Roosevelt's Letters to his Children*. Foreword by David McCullough. New York: Random House, 1995.

Kluger, Richard. *Simple Justice: The history of Brown v. Board of Education, the epochal Supreme Court decision that outlawed segregation, and of black America's century-long struggle for equality under law*. 2 vols. New York: Alfred A. Knopf, 1975.

Koenig, Louis W. *Bryan: A Political Biography of William Jennings Bryan*. New York: G. P. Putnam's Sons, 1971.

Kohlsaat, H. H. *From McKinley to Harding, Personal Recollections of Our Presidents*. New York: Charles Scribner's Sons, 1923.

Lane, Ann. J. *The Brownsville Affair: National Crisis and Black Reaction*. Port Washington, N.Y.: National University Publications, Kennikat Press, 1971.

Lardner, John. *White Hopes and Other Tigers*. Philadelphia: Lippincott, 1951.

Lee, Capt. Arthur H. "The Regulars at El Caney." *Scribner's Magazine* (October, 1898), 24:403–13.

Leech, Margaret. *In the Days of McKinley*. New York: Harper & Bros., 1959.

Leopold, W. Leonard. *Elihu Root and the Conservative Tradition*. Boston: Little, Brown, 1954.

Lewis, David Levering. *W. E. B. Du Bois: Biography of a Race, 1868–1919*. New York: Henry Holt & Co., 1993.

Link, Arthur S. *Wilson: The New Freedom*. Vol. 2. Princeton, N.J.: Princeton University Press, 1956.

————. "Woodrow Wilson: the American as Southerner." *The Journal of Southern History* (February, 1970), 36:3–17.

———— et al., eds. *The Papers of Woodrow Wilson.* 69 vols. Princeton, N.J.: Princeton University Press, 1966–93.

Lodge, Henry Cabot. *Selections from the Correspondence of Theodore Roosevelt and Henry Cabot Lodge 1884–1918.* 2 vols. New York: Charles Scribner's Sons, 1925.

Logan, Rayford Whittington. *The Betrayal of the Negro, from Rutherford B. Hayes to Woodrow Wilson.* New York: Collier Books, 1965.

Longworth, Alice Roosevelt. *Crowded Hours.* New York: Charles Scribner's Sons, 1933.

Lorant, Stefan. *The Life and Times of Theodore Roosevelt.* Garden City, N.Y.: Doubleday, 1959.

McCullough, David. *Mornings on Horseback.* New York: Simon & Schuster, 1981.

McFeely, William S. *Grant: A Biography.* New York: W. W. Norton, 1981.

McGreary, M. Nelson. *Gifford Pinchot: Forester-Politician.* Princeton, N.J.: Princeton University Press, 1960.

McReynolds, Edwin C. *Oklahoma: History of the Sooner State.* Norman: Oklahoma University Press, 1962.

Marcus, Geoffrey. *The Maiden Voyage.* New York: Viking Press, 1969.

Mark Twain's Letters Arranged with comment. Edited by Albert Bigelow Paine. New York: Harper & Brothers, 1917.

Martin, Albro. *Railroads Triumphant.* New York: Oxford University Press, 1992.

Mayer, J. P., ed. *The Recollections of Alexis de Tocqueville.* Translated by Alexander Teixeira de Mattos. New York: Meridian Books, 1959.

Meier, August. *Negro Thought in America, 1800–1915; Racial Ideologies in the Age of Booker T. Washington.* Ann Arbor: University of Michigan Press, Ann Arbor Paperbacks, 1966.

————, Elliot Rudwick. *Black History and the Historical Profession, 1915–1980.* Urbana: University of Illinois Press, 1986.

Miller, ("Fishbait"), William Mosley. *Fishbait: The Memoirs of the Congressional Door-keeper,* as told to Frances Spatz Leighton. New York: Warner Communications, by arrangement with Prentice-Hall, 1978.

Miller, Zane L. *Boss Cox's Cincinnati: Urban Politics in the Progressive Era.* New York: Oxford University Press, 1968.

Minger, Ralph Eldin. *William Howard Taft, The Apprenticeship Years, 1900–1908.* Urbana: University of Illinois Press, 1975.

Morgan, H. Wayne. *From Hayes to McKinley: National Party Politics, 1877–1896.* Syracuse: Syracuse University Press, 1969.

————, ed. *The Gilded Age.* Syracuse: Syracuse University Press, 1971.

Morison, Elting E, ed., with John Blum et al. *The Letters of Theodore Roosevelt.* 8 vols. Cambridge, Mass.: Harvard University Press, 1951–54.

————. *Turmoil and Tradition, A Study in the Life and Times of Henry L. Stimson.* New York: Atheneum, 1964.

Morris, Charles. *The War with Spain.* Philadelphia: Lippincott, 1889.

Morris, Edmund. *The Rise of Theodore Roosevelt.* New York: Coward, McCann & Geoghegan, 1979.

———. "Theodore Roosevelt, President." *American Heritage* (June/July, 1981), 4:15.

Morris, Sylvia Jukes. *Edith Kermit Roosevelt: Portrait of a First Lady.* New York: Coward, McCann & Geoghegan, 1980.

Mowry, George E. *The Era of Theodore Roosevelt 1900–1912.* New York: Harper & Brothers, 1958.

Muzzey, David Saville. *James G. Blaine: A Political Idol of Other Days.* 1934. Reprint. Port Washington, N.Y.: Kennikat Press, 1963.

Myrdal, Gunnar, with the assistance of Richard Sterner and Arnold Rose. *An American Dilemma: The Negro Problem and Modern Democracy.* 2 vols. New York: Harper & Brothers, 1944.

Nankivell, John H. *History of the Twenty-fifth Regiment, United States Infantry, 1869–1926.* 1927. Reprint. New York: Negro Universities Press, 1969.

Nevins, Allan. *Grover Cleveland: A Study in Courage.* New York: Dodd, Mead, 1934.

———. *John D. Rockefeller: The Heroic Age of American Enterprise.* 2 vols. New York: Charles Scribner's Sons, 1940.

———, ed. *Selected Writings of Abram S. Hewitt.* Introduction by Nicholas Murray Butler. Morningside Heights, N.Y.: Columbia University Press, 1937.

Novick, Sheldon M. *Honorable Justice, The Life of Oliver Wendell Holmes.* New York: Dell Publishing, 1990.

Oates, Joyce Carol. *On Boxing.* Garden City, N.Y.: Dolphin/Doubleday. 1987.

Paine, Albert Bigelow, ed. *Mark Twain's Letters.* New York: Harper & Brothers, 1917.

Payne, Darwin. *The Man of Only Yesterday: Frederick Lewis Allen.* New York: Harper & Row, 1975.

Phillips, David Graham. *The Treason of the Senate.* Edited with an introduction by George E. Mowry and Judson A. Grenier. Chicago: Quadrangle Books, 1964.

Pinchot, Gifford. *Breaking New Ground.* New York: Harcourt, Brace, 1947.

Porter, Glenn. *The Rise of Big Business, 1860–1910.* New York: Thomas Y. Crowell Company, 1973.

Pringle, Henry F. *The Life and Times of William Howard Taft.* 1939. Reprint. 2 vols. Hamden, Conn.: Archon Books, 1964.

———. *Theodore Roosevelt.* New York: Harcourt, Brace, 1931.

Pyron, Darden Asbury. *Southern Daughter: The Life of Margaret Mitchell.* New York: Oxford University Press, 1991.

Quarles, Benjamin. *The Negro in the Making of America.* New York: Collier Books, Macmillan, 1987.

Quillin, Frank. *The Color Line in Ohio: A History of Prejudice in a Typical Northern State.* 1913. Reprint. New York: Negro Universities Press, 1969.

Riis, Jacob A. *Theodore Roosevelt The Citizen.* New York: The Outlook Co., 1903.

Rixey, Lillian. *Bamie: Theodore Roosevelt's Remarkable Sister.* New York: David McKay, 1963.

Robinson, Corinne Roosevelt. *My Brother Theodore Roosevelt*. New York: Charles Scribner's Sons, 1921.

Roosevelt, Theodore. *An Autobiography*. New York: Charles Scribner's Sons, 1913.

———. *Diaries of Boyhood and Youth*. New York: Charles Scribner's Sons, 1928.

———. *Letters from Theodore Roosevelt to Anna Roosevelt Cowles 1870–1918*. New York: Charles Scribner's Sons, 1924.

———. *The Works of Theodore Roosevelt*. 19 vols. Homeward Bound Edition. New York: Review of Reviews, 1910.

———. *The Works of Theodore Roosevelt*. 24 vols. Memorial edition. Edited by Joseph Bucklin Bishop. New York: Charles Scribner's Sons, 1923–26.

Rothman, David J. *Politics and Power: The United States Senate 1869–1901*. Cambridge, Mass.: Harvard University Press, 1966.

Rudwick, Elliott. M. *Race Riot at East St. Louis, July 2, 1917*. Foreword by Oscar Handlin. Cleveland and New York: World Publishing Co., Meridian Books, 1966.

———. *W. E. B. Du Bois, Propagandist of the Negro Protest*. Preface by Louis R. Harlan. New York: Atheneum, 1968.

Russell, Francis. *The President Makers from Mark Hanna to Joseph P. Kennedy*. Boston: Little, Brown, 1976.

———. *The Shadow of Blooming Grove: Warren G. Harding in His Times*. New York: McGraw-Hill, 1968.

Safire, William, *Safire's New Political Dictionary, The Definitive Guide to the New Language of Politics*. New York: Random House, 1993.

Salvatore, Nick. *Eugene V. Debs: Citizen and Socialist*. Urbana and Chicago: University of Illinois Press, 1982.

Sasaki, Takahiro. "Race or Individual Freedom: Public Reactions to the Roosevelt-Washington Dinner at the White House in October, 1901." M.A. thesis, University of North Carolina, Chapel Hill, 1984.

Schlereth, Thomas J. *Victorian America: Transformations in Everyday Life 1876–1915*. New York, HarperCollins, 1991.

Schwartz, Bernard. *A History of the Supreme Court*. New York: Oxford University Press, 1995.

Semonche, John E. *Ray Stannard Baker, A Quest for Democracy in Modern America 1870–1918*. Chapel Hill: University of North Carolina Press, 1969.

Sherman, John. *Recollections of Forty Years in the House, Senate and Cabinet: An Autobiography*. 2 vols. Chicago, London, New York, Berlin: Werner Co., 1895.

Sherman, William Tecumseh. *Memoirs*. New York: Library of America, 1990.

Simkins, Francis Butler. *Pitchfork Ben Tillman, South Carolinian*. Baton Rouge: Louisiana State Univeristy Press, 1967.

Slayden, Ellen Maury. *Washington Wife: Journal of Ellen Maury Slayden from 1897–1919*. New York: Harper & Row, 1962.

Slotkin, Richard *Gunfighter Nation: The Myth of the Frontier in Twentieth-Century America*. New York: Atheneum, 1992.

Smith, Page. *John Adams*. 2 vols. Garden City, N.Y.: Doubleday, 1962.

Socolofsky, Homer E. and Allan B. Spetter. *The Presidency of Benjamin Harrison.* Lawrence: University Press of Kansas, 1988.

Stallman, R. W. *Stephen Crane.* New York: George Braziller, 1968.

———, and E. R. Hageman, eds. *The War Dispatches of Stephen Crane.* New York: New York University Press, 1964.

Steffens, Lincoln. *The Autobiography of Lincoln Steffens.* New York: Harcourt, Brace, 1931.

Stevens, George E. *The City of Cincinnati.* Cincinnati: George S. Blanchard, 1869.

Stoddard, Henry L. *As I Knew Them, Presidents and Politics from Grant to Coolidge.* New York: Harper & Brothers, 1927.

Stoddard, Lothrop. *Master of Manhattan: The Life of Richard Croker.* New York: Longmans, Green & Co., 1931.

Sullivan, Mark. *Our Times: The United States, 1900–1925. Turn of the Century.* 6 vols. New York: Charles Scribner's Sons, 1926.

Swanberg, W. A. *Citizen Hearst: A Biography of William Randolph Hearst.* New York: Charles Scribner's Sons, 1961.

———. *Pulitzer.* New York: Charles Scribner's Sons, 1967.

Swindler, *William F. Court and Constitution in the Twentieth Century: The Old Legality 1889–1932.* Vol. 1. Indianapolis: Bobbs-Merrill, 1969.

Taft, Mrs. William Howard. *Recollections of Full Years.* New York: Dodd, Mead & Co., 1917.

Teague, Michael. *Mrs. L.: Conversations with Alice Roosevelt Longworth.* Garden City, N.Y.: Doubleday, 1981.

Teichman, Howard. *Alice: The Life and Times of Alice Roosevelt Longworth.* Englewood Cliffs, N.J.: Prentice-Hall, 1979.

Terrell, Mary Church. "A Sketch of Mingo Saunders [*sic*]." *The Voice.* March, 1907. 128–31.

Thayer, William Roscoe. *The Life and Letters of John Hay.* 2 vols. 1915. Reprint. 1915. Boston: Houghton Mifflin, 1908.

Thornburgh, Emma Lou. "The Brownsville Episode and the Negro Vote." *Mississippi Valley Historical Review* 44:469–93. December, 1957.

Timmons, Bascom N., ed. *Charles G. Dawes: A Journal of the McKinley Years 1893–1913,* Chicago: The Lakeside Press, R. R. Donnelley & Sons, 1950.

Tinsley, James Aubrey. "The Brownsville Affray." M.A. thesis, 402747. Davis Library. University of North Carolina, Chapel Hill, 1948.

———. "Roosevelt, Foraker, and the Brownsville Affray." *Journal of Negro History* 41:43–65, January, 1956.

Tipple, John. "Big Businessmen and a New Economy." In *The Gilded Age,* edited by H. Wayne Morgan, 13–30. Syracuse: Syracuse University Press, 1971.

Vandiver, Frank W. *Black Jack: The Life and Times of John J. Pershing.* 2 vols. College Station: Texas A&M University Press, 1977.

Villard, Oswald Garrison. *Fighting Years: Memoirs of a Liberal Editor.* New York: Harcourt, Brace & Co, 1939.

Walters, Everett. *Joseph Benson Faraker: An Uncompromising Republican*. Columbus: Ohio History Press, 1948.

Weaver, John D. *The Brownsville Raid*. College Station: Texas A&M University Press, 1992.

———. *Warren, The Man, The Court, The Era*. Boston: Little, Brown, 1967.

Weinberg, Authur, ed. *Attorney for the Damned*. New York: Simon and Schuster, 1957.

Welch, Richard E., Jr. *The Presidencies of Grover Cleveland*. Lawrence: University Press of Kansas, 1988.

Wells, H. G. *The Future in America*. New York: Harper & Bros., 1906.

Werner, M. R. *Tammany Hall*. Garden City, N.Y.: Doubleday, Doran, 1928.

Wesley, Charles H. *The Quest for Equality: From Civil War to Civil Rights*. Association for the Study of Afro-American Life and History. New York: New York Publishers Co., 1968.

Westin, Alan F. *An Autobiography of the Supreme Court*. New York: Macmillan, 1963.

Wheeler, Major-General Joseph. *The Santiago Campaign 1898*. Freeport, N.Y.: Books for Libraries Press, 1970.

White, Walter. *A Man Called White*. New York: Viking Press, 1948.

White, William Allen. *The Autobiography of William Allen White*. New York: Macmillan, 1946.

Williams, R. Hal. *Years of Decision: American Politics in the 1890s*. New York: Alfred B. Knopf, 1978.

———. *"Dry Bones and Dead Language": The Democratic Party*. In *The Gilded Age*. Edited by H. Wayne Morgan. Syracuse: Syracuse University Press, 1971.

Williams, T. Harry, ed. *Hayes: The Diary of a President 1875–1881, Covering the Disputed Election, the End of Reconstruction, and the Beginning of Civil Service*. New York: David McKay, Inc., 1964.

Winkler, John K. *William Randolph Hearst: A New Appraisal*. New York: Hastings House, 1955.

Wister, Owen. *Roosevelt, The Story of Friendship, 1880–1919*. New York: Macmillan, 1930.

Woodward, C. Vann. *The Future of the Past*. New York: Oxford University Press, 1989.

———. *Origins of the New South, 1877–1913*. Baton Rouge: Louisiana State University Press, 1951, 1971.

———, ed., *Mary Chestnut's Civil War*. New Haven, Conn.: Yale University Press, 1981.

Index

Chattanooga, Tenn., 62; Foraker speech, 111–13

Chicago Courier, (1971) exoneration crusade, xiii

Chicago Defender, exoneration crusade, xiii. *See also* Saunders, Doris; Wall, Frederick

Chickamauga, 8, 62, 186

child labor, 163

Choate, Joseph H., 57

Cincinnati, Ohio, 4, 11–12

civil rights: (1883) Harlan's dissent, 158; (1889) black suffrage traded for tariff, 44–45; (1964), Lyndon Johnson wipes out Jim Crow polling places, 45

civil service: reform of, 17–18; "Rutherfraud" Hayes, 17; Roosevelt, "a reform fraud," 25; appointed to U.S. Civil Service Commission, 43–44

Clansman, The. See *Birth of a Nation, The*

Clark, Joel Bennett (Champ), 126

Clark, Mark, xviii

Clayton, C. B., 190

Clayton, Eva, 83

Cleveland, Grover: (1882) New York governor, 21–22; (1884) presidential candidate, "woman scrape," 25–26; elected by South's disfranchised blacks, 26–27, 28; "no rebel flags," 25–26; (1887) bold use of tariff issue, 38; (1892) re-elected, 48–49; retains Commissioner Roosevelt, 50; praises Foraker's Brownsville crusade, 133; puts ex-Klansman on Supreme Court, 158. *See also* Halpin, Maria; White, Edward D.

Clinton, William J., 83

Cockran, William Bourke, 156

Cody, Buffalo Bill, 64

Cole, Ralph D., 178

Colombia, isthmanian canal, 92–93. *See also* Panama Canal

Columbia Law School, 19

Combe, Frederick J., 106

Conkling, Roscoe: (1876) Roosevelt's father opposes, 14; loses to Hayes, 16, 17–18, 152; (1884), helps defeat Blaine, 23–24, 26; and corporations, 78–79. *See also* Platt, Thomas C.

Constitution: (1868) 14th Amendment ("equal protection"), 16, 136–37; corporations as persons, 78–79; (1870) 15th Amendment (race no bar to vote), 12, 16, 27, 126–37; (1913) 17th Amendment (di-rect election of U.S. Senators), 177–78; (1919) 19th Amendment (woman suffrage), 196. *See also* Electoral College

Constitution League, 117–19, 137

Coolidge, Calvin, (1923) inherits White House, 196

Corbett, James John, 164

Cornelius, Jack, xvii–xix, 210–11

Cornell University, 9

Cortelyou, George, 87

Cowles, Anna Roosevelt (sister, "Bamie," "Bye"): early years, 6; father's death, 18; mother's death, 22; Theodore remarries, 30–31; shares his first White House meal, 88; correspondent, 185

Cowles, William S. (Anna Roosevelt's husband), 88

Cox, George B., 37, 45–46, 57

Cox, James M., 196

Cox, Minnie M., 107

Cox, Wayne W., 107

Crane, Stephen, 70

Crane, Winthrop Murray, 142

Crisis, The (NAACP): (1910) Taft Doctrine racist, 158; (1913) Jim Crowism "on its way to becoming permanent," 175. *See* Du Bois, William E. B.

Crixell, Joseph, 106

Crixell, Teofilo, 106

Croker, Richard, 31, 82

Cromie, Robert, xiii

Cronkite, Walter, 209–10

Crum, William D., 151, 157

Cuba, (1906) trouble in, 110–11, 113. *See* Spain, war with

Culberson, Charles A., 105

Czologosz, Leon, 87

Daggett, A. S., El Caney, 71–72, 204; court of inquiry, 148

Dakota Territory, 43, 61. *See also* Roosevelt, Theodore

Dana, Paul, 63

Daniels, Josephus, 181

Davis, Richard Harding, 68

Davis, Varina, 112

Dawes, Charles G., 52, 61

Dayton, W. L., 4

death penalty (1908), 145

Debs, Eugene V., 173

Delano, Sara, 18. *See* Roosevelt, Mrs. James (Franklin's mother)

Standard Oil letters, breaks with Taft, 139–44; (1909) loses Senate seat, 146; "great gifts," "statesmanship," xxi, 142
——Brownsville crusade: (1906–1910): xxi–xxii; (1907) Gridiron Club confrontation, 123–26; Senate hearings, 128–31; (1908) reenlistment bills, 131–32; "They ask no favors," 132; parts company with Taft, 136; (1909); A.M.E. farewell tribute, 155–56; (1909–10) court of inquiry, 145–46; (1972) soldiers exonerated, xvi; (1973) restitution, xvii–xxi. *See also* Brownsville Affray
——(1908–17): congratulates Taft, gets humiliating response, 138; Roosevelt's reaction to Standard Oil letters, 142–43, 144; (1909) Foraker's parting shot, 155; (1910) attacks Roosevelt's New Nationalism, 167; (1914) runs for Senator under new 17th Amendment, loses, 177–78; (1915) denounces *The Birth of A Nation*, 180, 182–83; (1916) Roosevelt's conciliatory letter, 185–86; (1917) obituary of the "bulldog of politics" ignores Brownsville crusade, 185; *Notes of a Busy Life*, xii, 180, 183, 197. *See also*, Brownsville Affray and Walters, Everett
Foraker, Julia Bundy: (1847) birth, Republican heritage, 5, 10; (1867–70) courtship and marriage, 9–10; children, 31–32; (1889) comfortable with husband's defeat, 47–48; war was "Yellow Fever," 62–63; Roosevelt as White House host, 91–92; Gridiron dinner, "when you strike at a king . . ." 127–28; Roosevelt makes an unacceptable offer, 133; Archbold letters, 140–41; Foraker, Roosevelt and Taft in retrospect, 197
Foraker, Julia (daughter), 31, 32
Foraker, Louise, (daughter), 31–32
Foraker, Margaret Reece (senator's mother), 4, 32
Foraker Act (1900), 75, 77–78
Fort Brown, Tex. *See* Brownsville Affray
Fort Missoula, Mont., 61
Fort Niobrara, Nebr., 87, 105, 130
Fort Reno, Okla., 86–87
Fort Shaw, Montana Territory, 61–62
Fort Snelling, Minn., 61
Fortune, T. Thomas, 76
Foster, Charles ("Calico Charlie"), 23
Franklin, John Hope, 194, 244

Fraser, Donald M., 206
Free Soil Party, 3–4
Frémont, John C., 4
Freud, Sigmund, 5
Froehlke, Robert F., xvi, xviii

Garfield, James A., (1880–81) elected president, 20; assassinated, 19, 20, mentioned, 39
Garfield, James R. (son), 159, 167
Garlington, Ernest A., 129–30
Garrison, William Lloyd, 196
Gavit, John Palmer, 176–77
George, Henry, 31
Gompers, Samuel, 188, 191
Gould, Lewis L., xxi, 75
Gracie, Annie Bulloch, 6
Gracie, Archibald, 186
Grand Army of the Republic, 37
Grant, Ulysses S., 9–10, 112
Gridiron Club, (1907) Roosevelt-Foraker duel, 125–28
Griffith, David Wark. See *Birth of a Nation, The*
Groton School, 123–24
Guillmant, Pierre, xiii
Guiteau, Charles J., 20

Hackett, Francis, 182
Hagedorn, Hermann, 187–88
Halpin, Maria, 25–26
Halstead, Murat, 41
Hamilton, Alexander, 23
Hancock, Winfield Scott, (1880) Democratic candidate, 20
Hanna, Dan R. (son): (1914) Foraker "out of date," 178; (1920) reassesses Harding, 195
Hanna, Marcus A.: (1884) allied with Foraker, 23; (1887) opponents, 37; (1890) declares Foraker politically "dead", 48; (1895) backs McKinley for president, 178; (1896) Foraker escorts Ohio's "junior senator," 56; (1889) Roosevelt's aspirations, 74–75; (1900) asks Foraker to draft GOP trust plank, 79; (1904) dispute over Roosevelt's nomination, 95–96; death, 96–97; both Forakers eulogize, 97
Harbaugh, William Henry, 60, 74
Harding, Abigail (sister), 163, 179
Harding, Amos and Hulda (said to be president's West Indian parents), 196
Harding, Florence Kling (wife), 179, 195–96
Harding, Warren G.: (1910) runs for gover-

competitor with the *Journal*, 60. *See also* New York World

Pullen, Franklin W., Cuba, 65–67

Purdy, Milton D., 245

Quay, Matthew S., 45

Quigg, Lemuel, 74

race relations: riots and lynchings, 75, 85; (1906); and muckrakers, 101; Atlanta; 114–15; (1917) East St. Louis, Illinois, 188–91; (1917) Houston, Texas, 191–94. *See also* Brownsville Affray

railroads, regulation of, 102, 126. *See also* Elkins Antirebate Act; Hepburn Act

Rainey, Joseph H., 17

Reid, Whitelaw, 44, 92

Reno, Jesse Lee, 86

Reno, Nev., (1910) Jeffries-Johnson fight, 164–65

Riis, Jacob, 51, 53

robber barons, 78

Roberts, Fred, xiv

Robinson, Corinne Roosevelt (Roosevelt's sister, "Conie"), 6, 18, 22, 50

Robinson, Douglas (Corinne's husband), 88

Rockefeller, John D., 78

Rogers, Henry H., 126

Roosevelt, Alice Lee (daughter). *See* Longworth, Alice Roosevelt

Roosevelt, Alice Lee (first wife), (1880) marriage, 18; (1884) death, 22

Roosevelt, Anna (sister, "Bamie," "Bye"). *See* Cowles, Mrs. Anna R.

Roosevelt, Archibald (son), 90; World War I, 186–87

Roosevelt, Corinne (sister, "Conie"). *See* Robinson, Mrs. Corinne R.

Roosevelt, Mrs. Edith Kermit Carow (second wife): childhood friendship, 10–11; (1886) marriage, 30; politics, 50; (1898) near-fatal illness, 60; White House hostess, 92; (1909) last days as First Lady, 152–53; back in private life, 159

Roosevelt, Elliott (Theodore's brother), 22

Roosevelt, Elliott (Theodore's son), 6

Roosevelt, Ethel (daughter), 187

Roosevelt, Franklin Delano, 18, 196

Roosevelt, James A. (Theodore's uncle, Franklin's father), 18

Roosevelt, Kermit (Theodore's son), 90, 92–93; Groton debates Brownsville, 123–24;

(1908) father on Taft campaign, 135; expecting Foraker attack, 144; World War I, 187

Roosevelt, Martha Bulloch (Roosevelt's mother), southern roots, 6–7

Roosevelt, Quentin (son), (1918) death, 187–88

Roosevelt, Sarah Delano (Franklin's mother), 18

Roosevelt, Theodore (father), Lincoln Republican, 6; combat left to a substitute 7–8; son's body build-up, 10–11; (1876) first political speech, 14; Conkling squelches a political appointment, 17, 152; (1878) death, 18

Roosevelt, Theodore (son), (1856–75); parents birth, siblings, southern roots, 6–7; health, 10–11; books, birds and Edith Carow, 11; (1876–80) Harvard nonconformist, 15; (1878) father's death, 18; (1880–81) marries Alice Lee, wins silk stocking legislative seat, 18, 19; (1882–85) "Cyclone Assemblyman," death of wife and mother, 21–22; Dakota Badlands, buffalo dance, 30; (1886) "Rancher" marries Edith Carow, 30–31

———Returns to public service: (1889) civil service commissioner, 44, 50; (1893) bows out of mayor race, 50; (1895) police commissioner, "bound for the presidency," 51, 53; (1897–98) Assistant Secretary of the Navy, 56–58, 60–61

———War with Spain: (1895), "must have a commmission," 51; (1895) country needs war," 53; (1897) "supreme triumphs of war," 58; a "righteous war," 63; "one foe . . . as good as another, 64; (1898) "joy in battle, 64; Rough Riders,63; "Wood's Weary Walkers," 64–71; "crowded hour," 70, 72; Kettle Hill, 69–71; angers black readers, 70–71. *See also* blacks, in military service; Dunne, Finley Peter; Spain, war with

———Road to the Presidency, (1901) Governor, New York, 73–74; racial views, 65, 74, 98; possible "presidential candidate," 75; Philippines, 76, 83; vice presidency, "that madman," 80–81: (1901) inherits the White House, "gleeful moment," 87–88; dines with Booker T. Washington, 90–91, 99; regard for Foraker, 92; (1902) Holmes, first Supreme Court appointee, 94, (1904)